WHAT MAKES LIFE
WORTH LIVING?

To Yoko,
who makes my life worth living,

WHAT MAKES LIFE WORTH LIVING?

How Japanese and Americans
Make Sense of Their Worlds

GORDON MATHEWS

UNIVERSITY OF CALIFORNIA PRESS
BERKELEY   LOS ANGELES   LONDON

This book is a print-on-demand volume. It is manufactured
using toner in place of ink. Type and images may be less
sharp than the same material seen in traditionally printed
University of California Press editions.

University of California Press
Berkeley and Los Angeles, California

University of California Press, Ltd.
London, England

© 1996 by
The Regents of the University of California

Library of Congress Cataloging-in-Publication Data

Mathews, Gordon.
    What makes life worth living? : how Japanese and Americans
make sense of their worlds / Gordon Mathews.
      p. cm.
    Includes bibliographical references and index.
    ISBN 0-520-20132-9 (alk. paper).—ISBN 0-520-20133-7
(pbk.:
alk. paper)
    1. Social values—Japan. 2. Quality of life—Japan. 3. Social
values—United States. 4. Quality of life—United States.
5. Conduct of life. I. Title.
HN723.5.M355 1995
303.3'72—dc20   95-22263
                                                         CIP

Printed in the United States of America

Contents

Preface

This book is about how people in Japan and the United States struggle to find lives worth living through their commitments to what they value most in their lives: their families, or work, or dreams, or political ideals, creative endeavors, or religious beliefs.

There is a term in Japanese, *ikigai*, which means "that which most makes one's life seem worth living." Although American English has no clear equivalent to this term, *ikigai* applies not only to Japanese lives but to American lives as well. *Ikigai* is what, on a day-to-day and year-to-year basis, each of us most essentially lives for, be it lover, dream, booze, or God. In this book, I explore through *ikigai* the different, culturally shaped ways in which people comprehend their lives in Japan and the United States. I also explore how people in both societies in this late modern age strive in common to understand the underlying meaning of life.

I do this by comparing the personal accounts of nine pairs of Japanese and Americans (selected from a hundred sets of interviews I conducted in Japan and the United States in 1989–91), discussing their different pursuits of "a life worth living." The people in these pairs are different in their culturally shaped values and in the rules and limits of their societies. But they are also similar: they see the world in parallel ways, because of both the underlying similarities of their sociocultural worlds and their own individual similarities, transcending cultural difference.

My hope is that readers of this book will learn something about

Japan and the United States, but also about themselves. This book is
not about Japan as "other," an exotic, inscrutable place on the other
side of the world; rather, it is about Japanese and Americans as selves,
trying, like all of us, to make sense of their lives and worlds. This
effort to make sense of life is not just that of the people whose accounts appear in this book; it is also the endeavor of I who write this
book, and perhaps too of you who read it.

I am greatly indebted to the many people and institutions that have
made this book possible. The first draft of the book was a doctoral
dissertation, written in the Department of Anthropology at Cornell
University. I couldn't have written it were it not for the generosity of
a number of sources of funding. The National Science Foundation
supported me for three years, enabling graduate coursework and my
American fieldwork. The Fulbright-Hays Program funded my Japanese fieldwork, and the Spencer T. and Ann W. Olin Foundation at
Cornell University provided additional funding over a five-year period. The Reischauer Institute of Japanese Studies at Harvard University gave me a year of postdoctoral funding, during which I turned
my dissertation into this book. I marvel at my good fortune at being
able to spend the past five years laboring in no office or factory to
pay my rent, but doing research and writing to my heart's content. It
is for the reader to judge whether this book merits the support that
has been given me by these institutions. I hope you'll find that it is
worth their—and indirectly your—money.

Yoshida Shigeru first brought me to Japan in 1980 (going so far as
to get drunk with immigration officials to smooth the way for my
working visa), and first taught me Japanese. Rich Randolph, at the
University of California, Santa Cruz, first introduced me to anthropology, when I wandered into his office in 1985 wondering what I
should do with my life. Were it not for these two people, this book
would not have been written.

My doctoral committee at Cornell gave me much aid in formulating the ideas of this book. Robert J. Smith has taught me a great deal
not only about Japan, but also about how to write; I treasure his red
exclamation marks covering my drafts. I'm also grateful that for all

the doubts he almost certainly felt about my project, he stood with me all the way. Carol Greenhouse didn't allow me to slight in any way the American side of my research; I value her advice and friendship over the years. Steve Sangren would have preferred that this work be more theoretically rigorous; what rigor it has owes much to his advice.

Other professors at Cornell have also given me valuable advice. Vic Koschmann has kept me honest with his occasional doses of postmodern skepticism. Bernd Lambert has helped me to stay grounded in anthropology. Bob Ascher has read through the manuscript and provided detailed criticism and suggestions, most of which I've followed. He has truly understood what I am trying to do in my work; for that, and for his friendship as a kindred spirit, I'm grateful.

Other people also provided great help. Itō Naoki and Sasada Iwao were invaluable in finding Japanese research materials (the newspaper articles discussed in chapter 1 were provided me by Itō-san). These two served as my media antennae while I did research in Japan, and after I left Japan as well. James Roberson provided helpful criticism of my manuscript, and Kuwakado Chō, Joshua Roth, Jan Zeserson, and Hino Midori gave me new insights over the course of many long conversations. The three anonymous readers for the University of California Press provided accurate, large-scale criticism, and at several points prevented me from making a fool of myself in print—although, having not taken all their advice, I may be a fool yet. The editors at the University of California Press—Sheila Levine, Monica McCormick, Rose Anne White, and Laura Driussi—have been helpful; the copy editor of the manuscript, Mark Pentecost, worked diligently and sensitively to make this book more readable. On a more personal note, Ron Fenner has provided a quiet place to work over the past few years (but for the cat he bequeathed us, and its midnight gifts of mice). My wife Yoko remains my *ikigai*. Aside from her immense help with the translation of accounts, there is her enduring love and friendship. Without that, what worth would be these words on paper?

Finally, I am deeply indebted to my informants, the people I talked with for this book. They told me the story of their lives with an openness and a wisdom that taught me not only about Japanese and American selves and cultures, but also about how to live. Several of these people were crucial in locating additional informants and in aiding my research in innumerable ways large and small. I would very much like to cite their names, but to do so would compromise the anonymity of those whose accounts appear in this book, and so I remain silent. If ever you read this, you know who you are: I can't thank you enough for your help and your trust.

A note on names. All names of people whose accounts appear in this book are pseudonyms. Other nonessential details of their lives have also been disguised, so that they will be unrecognizable. Japanese names appearing in this book, whether of authors or of people I interviewed, are given in Japanese form, of surname first and given name second.

Part One

The Cultural Foundations of *Ikigai*

Introduction:
What Makes Life Worth Living?

What Makes Life Worth Living?

Life is but "futility of futilities," proclaims the book of Ecclesiastes in the Old Testament. "All life is suffering," holds the first of Buddha's Four Noble Truths. If these statements are true (a big "if," and yet who of us can say without hesitation that life is more joyous than painful, more fascinating than tedious), then how do we get through life? What makes our lives worth living?

Philosophers from William James, who held that if you "believe that life *is* worth living ... your belief will help create the fact" ([1897] 1956, 62), to Albert Camus (1955), who argued that life is worth living not despite but *because* it has no meaning, have tried to answer this question. But answers given by writers of fiction and song offer a more concrete starting point. Bruce Springsteen's song "Reason to Believe" (1982) depicts, among other futilities, a man poking a dead dog with a stick, trying to bring it back to life, a woman vainly awaiting the return of a husband who deserted her long ago, and a baby baptized and buried an instant later as an old man. The refrain of the song says, "Still at the end of every hard-earned day, people find some reason to believe." But this "reason to believe" is an illusion, the song seems to say: there is apparently no "reason to believe" in life's worthwhileness, no "reason to believe" that all will be well in the end. Still, the song's characters keep on believing—believing, or at least hoping, despite all the evidence to the contrary.

3

One reason for our perseverance in life is thus blind faith, or at least blind hope, according to Springsteen's song. A second reason is implied in a passage from a story by the Japanese writer Kuroi Senji:

> "Are you satisfied with that [work] . . . that you did?"
> "Am I satisfied? I guess I'd have to say that I'm not satisfied. But then, I don't work in order to be satisfied." . . .
> "Then why do you work?"
> "I wonder why. Come on! . . . How can I answer that? It's no use asking that kind of question." (Kuroi 1990, 198–99)

Of course we work to pay the bills; but beyond this, Kuroi's character seems to hold, we work and live because this is what people do. There's no use questioning it, just do it. In John Updike's *Rabbit Is Rich,* Rabbit Angstrom talks with his son in a similar way:

> "Look, Nelson. Maybe I haven't done everything right in my life. I know I haven't. But I haven't committed the greatest sin. I haven't laid down and died."
> "Who says that's the greatest sin?"
> "Everybody says it. . . . It's against Nature, to give up, you've got to keep moving." (Updike 1982, 356)

From these words, a lack of imagination coupled with the drive to keep moving seems to be the imperative at the root of day-to-day, year-to-year existence: all one can do is keep plugging away at life.

As ethnographers have shown, this perseverance may be accompanied by the consolations of fantasy. John Caughey found that in characteristic American fantasies, "the individual departs from the real social world, where he or she is average and recognition is slight and grudging, enters a 'glamorous' and media-glorified career field, and becomes . . . 'somebody,' 'a god to millions,' through the mass recognition of others" (Caughey 1984, 168). Thomas Rohlen found that the Japanese high school students he studied immersed themselves in their comic-book fantasies to make their exam-crammed reality tolerable: "The private world of Japanese [high school] students is one full of imaginings and often bizarre images. One needs only to glance through the comic books that are so popular among teenagers to realize that they have a fondness for the extraordinary, the weird, and the obscene that stands in stark contrast to their outward conduct" (Rohlen 1983, 109).

These investigators imply that fantasy is what makes our lives bearable. Maybe we're all Walter Mittys, dreaming of worlds in which, unlike the mundane realities of our actual lives, we are heroes.

But is this all that keeps us persevering: blind faith, dumb habit, the drive to keep moving, the sop of fantasy? Is it only our refusal to see life as it is that keeps us from wading deep into the ocean by the millions and throwing ourselves off buildings en masse?[1]

Perhaps not. Inertia and fantasy are negative explanations for people's perseverance to life, but there's also a positive explanation. Most people, it seems, have a sense of commitment to some facet of their world—perhaps their work, or their family, or their dream, or their religious belief—that gives them a reason to believe in the worthwhileness of their lives.

In Japan, this sense of commitment is called *ikigai,* a word that can be glossed as "that which most makes one's life seem worth living". Surveys of *ikigai* show that men tend to say they find *ikigai* in work or in family, women in family and children. Young people tend to say they find *ikigai* in future dreams, old people in past memories or in present family or hobby. A minority of people say they find *ikigai* in religious belief or in creative endeavors; some say they have no *ikigai*. There is much argument over the meaning of *ikigai* in Japan today, as we'll see; but most people seem able to specify, at least for the pollsters, what makes their lives seem worth living.

In the United States, there is no term fully comparable to *ikigai,* but the idea of *ikigai* seems readily comprehensible to Americans. Consider the line in so many love songs: "Baby, baby, I can't live without you"—in other words, you are what makes my life worth living. Or consider a Sunday comic strip I once saw. Its character moves through his day's drudgeries—traffic jams, piles of paperwork, unpleasant words from the boss—muttering "Why do I put up with this?" Then he gets home and is greeted by the hugs of his little daughter, and he understands: his child is what makes it worth putting up with. Indeed, many Americans may put up with the indigni-

---

1. Baumeister notes psychological research showing that depressed people in the United States perceive themselves more accurately than nondepressed people: "Most people seem to achieve happiness by systematically distorting their perception of themselves and their circumstances" (1991: 225). Goleman (1985) and Becker (1973) also discuss how "vital lies" enable us to remain secure and happy.

ties and drudgeries of life for the sake of something—children, lover, work, dream, or God—that makes their lives seem worth it all.

Ikigai is thus a direct answer to the question, what makes life worth living. And yet, this answer is not final, but only provisional. One who lives for work will soon enough retire, or get laid off; one's lover may leave; children will grow up and be gone; one's dreams may fade; God may disappear. One will eventually die, and what will it all mean then? Meanwhile, there are always doubts: "Does she really love me?" "Is this work worth spending my life on?" "Shouldn't my children be free of me?" "Where is the God to whom I pray?" *Ikigai* is essentially insecure; in Japan and the United States alike, it is not the end but the very beginning of the pursuit of a life worth living.

What makes life worth living? For much of my life, I've been asking myself this question. As a child, I remember thinking that life wasn't much fun; I escaped through books. At age seven, I came down with diabetes and needed daily shots of insulin thereafter. Doctors told me that if I didn't take care of myself, I would die young, and I soon convinced myself that I would. I vowed to write, and thereby last beyond myself; I tried to set all that happened to me on paper, as if to transcribe a life worth living from a life that I suspected wasn't.

At fifteen, I discovered LSD and another world that I believed to be better than this one. For several years, I would come home from school and sleep, then rise as my parents and siblings slept, to trip in my basement shrine: candles, plants, a charred sculpture, picture books of explorers' journeys, and piles of tattered currency from around the world (bought from an ad in *Boy's Life*). After high school I went to college, then left to write a novel about a man who bricks himself up in a room and creates a universe. For a year I lived in a cubicle in a pensioners' hotel, swallowing LSD and envisioning other worlds, until finally, still sane, I gave this up and decided to reenter the world of other human beings.

It took me years to do that—among other things, the idea of *making love* to *another human being* seemed impossible, a chimera—but eventually I became more or less resocialized into the world.

Nonetheless, that world still seemed false at core. As books like those of Ernest Becker (1971, 1973, 1975) showed me, our deepest human meanings are built upon our "denial of death," our futile efforts to become symbolically immortal, through money or success or patriotism—or through writing one's thoughts on piles of paper that, after all, are only paper. Could it be that our lives are most deeply based on lies? How could one find a life worth living in such a world?

Indeed, when I looked around in those years, I found the meanings that people seemed to live by insufficient. As books such as Studs Terkel's *Working* (1972) revealed, many Americans work hard but don't like their jobs; the janitor, the waitress, the salesman, the lawyer may work for the sake of a paycheck to enjoy in their leisure hours. But television is the most common American leisure activity—could television be what makes life worth living? Love songs told me "all you need is love," but some half of contemporary marriages end in divorce. Most Americans say they believe in God; but while for some God may indeed provide the basis for a sense of life worth living, for many people I knew God seemed to exist only for an hour or two on Sundays.

Because life in the United States didn't promise much of an answer—because writing seemed false, and my peers' paths of doctor, lawyer, merchant chief seemed futile—I decided to search somewhere else. I went to live in Japan in 1980 because I had been offered a job teaching in an alternative English school, but also because I wondered if Japanese might be able to answer my question. I soon enough came upon the term *ikigai* and found that to many Japanese their *ikigai* was clear: their total commitment to their families and companies. Yet, the longer I was in Japan, the more I saw that for many this commitment seemed unsatisfactory: the employee laboring for a company he hated but couldn't quit; the mother pushing her children to excel in an examination system she detested; the youth dreaming dreams certain to be crushed. In Japan too, what makes life worth living seemed problematic: Why go through with life?

Graduate school, with all its professional specialization, is hardly a place for the pursuit of existential questions, but in cultural anthropology I found a haven where I could indeed pursue such questions. I began graduate training at Cornell University in 1987, seeking to explore what makes life seem worth living in Japan and the United States. In 1989–91, I interviewed fifty-two Japanese in a northern Japanese city and fifty-two Americans in a western American city, talking with them about their work, their families, their religious beliefs, their dreams, hopes, and fears, and their *ikigai*. This book, a revision of my doctoral dissertation, contains the accounts of some of these people and my reflections about what they told me. The book is empirical in its approach and steeped in theories from social science. Underlying this, it is personal. What can the Japanese and Americans I talked with teach me about what makes life worth living?

Let me here tip my hand, to say that they could teach me nothing unequivocal. There's no light at the end of the tunnel, making all clear and well. But there is a glimmer of hope in what they taught me about the ultimate basis of *ikigai:* the meaning of life, as much as we can know it. It's only a glimmer, but it's all we can have, as I will try to show you before this book ends.

The Structure and Aims of This Book

This book is an exploration of *ikigai* in Japan and the United States. I first examine the cultural meanings of *ikigai* (part 1), then analyze *ikigai* in Japanese and American lives (part 2), and then explore the relation of *ikigai* to the meaning of life in the late modern world (part 3).

In chapter 1 I discuss how the dominant meanings of *ikigai* in Japanese print media are *ittaikan* and *jiko jitsugen*, "commitment to group" and "self-realization"; in chapter 2 I examine the parallel cultural tension in the United States between "self-realization" and "commitment" as ideals of how to live. In chapter 3 I turn from media to people and discuss how I conducted interviews and constructed accounts, and how Japanese and Americans can be compared in their pursuits of lives worth living.

In part 2, the bulk of the book, I look into the words and worlds of nine pairs of Japanese and Americans. Chapter 4, "*Ikigai* in Work and Family," examines the personal accounts of a committed Japanese bank manager and an alienated American airline pilot who both live for their work; two mothers, a married homemaker and a divorced administrator, who live for their children; and a Japanese company employee who dreams of finding his true self and an American who quit his high-stress job to devote himself to his family. In the chapter's commentary, "*Ikigai* and Gender," I elaborate on the familial division of *ikigai* in Japan (work for men, family for women) and the struggle of many Americans to overcome this division.

Chapter 5, "*Ikigai* in Past and Future," considers two young women who dream of a moneyed future that one cultivates and the other avoids; two young men who dream of quitting their mundane jobs to follow their "callings"; and two older women not far from death, one seeking to remain with her family in this world, the other looking ahead to God in the next. In "*Ikigai* and Dreams," I discuss how all *ikigai* are based in culturally and historically shaped dreams of the future.

In chapter 6, "*Ikigai* in Creation and Religion," I consider a Japanese calligrapher and an American novelist who find *ikigai* in their creative endeavors; a Japanese bank employee and an American policeman who find *ikigai* in their religious faiths; and an Ainu activist who dreams of resurrecting Ainu culture and an African-American schoolteacher who feels she has no more dreams left to dream. In "*Ikigai* and Significance," I analyze *ikigai* as the attempt to create and sustain a sense of the enduring significance of one's life.

Part 3 sets forth a cross-cultural theory of *ikigai*. In chapter 7 I examine how the people portrayed in part 2 culturally formulate their *ikigai* and socially negotiate their *ikigai* with the people around them, and I look at the institutional channeling of *ikigai* in Japan and the United States. Chapter 8 explores the linkage of *ikigai* to the larger meaning of life and the collaboration of self and society in maintaining this linkage. I consider Japan and the United States as societies lacking common frameworks of ultimate meaning, and show how the people in part 2 construct personal senses of ultimate meaning—senses that might not be true but that then again just *might* be true.

I have three aims in this book. First, I want to introduce to my readers the Japanese concept of *ikigai*. The conflict over the meaning of *ikigai* in Japan today is finally a conflict over how Japanese should live their lives at present and in the future. In this sense, *ikigai* can serve as a window into Japanese society, in all its continuities and transformations.

But *ikigai* has implications beyond Japan. My second aim is to show that *ikigai* is not only a Japanese cultural concept but a cross-cultural concept as well, explicating American as well as Japanese lives. Through *ikigai* selves in Japan and the United States comprehend their most essential link to their social worlds; through it they find lives worth living within their different societies. In this sense, *ikigai* becomes a means of seeing culture from the perspective of its inhabitants, of seeing how culturally shaped selves use their culture to comprehend what they live for.[2]

Ikigai in this sense can serve as a means of understanding Japanese and American cultures in a fuller way. Writings about Japan sometimes seem to oppose a unitary Japanese culture to a unitary American culture, a distinct "other" as opposed to "self," "them" as opposed to "us." But this is illusory, I believe. As this book's accounts show, members of different cultures—two mothers worrying about their teenage children's college prospects, two young men dreaming large dreams shadowed by reality's constraints, or two old women battling life-threatening illnesses and wondering what fate awaits them beyond this world—may in their pursuit of *ikigai* resemble one another more than they resemble the vast majority of their own countrymen and women. This reflects the importance of personal factors such as gender, age, and religious belief in shaping the parallel formulations of *ikigai* for my pairs of Japanese and Americans. It also reflects the

2. As much as possible, I avoid technical theorizing in this book. Nonetheless, a few definitions, based in phenomenology, may be in order. I define *self* as "locus of consciousness," and I maintain that selves of different cultures, despite different cultural moldings, may be compared as physically separate consciousnesses experiencing the world in part through that separation. I define *society* as a "totality of linguistically and institutionally connected selves and their social creations, appearing to each self as the social world lying beyond self and its immediate others." I conceive of *culture* as "the multitude of processes through which selves shape society and society shapes selves within a given linguistic and institutional matrix." My definition of self, in particular, may raise the hackles of both postmodernists and ethnopsychologists, but because it allows me to make the most sense of the people I interviewed, I adhere to it steadfastly.

underlying commonality of Japan and the United States, two societies that are not simply cultural antipodes, but also parallel representatives of "late modernity," a parallel that each of my pairs illustrates in microcosm.

The final aim of this book is, once again, to explore the question, "What makes life worth living?" In this book I hope to offer, through the concept of *ikigai* and through a theory of late modern culture based in the self's pursuit of *ikigai,* a means of comprehending how Japanese and Americans make up the meanings of their lives. I am trying to link the social-scientific discipline of cultural anthropology to the larger existential questions of philosophical anthropology, questions bearing not just upon others in distant, exotic places, but upon you and me as well. What enables us to experience our lives as worth living? How shall we shape the meanings of our lives? These philosophical questions are socially and culturally rooted, and I believe cultural anthropology, as the intersubjective science of human beings, is most suited to address them.[3] In this book, I seek to make at least the rough beginnings of such an address.

3. The kind of philosophical anthropology I advocate is discussed from a social-scientific standpoint by Ernest Becker in *The Birth and Death of Meaning* (1971), and from a philosophical standpoint by Martin Buber in his essay "What is Man?" ([1938] 1965).

Chapter One

The Varieties of *Ikigai* in Japan

Ikigai in Japanese Print Media

While living in Japan during the 1980s, I often came across the word *ikigai*, a word that both intrigued and puzzled me. Japanese dictionaries define *ikigai* in such terms as *ikiru hariai, yorokobi, meate* (something to live for; the joy and goal of living) (*Nihongo daijiten* 1989, 96) and *ikite iru dake no neuchi, ikite iru kōfuku, rieki* (a life worth living, the happiness and benefit of being alive) (*Kōjien* 1986, 109).[1] David Plath (1980, 90) has provided a "rough gloss" of the question "What's your *ikigai?*" as "What is it that most makes you feel life is worth living?"[2] Japanese opinion surveys (for example Mita 1984, 59–66) indicate that Japanese men and women in their twenties tend to find their *ikigai* in leisure activities or in future dreams of work or marriage; men over thirty in work or in family and children; and most women over the age of thirty in family and children.

---

1. As these definitions imply, *ikigai* may be conceived of either as the "object" that makes one's life seem worth living (*ikigai taishō*)—one's work or family or dream—or as the feeling that life is worth living (*ikigai kan*), the former being the emphasis of this book. This distinction is made by many Japanese writers on *ikigai* (Kamiya 1980a, 15; Kobayashi 1989, 25; Sorita 1981, 20). The term *ikigai* seems to have rough counterparts in other languages: for example, the French *raison d'être* and *joie de vivre* seem roughly to parallel *ikigai taishō* and *ikigai kan*. But as Kamiya argues (1980a, 14–15), *ikigai* is less philosophical and more intuitive in its nuances than are comparable terms in Western languages.

2. Plath (1980, 90–91) and Lebra (1984, 162, 213, 216) discuss Japanese *ikigai* in English, in terms of the life course of the Japanese company employee (Plath) and the meaning of motherhood in Japan (Lebra).

But when I asked my Japanese friends what their *ikigai* was, they said that they had no idea. When I challenged one friend on his inability to respond to my question, he maintained that those people answering the *ikigai* surveys so positively didn't know what their *ikigai* really was. Work and family could never be real *ikigai*, he said; the only people with real *ikigai* were a few poets, and possibly Mother Teresa.

How can this discrepancy be explained? As I will show in this chapter, the opinion surveys and my friend's disparagement of those surveys reflect opposing conceptions of *ikigai* in Japan today and opposing views of how life should be lived.

The term *ikigai* is composed of three Chinese characters: 生（き）(*iki*) and 甲斐 (*kai*). At present, *kai* is generally written in *hiragana* (Japanese phonetic syllabery) to form 生きがい. *Iki* refers to "life"; *kai* is a suffix meaning roughly "the realization of what one expects and hopes for." The term has a long history, appearing as far back as the fourteenth-century *Taiheiki*, as well as in such early twentieth-century works as Natsume Sōseki's 1912 novel *Kōjin* (*Nihon kokugo daijiten* 1972, 658); but the contemporary Japanese works on *ikigai* that I've studied say little about the history of the term or about *ikigai* as conceived in the past. In the decades following World War II, there was considerable debate in the Japanese press as to "whether soldiers cried out for their mothers or invoked the name of the emperor as they lay dying" (Smith 1983, 36), debate, in our terms, as to whether these soldiers' *ikigai* (or *shinigai*: not "what one lives for" but "what one dies for") was rooted in nation and emperor or in their own mothers and wives. Some contemporary writers on *ikigai* argue that before the war *ikigai* was indeed rooted in emperor and nation and became privatized, rooted (for men) in the advancement of career and company, only after the war (Noda 1988, 23); but it's difficult to know the extent to which such a past was real or has been mythologized on the basis of a different present. The only *ikigai* survey data I've come across from this prewar period (surveys of young conscripts reporting for induction into the military in 1931 and 1940) indicate that for many their *ikigai* did lie in "sacrifice for the nation"

(Mita 1984, 57). But given the setting in which these surveys took place, their data seem suspect.

"In the period immediately after the war," writes Kamiya Mieko, "everyone was frantically searching for enough to eat. Probably no one had time to think about *ikigai*" (1980a, 273). It was only after Japan's economy had begun expanding and its standard of living rising that questions of *ikigai* began to be addressed; by the early 1970s, Kamiya was commenting on the "flood" of books and articles on *ikigai* (1980b, 11); a decade later, Sorita wrote of the "boom" in media discussions of *ikigai* (1981, 17–18). This interest in *ikigai* continues today. Bookstores may carry a dozen tracts on *ikigai;* during an eighteen-month period in 1989–90, the period of my Japanese research, four major newspapers—*Asahi Shinbun, Tōkyō Yomiuri Shinbun, Nihon Keizai Shinbun,* and *Hokkaidō Shinbun*—ran some fifty articles dealing in some way with *ikigai.*

Why this *ikigai* "boom"? One reason is the increase in life expectancy in Japan over the past fifty years, rendering problematic the lifelong adherence to *ikigai* such as work or family, one's company or one's children. At present, men's average life expectancy in Japan is 76.1 years, women's 82.1, both the longest in the world. From retirement, men have on average more than two decades left to live; women, following their youngest child's completion of school, have three decades or more (Misawa and Minami 1989, 215–17). What the elderly will do with these extra decades of life, how they will find something to live for, is a social problem of pressing importance in Japan. This is all the more so because of the gradual waning of the three-generational family as the norm—in 1960, 87 percent of elderly Japanese lived with a married son; by 1985, only 65 percent did (Misawa and Minami 1989, 221)—and also because of the great increase of the elderly in the Japanese population. "Until the middle of the 20th century only about 1 out of 20 Japanese was over age 60. Today [1983] the figure is more than 1 in 10; by the year 2000 it will be 1 in 5" (Plath 1983).

Reflecting this problem, twenty of the fifty newspaper articles about *ikigai* were on the *ikigai* of the elderly. Among other matters, these articles discuss company policies through which employees are aided in planning their postretirement *ikigai;* the creation of *ikigai* for the elderly through government employment, high technology, or counseling centers; seminars advocating that old people actively seek their own *ikigai;* and the strains old people may feel when bereft of *ikigai,* strains that may lead to suicide.

The problem of finding *ikigai* in old age is reflected in the plight of the *Shōwa hitoketa* men, those born in the first ten years of the Showa Era (1926–35). On the backs and work ethic of this generation, which reached adulthood in the decade after the war, the Japanese "economic miracle" was built; it is this generation which, as the mocking popular wisdom goes, "can't dance, can't speak English, only know how to follow orders, eat everything on their plates, and find their *ikigai* only in work" (Minami 1989, 118–19; also Plath 1980, 118). When these *Shōwa hitoketa* men retire, after forty years of devotion to nothing but work, what will they do with themselves? Can they find new *ikigai* by which to live, or will they only become *sodai gomi* ("oversize garbage" that a wife lugs to the curb to be taken away), *nure ochiba* ("wet fallen leaves" that stick fast however much the wife may try to sweep them away), or *washi otoko* ("me-too men," who insist on following their wives everywhere because they have nothing else to do)? The proliferation of scornful labels for retired, *ikigai*-bereft *Shōwa hitoketa* husbands illustrates the problem this generation of men is becoming for its wives, if not yet for Japanese society as a whole.

A second reason for the *ikigai* "boom" lies in Japan's affluence. The vertiginous transformation of Japan from utter poverty to unimaginable wealth is well illustrated by a passage from a 1990 *Newsweek* article on "Japan's Big Spenders":

One of the women at the Mitsukoshi diamond party [a party given by Mitsukoshi Department Store for its best jewelry customers]—she wore a ring worth nearly $7 million—had a sister who died of starvation in 1946. The wife of a real-estate entrepreneur, she still can't shake the idea that Japan's affluence is somehow ephemeral. As the Yomiuri Shimbun [*sic*] wrote, "It was only a decade ago when her life began to go up. Her husband makes money by selling land, but she often feels that someday these [paper yen notes] will again be worthless." Nowadays, when she can't sleep at night, "she stares at the ring and how it shines, and her fear slowly goes away." (Powell 1990)

For many, this affluence seems to have brought not only bemused amazement, but also a greater questioning. "Now that I have all the goods I've ever wanted, how shall I live?" Recent Japanese books discuss "the paradox of affluence" (Hirooka 1986) and "the psychopathology of affluence" (Ōhira 1990); television documentaries such as the *Shin Nihonjin no jōken* (Conditions of the new Japanese) series (NHK 1992) call for a reexamination of Japanese values.[3] Noda Masaaki (1990) has argued that as Japan becomes a mass-consumption society, people can no longer find the meaning of their lives in socially given goals such as getting promoted or raising children, but seek instead an individual meaning. This potential shift in values is reflected in the remaining thirty newspaper articles on *ikigai* that I collected.

These articles often conflict with *ikigai* surveys. Surveys indicate that many men find their *ikigai* in work,[4] but several articles indicate that *ikigai* as found in work is insufficient or even dangerous (for example, *Nihon Keizai Shinbun* 1990, reporting that work as *ikigai* can lead to psychological depression). According to surveys, women most often find *ikigai* in family and children, but several articles (for example, *Tōkyō Yomiuri Shinbun* 1989; 1990) argue that children should not be a mother's *ikigai*, but should be allowed to develop their own independence. Many articles discuss the creation of *ikigai* for old people by government agencies; but others (*Hokkaidō Shinbun* 1989b) hold that *ikigai* must be found by old people for themselves. Many articles discuss companies' efforts at *ikigai* planning for employees; others, however, ridicule this effort: "Why must play and hobbies be thought of within the framework of the company? Play is supposed to be the most individual of activities" (*Asahi Shinbun* 1990b).

---

3. Japan has been in economic recession in the four years since I conducted my research there, and the questioning brought by affluence seems at present muted. Over the long term, however, Japan's affluence will surely continue, as will too the questioning of *ikigai* that affluence brings with it.

4. In recent Japanese *ikigai* surveys, family often eclipses work as men's most widely held *ikigai*. My interpretation of this is that family as *ikigai* tends to indicate men's sense that they must devote themselves to work in order to support their families, rather than that they should be devoted to their families as opposed to work.

Ikigai as Commitment to Group
and as Self-realization

We thus see what seem to be contradictory conceptions of *ikigai*. For many months during my research, I couldn't specify what these conceptions were, until I found, in conflicting newspaper articles, labels exactly fitting them. The first article, *"Ikigai—jibun no kanōsei, kaikasaseru katei"* (*Ikigai:* the process of allowing the self's possibilities to blossom), by Kobayashi Tsukasa in *Nihon Keizai Shinbun*, 4 April 1990, makes this statement:

> Some people say, "My work is my *ikigai*." But these people are confusing *hatarakigai* [the sense that one's work is worth doing] with *ikigai* [the sense that one's life is worth living]. Some people hold that *gētobōru* ["gateball," croquet, the stereotypical pastime of old people in Japan] or raising chrysanthemums, or writing *haiku* is their *ikigai;* but that's just *asobigai* [play that is worth doing], not *ikigai* [life that is worth living]. Real *ikigai* is more than that. . . .
>
> People can feel real *ikigai* only when, on the basis of personal maturity, the satisfaction of various desires, love and happiness, encounters with others, and a sense of the value of life, they proceed toward self-realization [*jiko jitsugen*]. (Kobayashi 1990)

The key to Kobayashi's definition of *ikigai* in this passage is *jiko jitsugen*, the foreign-sounding translation of "self-realization" or "self-actualization" (Kobayashi cites Abraham Maslow, the key Western theorist of "self-actualization"). *Jiko jitsugen* is the label we will apply to the first of our two contrasting conceptions of *ikigai*.

The second article, appearing anonymously in *Nikkei Sangyō Shinbun*, 29 October 1990, is entitled *"Josei no kizoku ishiki, ikigai motome bunsangata ni"* (Women's sense of belonging: seeking *ikigai* in many areas). "Japan is said to be a country in which group consciousness is especially strong," the article begins. "As compared to men, who overwhelmingly tend to be 'company men,' what sense of belonging do women have?" The article then discusses survey data showing that although men tend to find their sense of belonging in work and family, women have more diverse sources of belonging, not only from family and work, but also "culture circles," sports clubs, and neighborhood associations. For our purposes, the importance of the article lies in its equation of the words *ikigai* and *ittaikan,* terms it uses interchangeably. *Ittaikan* means "sense of belonging to, sense of oneness with"; *ittaikan* is the term with which we will label our second conception of *ikigai.*

Ittaikan (sense of oneness with or commitment to group and role) and *jiko jitsugen* (self-realization) are the conflicting Japanese conceptions of *ikigai* through which we can understand my friend's comments reported at the beginning of this chapter: the surveys reflect *ittaikan* as *ikigai,* and my friend *jiko jitsugen.* These conflicting conceptions also help to explain the contradictions in the newspaper articles and surveys. If *ikigai* is *ittaikan,* then a wife and mother's *ikigai* should be the family of which she is a member, the children which, by her role in the family, it is her charge to nurture. A husband and father's *ikigai* should be the family it is his role to support and the work and company that enable him to do so. Companies should help plan their employees' present and future *ikigai;* because employees belong to their companies for much of their lives, their companies have the responsibility to provide them future loci of belongingness after they retire. The elderly, especially if they can no longer find belongingness in family, should strive to find belongingness in *gēto-bōru* (croquet) groups or in old people's recreation centers.

If, however, *ikigai* is *jiko jitsugen,* then *ikigai* as work for the company is suspect, for that work is unlikely to have been an occupation that is one's true calling; true *ikigai* can't be found in serving simply as a cog in the corporate machine. *Ikigai* can perhaps be found by a woman or man in family and children if one's true fulfillment as a human being comes from nurturing one's family, but not, for example, if a woman is immersed only in the social role of mother. *Ikigai* can't be found in hobbies; something like tea ceremony could be one's *ikigai* only if one were to devote one's life to it rather than practicing it as a pastime. Companies can't provide *ikigai;* indeed, nothing outside the self can provide *ikigai.* In short, while *ikigai* as *ittaikan* carries with it the premise that selves are most essentially their social roles, *ikigai* as *jiko jitsugen* carries with it the premise that there is an underlying self more essential than social role.

Ikigai as *ittaikan* is most fully expressed (although he doesn't use the term *ittaikan*) in a book by the Buddhist religious leader Niwano

Nikkyō, *Ningen no ikigai* (Human *ikigai*), published in 1969 and now in its sixteenth printing. Family is the most common Japanese *ikigai,* holds Niwano, but the family should be a place not only for "consumption" and relaxation, but also for "production," responsibility, and self-sacrifice (1969, 103–5). "The husband should work to support his family; the wife should maintain the home, help her husband, and raise the children—this is how they . . . can be most fulfilled" (130–31).

No work is trivial, writes Niwano; any work can be *ikigai;* one simply needs to look at the larger picture to see its true significance. "Just as swimmers and runners can strive to improve their records, so too can the ordinary worker strive to improve his efficiency . . . and thereby create *ikigai* in his work" (204). "Ideally everyone [i.e., every man] should find *ikigai* in work" (166); however, those who cannot find *ikigai* in work should strive to find a leisure activity that will provide *ikigai* (170). Niwano tells of a government official who worked as a little-league baseball umpire and found his *ikigai* in that way, as well as of amateur astronomers who discovered new comets, finding *ikigai* in that pursuit (171–74). The elderly especially should attempt to find *ikigai* in being useful to others, in "doing for others rather than in having things done for them" (233). If, however, there is no work or service to be performed, no family to aid, there is at very least one's hobby to be developed as *ikigai* (248). "A beautiful society," concludes Niwano, "is one in which everyone sacrifices self for the good of society" (266); the way to find *ikigai*, Niwano holds, is to use up oneself for others (269).

If Niwano emphasizes the group over the individual, self-sacrifice over self-expression in his conception of *ikigai*, Kamiya Mieko, in her *Ikigai ni tsuite* (About *ikigai*), first published in 1966, reissued in 1980, and now in its twelfth printing, emphasizes the exact opposite. Kamiya, a Christian and a physician well known in Japan for her many books, holds that *ikigai* cannot be found merely by adapting oneself to a social role: "However good a mother you may appear to be in others' eyes, if you act as a mother only from custom or duty . . . being a mother cannot be your real *ikigai*" (1980a, 80). Indeed, "Some people seek their *ikigai* in deliberately destroying social stability . . . in throwing aside social position to become missionaries or in leaving their families to become adventurers in foreign lands" (52). *Ikigai,* she writes, is that which gives one a true sense of life satisfaction; it is pursued not for utility but for its own intrinsic fascination, and it is absolutely individual (79–81).

Kamiya's conception of *ikigai* is colored by her readings of existentialism. "Without being conscious of it," she writes, "people ceaselessly question themselves through all their experiences as to what their lives really mean. . . . If they cannot justify their lives . . . they cannot feel *ikigai*" (74–75). Finally, Kamiya seems to say, the essential human question is how one finds *ikigai* in a world of suffering and death. For Kamiya, the ability to confront death, realizing that money, fame, and attachments all must vanish, enables one to live with a sense of truly being alive (158–59).

Kobayashi Tsukasa's *"Ikigai" to wa nanika* (What is *"ikigai"?*) is in a sense Kamiya's work updated, but with a more combative tone vis-à-vis the norms of conventional Japanese society. Kobayashi, a psychiatrist at Sophia University's Institute of Counseling, tells his readers that a man who is merely a "work robot"—as are most of Japan's company workers, he would say—has not really lived, as he may find out on his deathbed (1989, 11, 20). Many company workers believe their work is their *ikigai,* but such beliefs, argues Kobayashi, are an illusion: "[Company employees] work hard, but they close their eyes to self-realization. They believe that their work is self-realization, but that is a misunderstanding. They are confident that their work supports their families, their companies, Japan, but when they retire it will make no difference to their companies—all many of these employees have been contributing to in their work is an increase in pollution" (53).

If most work can't serve as *ikigai,* neither can most hobbies: "You cannot simply say that . . . your *ikigai* is writing *haiku.* If, like Masaoka Shiki [famed nineteenth-century *haiku* poet], you quit college for the sake of *haiku,* and then, while struggling with tuberculosis and dying at thirty-six, still manage to leave behind a fabulous record of *haiku*—only then can you say that your *ikigai* is *haiku*" (216). Kobayashi does hold that family can be a valid *ikigai*—he writes of himself, "if it weren't for the love of my family and friends, my *ikigai* would vanish and maybe I would commit suicide" (214)—but the basis of that *ikigai* too is threatened, he implies, by contemporary Japanese values. Despite Japan's wealth, most people don't feel happy, Kobayashi asserts, because they try to attain happiness through material acquisitions rather than through freedom of the spirit, without which true *ikigai* can never be found (168).

These books, with their opposing conceptions of *ikigai*, show other contrasts as well. It's perhaps not coincidence that Niwano, the co-founder of a popular Buddhist religious organization (Risshō Kōsei-kai) in prewar Japan, uses no Western references (indeed, no references at all) and conceives of *ikigai* entirely in terms of the self's contribution to the group, whereas Kamiya, a Western-educated Christian, and Kobayashi, a psychiatrist, cite more Western than Japanese references and think of *ikigai* entirely in individualistic terms.

In their different conceptions of *ikigai*, these authors seem to have very different conceptions of the kind of society that Japan should become. Niwano's vision is of a democratic Japan (1969, 108), but one in which not the individual but the group is foremost, the individual unhesitatingly sacrificing himself for the ends of his group and his society. Kobayashi and Kamiya's vision is of a Japan in which the individual can pursue self-realization unimpeded by pressure to conform, a Japan which allows the individual primacy over the group. To put this contrast in starkest terms, if Niwano describes an idealized prewar Japan, one with discipline but without militarism and secret police, Kobayashi envisions a sanitized America, without crime, drugs, and cynicism, where people pursue their dreams free of society's coercion.

Ikigai in Japan's Present and Future

Through their words, these writers are attempting to bring to reality their different visions of Japan's future. Indeed, our two conceptions of *ikigai*, *ittaikan* and *jiko jitsugen*, are battling it out in Japanese media and minds over the direction of that future.

These different conceptions are apparent in the people I interviewed, each discussing with me for six hours or so *ikigai* in the context of work, family, life history, and religious belief. *Jiko jitsugen* is the concept of *ikigai* most forcefully advocated in today's Japanese print media, but the concept of *ikigai* that many of those I interviewed leaned toward was *ittaikan*. A wife and mother in her sixties (Murakami-san in chapter 5) said that "my *ikigai* has been my husband since I married him, and will be until I die"; a bank employee in his forties (Miyamoto-san in chapter 4) asserted that "my *ikigai* is my work. . . . I can't separate myself from Asahi Bank: I am what I am because of Asahi Bank, Asahi Bank is what it is because of me." A smaller number of those I spoke with held to *jiko jitsugen* as the form of their *ikigai*: as a company worker in his forties (Takagi-san in chapter 4) said, "My work can't be my *ikigai*. . . . My wife [and children] can't be my *ikigai* either. . . . I want to have an *individual purpose* to my existence! That's the ideal; if I look at my own life, it's far from that ideal."

But the majority of the Japanese I interviewed seemed to think of their *ikigai* neither as *ittaikan* nor as *jiko jitsugen,* but as ambiguously balanced in between. A housewife of forty (Wada-san in chapter 4) told me, "Since I got married, my family has been my *ikigai*. Being for my family is being for myself and being for myself is being for my family. I guess I sound like a very average person! . . . I've got to grow as an individual!" A company worker in his twenties said, "I guess this work is my *ikigai*. I have dreams—I'd like to win the lottery. But realistically. . . ." A rock musician turned construction worker told me, "I like myself because I'm working hard to support my family. But I hate myself for giving up my dream, my music. It's half and half."

Only one of the Japanese I interviewed claimed to have read about *ikigai* except in passing (she had read Kamiya Mieko's book), but most were well aware of *ittaikan* and *jiko jitsugen,* if not of these terms, then of the ideals of living for self or for group. For the most part, however, they did not align themselves entirely with either ideal but lived in a state of tension between them. This tension can be understood through considering the relation of self to society in Japan.

Anthropologists have written extensively about the Japanese self as group-oriented or sociocentric. Lebra, for example, writes that "the Japanese individual seems to feel really alive only when in a group" (1976, 27); "the individual Japanese is not a self-sufficient, autonomous whole but a fraction constituting a part of the whole" (105). Hamaguchi coins a new term for the Japanese self, *kanjin*, a person whose identity is located in the linkages between self and others, as opposed to the Western *kojin*, whose identity is located within one's autonomous self (Hamaguchi 1982, 1985).

As the accounts in this book indicate, Japanese do possess selves that are "not entirely sociocentric" (Smith 1991). If Japanese selves were entirely sociocentric, Kamiya's and Kobayashi's arguments would make no sense to their readers, and it would be difficult to understand how some of the Japanese I interviewed could have so fervently proclaimed their ideal of "self-realization." But Japanese sociocentrism, a sense of self as defined by its relation to others, was also apparent in the words of most of the Japanese I interviewed. This sociocentrism may be in part an intrinsic outgrowth of Japanese language and culture, but also in part the product of Japanese institutions—family, schools, companies—that serve to mold and polish selves to be sociocentric, a molding and polishing that most Japanese seem to accept but that some may resist.

In his discussion of "order in Japanese society," Rohlen notes (citing William Caudill) that whereas American mothers "generally regard the child as born dependent and therefore to be raised to greater independence," Japanese mothers are "inclined to view the child as born asocial with the implied goal of child-rearing to be teaching the child to integrate with others, to become social" (1989, 18); child-rearing patterns proceed accordingly (19–20). Early schooling, with its stress on *shūdan seikatsu* (group living), continues this emphasis, as do Japanese institutions throughout the first decades of life. As Rohlen writes,

> If we look closely at the developmental cycle, we find at every stage from nursery school to early employment the same basic routines reiterated and the same social lessons repeated time and again. Shared housekeeping chores, dress codes, group discussions, patterns of group assembly and movement . . . are relearned at each new entry point. . . . Emphasis is always on standardizing the basic practices and on understanding their moral implications in the context of *shūdan seikatsu*. (27)

The model of this social ordering is the family; however, "among adults attachment is rarely as certain or as complete as it is between parents and children" (31), and enormous efforts are made by companies to create and sustain senses of primary attachment among their employees (Rohlen 1974). Sometimes these efforts involve explicit psychological remolding of selves. Reynolds discusses Naikan therapy, whereby the patient is enjoined to remember all the sacrifices that mother, father, teachers, and employers have made on his or her behalf, and thus to feel a renewed sense of gratitude toward them. Not surprisingly, employers sometimes send their employees to this therapy. While sympathetic to Naikan, Reynolds notes the graffiti scrawled and carved in the treatment areas where patients are left to reflect on their lives: "Completely boring. . . . This kind of crap is unbelievable" (1983, 32). Kondo describes an "Ethics School" to which the owner of the factory where she did her fieldwork sent his employees. Although impressed by the persuasiveness of its training, Kondo sees it as engaged in "the disciplinary production of selves" (1990, 112), a "production" that would not be necessary if there wasn't resistance to the "factory as family" ideology the owner was attempting to instill.

There is an ongoing debate among students of Japan as to whether order in Japanese society can best be explained through a "cultural" model or an "authoritarian" one (Rohlen 1989, 9). Does order emerge primarily "from the bottom up" (from individuals' internalized cultural molding, which they view as "natural," intrinsic to themselves) or "from the top down" (from institutions' external coercion, which individuals view as extrinsic to themselves)? Lebra and Hamaguchi, as well as, implicitly, Smith (1983, 74, 81) and Kondo (1990, 26–33), seem to adhere to a "bottom-up" model in their discussions of an intrinsically sociocentric Japanese self. Sugimoto and Mouer (1982) adhere to a "top-down" model, arguing that Japan is not intrinsically group-oriented, but a controlled society in which the individual must conform to the group or be crushed.

There is a clear link between *ikigai* as *ittaikan* and the cultural, "bottom-up" model of Japanese order. To the extent that the cultural model of Japanese "sociocentrism" describes today's Japan, "commitment to group" will be the dominant form of *ikigai*. Because selves have been enculturated to be sociocentric, they articulate their *ikigai* as "commitment to group." This is an underlying assumption of Niwano's book. There is also a clear link between *ikigai* as *jiko jitsugen* and the authoritarian, "top-down" model of Japanese order. To the extent that Japanese sociocentrism is seen not as "natural" enculturation but as coerced conformity, "self-realization" will beckon as the promise of personal freedom in an unfree social world. This view is an underlying assumption of Kamiya's and especially Kobayashi's books. That the majority of those I interviewed seem committed to neither conception of *ikigai* but to rest uncertainly between them may indicate the partial validity of both models of Japanese social order. The reality of Japanese life today, as conceived of by those I interviewed, may lie in the conjunction of and tension between these models.

But Japan may now be undergoing a historic shift in its conceptions of *ikigai* and of how best to live. Apparently, the postwar decades of rebuilding Japan were most conducive to a definition of *ikigai* as *ittaikan,* but as Japan became more affluent, some began to question the ideal of living for the group, and a new conception of *ikigai* emerged, that of *ikigai* as *jiko jitsugen.* As of this writing, the newer definition seems to be "winning" in Japanese articles and books: *ikigai* as self-realization is advocated far more than *ikigai* as commitment to group. But as I have noted, most of those I interviewed did not formulate their *ikigai* in terms of *jiko jitsugen;* for many, *ikigai* was a matter of playing their roles at work and in family, despite ambiguities they felt about "commitment to group," and despite what the latest books say about "self-realization." How can we interpret this discrepancy?

One possibility is that there is a "lag time" between the ideas set forth in books and articles and the ideas of people in their workplaces and living rooms. Most adults, having grown up in a Japan in which *ittaikan* was an essential value, don't recognize *jiko jitsugen,* but perhaps they will. Perhaps the younger generation will serve as the bearer of *jiko jitsugen* as a new definition of *ikigai* and a new Japanese value. Writers such as Sengoku (1991), Hirooka (1986), Shimizu (1987), and Ōhira (1990) argue that affluence, for better or worse, really is creating a new Japan, weakening the earlier emphasis on work and production and increasing the emphasis on leisure, consumption, and self-realization, perhaps leading to a Japanese future very different from its recent past.

Another possibility is that the books and articles touting *jiko jitsugen* will continue to have little relevance to most people's lives. Social critics may write of self-realization, but most people will go on living, whether by choice or by coercion, on the basis of belonging to the group. In 1990, the Suntory Company ran an advertisement asking readers to send in their dreams of what they would most like to do in their lives; Suntory promised to fund and film the most interesting such dream. The irony is that although the lucky winner had his or her dream realized and publicized, the employees of Suntory, as of other companies, no doubt continued to work long hours under close supervision, living lives far from the "self-realization" so alluringly depicted in the advertisement. Perhaps these two contradictory conceptions of *ikigai* will continue to coexist in all their tension, *jiko jitsugen* connoting, for most Japanese, alluring, dangerous, all-but-unrealizable dreams, *ittaikan* the quotidian, safe, all-but-inescapable reality.

Chapter Two

Individualism, Community, and Conformity in the United States

American Print Media Equivalents to Japanese *Ikigai*

There are, in American English, no exact linguistic equivalents to *ikigai*. But there are cultural equivalents—phrases used in American print media roughly equivalent to the way *ikigai* is used in Japanese print media. Phrases such as "a life worth living" or "that which makes life seem worth living" hardly ever appear in American print media, but phrases such as "meaning" or "meaning of life" do appear, as in such recent books as Viktor Frankl's *Man's Search for Meaning* ([1959] 1984), A. J. Ayer's *Meaning of Life* (1990), Roy Baumeister's *Meanings of Life* (1991), and Jacob Needleman's *Money and the Meaning of Life* (1991). These books discuss "meaning of life" in two different ways. Ayer and Needleman deal with *the* meaning of life, a meaning presumably applying to the human condition as a whole. Frankl and Baumeister deal with *one's own* meaning of life, in terms resembling those in Japanese discussions of *ikigai*. Frankl describes "meaning of life" as unique and individual, just as Kamiya describes *ikigai*, and Baumeister examines "meaning of life" as found in work and love, corresponding to *ikigai* as depicted in Japanese surveys.

These books show that the idea of *ikigai* may be applicable to the

United States, but it seems that "meaning of life" can't serve as an American equivalent to the Japanese *ikigai*. *Ikigai* is a confusing term for many Japanese. "What's your *ikigai?*" is a question that puzzled my friends, as noted in the last chapter, but as our interviews proceeded, all Japanese I interviewed were able to answer the question. However, when I asked the Americans I interviewed, "What, for you, is the meaning of your life?" they were unable to answer (and in several cases were reduced to talking about the comedy group Monty Python, whose movie *The Meaning of Life* was for them the main connotation of the phrase). This isn't because the Americans I interviewed were uninterested in "meaning of life"—sales of books such as Frankl's show that millions of Americans are indeed interested—but because "meaning of life" seemed for them abstract and difficult to formulate; it lacked the practical connotations that *ikigai* had for many of the Japanese I spoke with.

I thus abandoned this question as a means of getting at "American *ikigai*." Instead, I learned to ask, "What relationship, activity, pursuit, or dream is most important to you in your life? What do you feel is the center of your life? What most makes your life seem worth living?" The Americans responded to these questions almost exactly as the Japanese responded to "What's your *ikigai?*" Nonetheless, these questions do not correspond to any American cultural equivalent to *ikigai;* they don't have the cultural specificity and salience that *ikigai* has for Japanese.

But this doesn't mean that Americans and Japanese can't be compared as to their enculturated conceptions of what makes life worth living. Several of the first dozen Americans I interviewed mentioned books that had shaped their senses of their lives, such as Gail Sheehy's *Passages* (1977), Robert Bellah and his coauthors' *Habits of the Heart* (1986), and M. Scott Peck's *The Road Less Traveled* (1978). Reading these books, I found that they show the same dichotomy as Japanese books and articles on *ikigai:* Sheehy and Peck advocate "self-realization" over "commitment to group and role"; Bellah et al. advocate "commitment to community" over "self-realization." In the United States, then, conflicting conceptions of "how one should live" parallel the conflicting conceptions that define *ikigai* in Japan.

In chapter 1, our investigation into *ikigai* led us to *jiko jitsugen* and *ittaikan*. In this chapter, we begin rather than end with American conceptions of "self-realization" and "commitment." The analyses in these two chapters will help us in part 2 to understand the different cultural vocabularies used by individual Japanese and Americans in comprehending their lives as lives worth living.

Individualism, Community, and Conformity, 1950–1990

In the United States, the tension between individual and group, between "individualism" and "conformity" for one who favors the individual, "individualism" and "community" for one who favors the group, has been noted by Tocqueville and by observers of American culture ever since. "The citizen of the United States is taught from infancy to rely upon his own exertions in order to resist the evils and the difficulties of life; he looks upon the social authority with an eye of mistrust and anxiety," wrote Tocqueville ([1835] 1990, 191), and yet "I know of no country in which there is so little independence of mind . . . as in America. . . . It seems at first sight as if all the minds of the Americans were formed upon one model, so accurately do they follow the same route" (263, 267). Robert Lynd wrote in 1939 that an "outstanding assumption in American life" was that "Individualism, 'the survival of the fittest,' is the law of nature and the secret of America's greatness; and restrictions on individual freedom are un-American and kill initiative. *But:* No man should live for himself alone; for people ought to be loyal and stand together and work for common purposes" ([1939] 1967, 60). More recently, William O. Beeman has found two underlying principles of American advertising: (a) be independent and (b) conform: "Every time we choose one brand of liquid detergent or motor oil over another, we are subtly being told both: 'you are unique and special' and 'you are in the company of the millions of others who choose this' " (1986, 64).

As these commentators all imply, one cannot think of individualism in American culture apart from community; the two are in dialectical relation (Varenne 1977). In social-scientific and popular analyses of American culture over the past few decades, one can see this dialectic as a pendulum that swings back and forth between emphasis on "individualism" and on "conformity"/"community." Analyses in the 1950s tended to emphasize the loss of individualism in conformity, in the 1960s and 1970s the glories of individual self-realization over all else, and in the late 1970s and 1980s the need to abandon hypertrophic individualism and return to a sense of community. Let me now discuss a few of these works.[1]

David Riesman et al.'s *The Lonely Crowd* (first published in 1950) and William H. Whyte Jr.'s *The Organization Man* (first published in 1956) depicted a shift in American culture and character in the postwar era, from (as their works were popularly interpreted) individualism to conformity. Riesman and his coauthors held that the basic mode of conformity was shifting in American society from "inner-direction," in which "conformity is insured by [the] tendency to acquire early in life an internalized set of goals" to "other-direction," in which "conformity is insured by [the] tendency to be sensitized to the expectations and preferences of others" (1953, 23). In this new world, the internal mode of social control shifts from "gyroscope" to "radar" (42), as the source of authority becomes not one's internalized parents but one's peer group and, behind it, the mass media (37, 106). *The Lonely Crowd* was mostly written as neutral social science, but many of the book's readers—it was a surprise bestseller—saw it as advocating an earlier, inner-directed individualism as opposed to the oppressive other-directed conformity of America in the mid-twentieth century.

Whyte argued that "a major shift in American ideology" was taking place: the Protestant Ethic was being transformed into the Social Ethic, "that contemporary body of thought which makes morally legitimate the pressures of society against the individual" (1957, 7). The Social Ethic includes the "belief in 'belongingness' as the ultimate need of the individual" (7); 'the organization man' adheres to this ethos as a justification for his existence, Whyte held, and is molded to it through business-oriented education, corporate norms,

---

1. American media are vast and complex; from each of these decades, books can be found that are opposite in emphasis from those I discuss. I choose the books I discuss because these seem to have most influenced American conceptions of individual and group over the past forty years; they seem most accurately to have captured the spirit of the decades in which they were written.

and a suburban community life mirroring at home the norms of the corporate workplace. Whyte's conclusions were modulated—"I do not . . . intend this book as a censure of the fact of organization society" (12)—but unmistakable: the individual "must *fight* The Organization" (448).

These two books describe what may have been the main American social current of their age. After the wrenching upheavals of the Great Depression and World War II, many Americans embraced the security offered by large organizations and built their lives around the principle of "fitting in" to their group. At the same time, however, these books owed their influence to what their readers saw as their rejection of that new American world; many read them as laments for lost American individualism.

Some of what was written in *The Lonely Crowd* and *The Organization Man* rings true forty years later: certainly the myth of the individual free of the constraints of large institutions is even more distant from American social reality now than it was forty years ago. For the most part, however, Riesman's and especially Whyte's analyses seem to describe an American world very different from that of today. Whyte described the young executive's litany as "be loyal to the company and the company will be loyal to you" (143). The *New York Times* recently reported on an executive whose father had worked for the same company for fifty years but who was himself recently laid off, telling his college-age son, "Forget about . . . loyalty. They're not going to be loyal to you. Don't be loyal to them" (Barringer 1992). In their book, *The New Individualists: The Generation after "The Organization Man"* (1991), Leinberger and Tucker interviewed the children of the men Whyte had interviewed and found that they had rejected the organizational ethos of their fathers to pursue their own paths to fulfillment. Difficult economic times have rendered this pursuit an unaffordable luxury for many, who now struggle to make a living with far less security and affluence than their parents enjoyed.

Indeed, although I interviewed many American corporate employees, I interviewed no one describing a world of "belongingness" such as Whyte depicted. If Whyte's book describes any society today, it's not the United States but Japan: many of the Japanese company workers I interviewed discussed enforced corporate "belongingness" in almost exactly the same terms that Whyte used. Why does Whyte's account from the American 1950s seem applicable to Japan today? An answer is suggested by the first two pairs of accounts in part 2. The Americans spent their youth in worlds resembling Whyte's, which in subsequent years dramatically shifted in their cultural premises; the Japanese, on the other hand, have lived in worlds that seem to have retained group-oriented cultural premises over the decades spanning their childhoods and their middle-aged adulthoods.

In the early 1950s, at roughly the same time that Whyte was describing the submergence of the individual in the group in America, psychologists such as Abraham Maslow were formulating a new "humanistic psychology" advocating individual growth over all else. The ultimate state of being, for Maslow, is "self-actualization": "the desire to become . . . everything that one is capable of becoming," in accordance with one's own internal genius (1970, 46).

Maslow's work had little immediate influence, but with the emergence of the American counterculture in the 1960s, ideas such as his came to be seen as promising individual salvation from the corruption of American institutions. This is apparent in Charles A. Reich's immensely popular *The Greening of America* (1970). Against "the impoverishment of life, the irrationality, violence, and claustrophobia of the American Corporate State" (218), the young, "emerg[ing] out of the wasteland of the Corporate State like flowers pushing up through the concrete pavement" (394–95), offer "a recovery of self" (5). For corporate consciousness, "society [and] . . . institutions [are] . . . the primary reality," but in the consciousness of the young, "the individual self is the only true reality" (225). For Reich, this unfettered individual self was America's great hope.

In the 1970s, this "recovery of the self" became the charge not of the oppressed young but of oppressed women (Ehrenreich 1983, 99–116). One of the most influential popular books in the "feminist self-realization" movement was Gail Sheehy's *Passages,* first published in 1976. Sheehy's "passages" in the lifecourse bear a psychological telos that she termed "gaining our authenticity": "the arrival at that felicitous state of inner expansion in which we know of all our potentialities and possess the ego strength to direct their full reach" (1977, 48–49). What this pursuit of authenticity meant, for Sheehy, was that the search for one's true self takes precedence over the playing of social roles such as "breadwinner" or "wife" (358); one must move "out of roles and into the self" (364). "Growing in tandem is virtually impossible in a patriarchal society, as ours has been," Sheehy writes (129), and goes on to wonder if divorce might not even be required in order to grow (208). Sheehy's ideal was the individual who doesn't become "stagnant," but who continues to grow, taking on new marriages and careers to foster that growth.

Whyte described an American world in which the group, the organization, took precedence over the individual. For Sheehy, on the other hand, not only did the individual take precedence over the group, but all commitments to group and role should be sundered if they do not further the self's growth into authenticity. This emphasis on self-realization continues to the present. To take just one of many examples, M. Scott Peck's *The Road Less Traveled* (1978)—a book that as of this writing has remained on the *New York Times* paperback bestseller list for the past ten years—holds that "the ultimate goal of life remains the spiritual growth of the individual" (168), with commitments to others being valid only if they foster such growth.

The focus on self in these books is hardly new in American culture. Self-realization, broadly construed, has long been an American goal, whether through religious salvation (as in the writings of Jonathan Edwards) or secular success (as in the writings of Benjamin Franklin). What is new is the discussion of self-realization in psychological terms. The idea that the self is the ultimate reality, its psychological fulfillment life's highest goal, can be glimpsed in the writings of Emerson, among others, but it was not until the 1970s that this idea was embraced by millions of Americans, as the bestseller lists over the past two decades indicate. Why might this have come to pass?

Social critics offer a number of explanations. Yankelovich (1982) notes how the traditional "giving/getting compact" of working hard and sacrificing one's pursuit of pleasure in return for a stable job and family life and a rising standard of living, gave way in the 1960s and 1970s to the idea of self-fulfillment apart from commitments to others. He attributes this to the booming American economy of this era, a time during which many Americans believed their affluence to be a natural birthright. Wolfe offers a similar view: "The saga of the Me

Decade [the 1970s] begins with . . . the thirty-year boom" beginning in the 1940s, which "has pumped money into every class level of the population on a scale without parallel in any country in history," enabling Americans to engage en masse in what Wolfe sees as the traditional aristocratic luxury of doting on the self (1983, 272, 277). Leinberger and Tucker argue that those born in the two decades after World War II, "reared in the purely expressive arena of the family, educated in schools that emphasized self-expression, and ex-horted to self-gratification by the media," formed the first American generation to "worship the self" (1991, 236, 239).

But the American emphasis has again shifted. Although books ad-vocating self-realization continue to find a wide audience, this pursuit was emphatically rejected in a number of influential books in the late 1970s and 1980s. In 1976, the same year that *Passages* was first published, Philip Slater noted that "individualistic thinking is . . . built upon the absurd assumption that the individual can be consid-ered separately from the environment of which he or she is a part" (1976, 15). This theme was elaborated upon by Christopher Lasch, in *The Culture of Narcissism* (1979).

Lasch argued that the narcissistic personality, fearful of all com-mitments and concerned only with the self and the attention that others pay it, has become dominant in American society. "The Ameri-can cult of friendliness conceals . . . a murderous competition for goods and position," a competition that "has grown more savage in an age of diminishing expectations" (1979, 124). Therapy, which has "established itself as the successor both to rugged individualism and to religion" (42), is how people attempt to escape this struggle: "Hav-ing no hope of improving their lives in . . . ways that matter, people have convinced themselves that what matters is psychic self-improve-ment" (29). "In a dying culture, narcissism appears to embody—in the guise of personal 'growth' and 'awareness'—the highest attain-ment of spiritual enlightenment" (396).

Lasch's argument was a reversal of Whyte's: rather than individu-als swallowed up in worship of the group, Lasch depicted individuals swallowed up in worship of the self. It seems difficult to believe that over a scant twenty years the United States could really have shifted as profoundly as these analyses seem to indicate. Nonetheless, there does seem to have been a basic shift in American cultural valuations of individual and group between 1956 and 1979, a shift that gave these works, with their opposite messages, such popular resonance.

A more restrained analysis of shifting American conceptions in the late 1970s was that of Daniel Yankelovich, who argued that, as opposed to an American ethic of self-denial in the 1950s and one of self-fulfillment in the 1960s and 1970s, a new ethic was emerging in the 1980s: "an ethic of commitment" (1982, 10). "In the postwar era it was widely assumed that the problems of production were solved and that the national task was simply to consume as much as we could. Inevitably, the emphasis on consumption led to a heightened concern with self—the ultimate object of consumer values" (43). In the 1970s, however, the growth of the American economy began to slow, and American standards of living began to suffer. "What happens," Yankelovich asks, "when the fabled growth machine begins to falter at the very moment that the population's . . . expectations have reached unprecedented heights?" (171). The clash of the psychology of affluence with an economy of restriction necessitated a "stepping off Maslow's escalator," a turning away from the self to a new ethic of "commitment to . . . the world" (231–40, 247).

The timing of Yankelovich's speculation was remarkably bad—the Reagan 1980s were hardly noted for the sense of social commitment they engendered in Americans' lives. Rather, "in the face of a shrinking economy, Americans grew ever more willing to mortgage the future in order to sustain the illusion of affluence, as debt—personal, corporate, and federal—climbed to staggering levels" (Leinberger and Tucker 1991, 272). But the yearning for commitment continued, as shown by the impact of Robert Bellah and his coauthors' 1985 book *Habits of the Heart.*

Americans, these authors argued, are incapable of speaking of commitment for its own sake, so strong is the hold of individualism upon our thinking. Our religious and moral beliefs are culturally rendered no more than personal preferences, unlinked to any standard greater than the self: "The meaning of one's life for most Americans is to become one's own person, almost to give birth to oneself . . . but what the ever freer and more autonomous self is free *for* only grows more obscure" (1986, 82). The contradiction of contemporary American individualism, *Habits of the Heart* argued, is that although Americans have trouble articulating it, the desire to share their lives with others in community remains unabated. The book concludes with a call to return to conceptions of the common good, to a "reconstituting [of] the social world" (286).

Habits of the Heart continues to be widely read today, its message perhaps appropriate to a 1990s era that has been called a "hangover" to the "30-year experiment in desublimation" of the 1960s, 1970s, and 1980s (historian Fred Siegel, quoted in Klein 1992, 19). As a *Newsweek* article recently summed up those decades,

Self-actualizing liberals have been obsessed with personal freedom to the point of self-immolation; predatory conservatives have been obsessed with commercial freedom to the point of pillage. . . . "Greed is good" was the '80s analogue to the '60s' "Do your own thing" (and the '70s' "You *can* have it all"). Many of the icons of the Reagan boom are now bankrupt or on parole. Their most visible legacy is the $4 trillion national debt that stands as a metaphor for the *moral* deficit incurred during the nation's 30–year spree. (Klein 1992, 19–20)

This moral deficit can be alleviated, the article holds, only through a return to commitment to others. But the problem with this conclusion, and with Bellah and his coauthors' vision of a new ethic of working for the common good, is that after decades of the pursuit of self, where is any basis for a common good to be found? A number of recent Christian books (Baldwin 1988; Wilson 1990; Swindoll 1991) offer a vision of ordered community in which child is to be obedient to parents, wife to husband, employee to employer, citizen to civil authorities, worshiper to church authorities, and most importantly, believer to God. But many, perhaps most Americans today, are not Christians in the mold of these works. The United States is a society of Christians, agnostics, and New-Agers, feminists and housewives, liberals and conservatives, of whites, blacks, Hispanics, and Asians, men and women, young and old, each seemingly with their own agenda. How is such a heterogeneous mix of peoples and values to come together to work for a *common* good? To the extent that this question remains unanswered, "community" must remain a chimera.

Individual, Group, and Change
in the United States and Japan

American print media and perhaps American culture at large thus seem to have moved, in decade-long swings of the pendulum, between emphasis on individual self-realization and emphasis on community; the same seems true in Japan, albeit with different timings. Underlying these pendular swings, however, there still seems to be a persistent cultural emphasis in the United States on the individual and in Japan on the group. In chapter 1 we saw that while "self-realization" is much discussed in Japanese media at present, it may be difficult to attain within Japanese society. By the same token, "community" seems much discussed in American media at present but difficult to attain within American society. Indeed, if in Japan "self-realization" seems the all-but-impossible dream and "commitment to group" the quotidian reality, in the United States, "commitment" and "community" seem the alluring dream, individual separateness the everyday reality. This is reflected in the words of the Americans I spoke with.

Only a few seemed to believe in the pursuit of self over all commitments to others advocated by Sheehy; only a few held to community as a ⌈panacea⌋ as thoroughly as did Bellah and his colleagues. Most comprehended their lives through a balance of the pursuit of self and commitments to others (particularly to family), ideas often in conflict in their minds. "I do love my family," a woman in her fifties told me. "But part of me wishes I'd made something of myself." A woman in her forties (Ms. Pratt in chapter 4) said, "I'm absolutely dedicated to my children. . . . [But] the center of my life is how I am as a human being. . . . It's sort of 'to thine own self be true.' " A man of thirty (Mr. Isaacs in chapter 5) said, "It's unlikely that I'd give up my dream" of quitting his work and pursuing his calling. "But my priorities may change as I have kids." The Americans I spoke with formed a spectrum between ideals of "self-realization" and "commitment," with those in the middle often alternating between these conceptions in interpreting their lives.

But underlying my informants' declarations of what they lived for, most Americans I interviewed seemed to comprehend their lives within a frame of taken-for-granted "individualism," as most Japanese seemed to comprehend their lives within a frame of taken-for-granted "groupism" (Lebra 1984, 294–95). I discussed in chapter 1 how anthropologists often depict the Japanese self as sociocentric. By the same token, social scientists often depict the American or Western self as individualistic. Dumont, for example, asserts that in the Western view the "individual is quasi-sacred, absolute; there is nothing over and above his legitimate demands; his rights are limited only by the identical rights of other individuals. He is a monad" (1970, 4). Roland writes that "the individualized self . . . is the predominant inner psychological organization of Americans" (1988, 8).

To return to the labels of chapter 1, this may be explicable through a "bottom-up" model. As opposed to the Japanese language, with its shifting personal pronoun equivalents dependent on the relative status and degree of intimacy between speaker and listener (Smith 1983, 77), English has an invariant first person pronoun: "I" remain "I," as opposed to "you," regardless of who "I" am speaking to; and this may shape selves who think of themselves as "I" apart from their interrelations with others. But this individualism may also be explicable through a "top-down" model. Many of the Americans I spoke with were shaped by social and institutional structures that left them little choice but to be "individualistic": women who seek individual careers because, given the prevalence of divorce, they can't trust their marriages to stay intact, and men who learn, through corporate layoffs, not to be loyal to their companies but to look out for themselves. These Americans may be individualistic less through an enculturation they see as "natural" than through harsh lessons from the social reality in which they live.

Comparing American and Japanese institutions, it seems apparent that American institutions are undergirded by the American cultural emphasis on the individual over the group, just as Japanese institutions are supported by the Japanese emphasis on the group over the individual. Consider, for example, immigration policy: The United States accepts relatively large numbers of immigrants, believing that they will help society by helping themselves; Japan accepts almost no immigrants, believing that they will upset the harmony of the existing

Japanese group. Consider corporate salary structure: Japanese companies have based salaries almost entirely on the basis of seniority, emphasizing group harmony and hierarchy over individual ability; American companies have tended to reward individual ability. Consider adult education: In the United States, the community college system makes adult education readily available to those who seek to upgrade their work skills and find better employment; in Japan, practical adult education is all but nonexistent outside one's company, reflecting the value that one should stay loyal to one's existing work group. Consider health care: Japan has national health insurance, protecting all members of the national group; the United States, holding health care and its financing to be an individual responsibility, does not. These examples involve particular socioeconomic factors, but underlying these factors are the different cultural emphases we've been discussing.

These different cultural emphases also seem reflected in the two societies' social problems. Many of Japan's problems seem traceable to an excess of emphasis on the group. Individuals may feel so weighted down by social constraints—the examination hell of high school students (Rohlen 1983, 77–110), the long working hours of company employees (Lummis and Saitō 1991), the intimidation suffered by opponents of the emperor system (Field 1991), the bullying of those who are in any way different—that individual freedom may seem all but unimaginable.[2] Many of America's problems seem attributable to an excess of emphasis on the individual. The high divorce rate (Hochschild 1989; Louv 1992, 42–65) and consequent fracturing of the family, the great disparity between rich and poor (Reich 1990), including the corporate executives who are paid salaries of millions while their companies lay off thousands of employees (Crystal 1990)—these may be interpreted as individuals seeking their own gain at the expense of the group and its harmony.

Problems such as these have led Japanese social critics to decry

2. The problem of *ijime*, or bullying in schools, has been discussed in hundreds of Japanese newspaper articles over the past decade, especially in 1985–86. In 1994–95, the suicide of several bullied youths once again led to media outcry.

the emphasis on commitment to group and instead encourage self-realization, and American critics to decry the emphasis on self-realization and selfishness, to encourage community and commitment. In the view of these critics, excessive Japanese groupism and excessive American individualism have led to social disease, whose cure is to emphasize the other, unmarked pole in the cultural dialectic: Japanese individualism and American groupism.

This can be seen in Japanese and American conceptions of "America" and "Japan." Japanese conceptions of self-realization are influenced by the ideas of Western psychologists such as Maslow, and in a larger sense by ideas of "America" as a land of individual freedom. American conceptions of community and commitment may be influenced by the emergence of Japan in many Americans' minds as a group-centered nation that "works" better than the individualistic United States. This was depicted by Halberstam (1986) in his account of the American and Japanese automobile industries and the triumph of the latter over the former in the 1980s. Just as some of the Japanese I spoke with seemed to think of the United States as a land of individualism unimpeded by social pressure, some of the Americans I spoke with seemed to think of Japan as a land of group harmony, free of American "me-first" selfishness (Johnson 1991; Feinberg 1993).

Linked to these different conceptions of "individual" and "group," "self-realization" and "commitment," are the economic situations of the two societies. As we have discussed (but see also Yamazaki 1987 and Bell 1976), Japanese and American theorists maintain that economic affluence leads to the cultural valuation of self-realization, economic difficulties to emphasis on community and commitment. Japanese self-realization differs in its meanings from American self-realization, as Japanese commitment differs from American commitment; the analysis of this chapter and the preceding one clearly demonstrates this, as on a more personal level, the accounts in part 2 will also. Nonetheless, it may be that our collective dreams of self-realization or of commitment are due, more than we wish to recognize, to the rise and fall of figures on economists' charts.

Chapter Three

The Comparison of Japanese
and American Selves

The Relation of Print to People

In the first two chapters, we looked at what Japanese and American print media say about what one should live for; in the chapters to come, we will look at the accounts of some of the Japanese and Americans I interviewed and the ways in which they comprehend their lives. In this chapter, I consider the relation of print media to the people I spoke with, outline how I conducted interviews and fashioned the accounts of part 2, and set forth a theory through which to compare Japanese and Americans in their pursuit of a life worth living.

What is the relation of the ideas expressed in Japanese and American print media to the ways in which Japanese and Americans conceive of their lives? Most people, it seems, don't much think about what most makes their lives worth living, whether in terms of "self-realization" or "commitment to group." Indeed, when I asked Japanese, "What's your *ikigai?*" or Americans, "What's most important to you in your life?" many claimed to have never thought about such a thing before. However, as they spoke about themselves over the course of our interviews, it became apparent that they had thought about such matters, but in more concrete terms than my questions addressed. In statements like, "My kids mean everything to me," "I wish I could quit my job and do something I really want to do,"

"When I'm playing my guitar, that's the greatest feeling in the world!" and "I pray to God each day to make me a better person," we see statements of *ikigai* that seem part of the daily and weekly thoughts of the Japanese and Americans I spoke with.

The books and articles discussed in the first two chapters, as a small part of Japanese and American mass media, both shaped and reflected the cultural vocabularies of those I interviewed. Only a few of my informants claimed to be directly influenced by books such as *Ikigai ni tsuite, Passages,* or *Habits of the Heart,* but all shared with these books common ways of conceiving of self and world. The Japanese thought about *ikigai* in terms of their personal dreams in conjunction with or in contradiction to the obligations of family and work; the Americans thought about their lives in terms of the pursuit of self-fulfillment, tempered by love for and a sense of responsibility toward family and community.

Those I interviewed comprehended their lives through the conceptions available to them "in the air" of their cultural worlds, but they did not do so unthinkingly. Rather, they actively chose those conceptions that most enabled them to sense that their lives were worth living, and they reformulated those conceptions in order to maintain that sense vis-á-vis the world around them. Although it's impossible to unravel the direct relation of mass media to the ways in which the people I spoke with comprehended their lives, it seems clear that both media and selves are created by and create an ever-shifting cultural vocabulary, one that shapes selves, but that is also shaped and manipulated by selves in their efforts to make sense of their lives.

Methods of Interviewing and Shaping Accounts

I conducted interviews in a city in northern Japan, September 1989–November 1990, and in a city in the western United States, December 1990–July 1991. These cities are similar in history and ambience, but the most compelling reason for choosing them was that I had friends in both. For the kind of intensive interviewing I sought to undertake, it wouldn't do to buttonhole strangers on streetcorners, imploring them to answer my hours of questions. Instead, I had my friends introduce me to a variety of different people they knew, and then used these people to introduce me to others, and those people to still others, until I had interviewed a wide range of different Japanese and Americans.

My choice of informants thus composed no "random sample"; I sought only to interview a diversity of Japanese and Americans who, I hoped, would candidly tell me of their lives. Almost all apparently did. In all honesty, I doubt that I would tell a stranger as much as they told me; I'm grateful to them for their trust. My own motives in listening were clear enough—I had research to conduct, a book I wanted to write—but why did these people choose to talk with me? One motive might have been simple kindness to an inquiring stranger: "Sure, I'll talk with you. What the hell!" Another motive might have been to be listened to. As one Japanese woman told me, "My husband, when I try to talk, just picks up his newspaper; my kids just say, 'Mom, I've already heard that story!' But at least you listen." Beyond this, those I spoke with told the story of their lives not just to me, but to themselves. Most seemed to welcome the chance to verbally reconstruct their lives, to see what those constructions looked like. And finally, many may have desired to see themselves in a book: even if one's identity is disguised, and even if the book merely gathers dust on library shelves, who of us would not want to be in print, in some sense alive beyond ourselves?

I interviewed fifty-two Americans and fifty-two Japanese, of various ages, occupations, and worldviews, in anywhere from two to five two or three-hour sessions.[1] Most interviews were conducted at people's homes, but also sometimes at work, in empty corporate conference rooms and classrooms after the school day, and sometimes in coffee shops and restaurants. All Japanese interviews were conducted in Japanese, all American interviews in English. Although my Japanese is grammatically far from perfect—I learned Japanese on the

---

1. The Japanese I interviewed included company employees, housewives, retirees, laborers, teachers, traditional craftsmen, and religious devotees; the Americans included teachers, policemen, research scientists, atheists, fervent Christians, jazz musicians, writers, a number of African Americans, Asian Americans, and Latinos, and several gays and lesbians. Those whose accounts appear in part 2 represent only a small swatch of those I interviewed; given limitations of space, I can include only a few of the many pairs of accounts I would like to have included.

street rather than in the language classroom—my listening compre-hension and ability to communicate were entirely adequate for my interviews.

In the interviews, I asked (1) questions about work, family, and present life ("Do you like your work? Would you work if you didn't have to? Are you happy you married the person you married? Tell me about your children," etc.); (2) questions about one's life up until the present ("What most stands out in your memory from when you were a child/in your teens, twenties, thirties?" etc., branching out to cover one's general picture of life: "What's been the happiest/saddest time of your life?"); (3) questions about one's envisioned future ("If all your dreams came true, what kind of life would you be leading? What kind of life do you hope/expect to be leading ten years from now?") and about aging and death ("Are you afraid of getting older? Of death? Do you have any religious belief?"); and (4) questions about *ikigai* ("What's your *ikigai*? How has it changed over the years?" etc. To discuss *ikigai* with Americans, I asked, "What rela-tionship, activity, pursuit, or dream is most important in your life? What do you feel is the center of your life? What most makes your life seem worth living?"). Although this was the general framework of my questions, each set of interviews was different in length and feeling and evoked different questions to suit each person's life, thoughts, and degree of loquaciousness.

I tape-recorded each interview. Following each set of Japanese interviews, I wrote out a preliminary English translation and then compiled an hour-long, edited Japanese interview tape, which my wife (who is Japanese and a professional translator) and I together worked up into a document in English of some thirty pages. I edited and transcribed American interviews into documents of similar length and tried to pair each with a Japanese counterpart.[2] Later,

2. I sometimes tried to pair my informants in advance. I'd ask my American friends, for example, "Do you know of a young man in his twenties with lots of dreams I might interview?" to match a Japanese I'd interviewed. But this effort was only rarely successful; most often, I paired informants only after I had completed interviews. In this sense, the comparability of Japanese and American accounts in this book doesn't arise from any elaborate attempt on my part to find comparable Japanese and Americans; rather, these pairs emerged from within my pool of a hun-dred Japanese and Americans chosen more or less haphazardly.

I edited each pair of interviews down to the accounts appearing in part 2.

I chose the nine pairs of accounts of part 2 for their compelling nature and for the kind of personal and cultural comparisons they make possible. It was a difficult choice, and my selection has been somewhat arbitrary. The people portrayed in this book, it is important to remember, are not cultural representatives, a weight they can't fully bear, but individual selves. Thus, to take just one example, the young Japanese woman portrayed in chapter 5 is more conservative than many Japanese women of her age; while she is not entirely atypical, it would be grossly distorting to see her not as "Nakajima Yuri" but as "a representative Japanese woman in her early twenties." (Indeed, I struggled to include in the book a less traditionally minded Japanese woman, but the pairings within the narrative sequence of the book didn't work out.) What is true for her is true for everyone in these pages: they represent only themselves. At points throughout what follows, I quote briefly from interviews with other informants, as well as from mass media, in order to gain a broader view of the issues being discussed.

I regret that I can include so few accounts. I also regret that I've had to edit the accounts in part 2 so drastically—I've included less than a tenth of what was actually said. The reader won't see the original narrative sequence of our interviews and won't see my questions within the accounts. What this means is that you who read will be unable to apprehend these people's accountings of themselves except through my reaccountings. My editing is necessary to make this book readable, but it comes at a price: you will know the people I spoke with only through my own intrusive editorial hand.

This leads to some key questions. Can Japanese and Americans be compared as I seek to compare them? More specifically: Can a concept such as *ikigai* validly be used to compare selves of different cultures? Can personal accounts from selves of different cultures speaking different languages validly be compared? Let me briefly address each question in turn.

The basic definition of *ikigai* in Japan today is "that which most makes one's life seem worth living." But *ikigai* may also be defined in an analytical, cross-cultural sense as "that which evokes one's deepest sense of social commitment," in that "what makes one's life worth living" inevitably stems from one's social world. This is true of both commitment to group and self-realization: whether one's *ikigai* is one's family or one's art, one's company or one's dream, one's spouse or one's God, one is projected through these *ikigai* into relations beyond the self. *Ikigai* is the self's formulation of what makes life seem worth living in terms of its most essential commitment to its social world. Part 2 depicts this sense of commitment in the lives of a few Japanese and Americans.

In this sense, we may indeed compare Japanese and American selves as to *ikigai*, but the accounts of part 2 are not transparent windows into selves but constructed texts. They are texts on several levels. First, the interviews involved not selves but self-presentations, socially exchanged (Goffman 1959; Linde 1993, 3–19). In a few cases—the most spectacular being that of a murder which irrevocably shaped my informant's life, as I learned only later—those I spoke with omitted crucial information. More often, their self-presentation was more subtle. As a young Japanese woman put it, "I wonder if I'm not saying too much that 'sounds good' in this interview. However much you want to tell your *honne* [true feelings], you also want to make yourself look good."

Beyond this, the interviews involved people answering my questions rather than speaking on their own terms; their accounts were thus shaped in ways that they themselves might never shape them. Furthermore, my Japanese accounts were translated, and all accounts were edited, both processes being inevitably distorting. Through the process of translation, half of my informants are made into beings of a different linguistic world, incomprehensible to themselves.[3]

I tried to narrow the gaps between texts and selves by coming to know many of those I interviewed over an extended period apart from our interviews, and by allowing those I spoke with to criticize and correct our interview tapes and my edited accounts.[4] But this is

3. For discussions of the essential impossibility of translation, see Whorf ([1941] 1988) and Steiner (1975). For a fuller discussion of the textual nature of life history accounts, see Watson and Watson-Franke (1985, 46–50) and Ricoeur (1979).

4. Six of the nine Americans whose accounts appear in part 2 received edited typescripts of our interviews; the others received cassette tapes of interviews. The

no guarantee that my accounts bear an accurate relation to their selves and their lives. It may be that my interviews are accurate representations of my informants' self-presentations, and yet in fact bear no real relation to what they think about most essentially in their lives. The unresolvable question remains: What relation do these texts bear to selves? I don't know. The accounts that follow portray, I think, real people in all their complexity rather than stick-figure embodiments of the questions I sought to have answered, the theories I sought to formulate. But this is for the reader to judge.

A Cross-cultural Theory of *Ikigai*

Assuming, then, that comparison of my Japanese and American informants' accounts of their lives and *ikigai* is indeed valid, what we now need is a theory through which these accounts may be compared.

The question of how selves comprehend their commitment to the social order was asked by Max Weber early in this century: "The real empirical sociological investigation begins with the question: What motives determine and lead the individual members [of communal society] . . . to behave in such a way that the community . . . continues to exist?" ([1925] 1964, 107). However, anthropologists have not generally dealt with this question. One reason relates to what is perhaps the most widespread concept of culture in anthropology since the 1970s: "an historically transmitted pattern of meanings embodied in symbols," "a traffic in . . . significant symbols" (Geertz 1973, 89, 45). This concept stresses the *public* nature of culture, culture not as found within the self, but as transmitted between selves. As Harris has discussed, this concept implies that culture within the self is unknowable: "While public, shared concepts must help to shape private

---

Japanese all received cassette tapes; four of the nine also received hour-long edited tapes of their interviews translated into English (but probably only one or two understood enough English to comprehend the tape). I urged my informants to read or listen to what I gave them and communicate their impressions; many did, offering minor corrections and suggestions for disguising their identities. As this book was being written, I wrote to all those appearing in part 2, offering them the chance to examine and edit their accounts. Although I've received a number of friendly letters in response, no one has taken me up on this offer.

experience, it remains doubtful whether anthropologists have means for gaining access to that experience as experience. . . . Hence, claims that we can know what it is like to be a self in a different society arouse skepticism" (1989, 601–2).

On one level, this caution is well taken: the anthropologist can't enter the informant's mind except through the social act of speech, of dialogue. At another level, it is questionable. Wagner, in commenting on Alfred Schutz's phenomenological sociology, has written that "even the socially most stereotyped cultural ideas only exist in the minds of individuals who absorb them, interpret them on the basis of their own life situation, and give them a personal tinge which the reporting anthropologists so often ignore" (1970, 17). In this view, it is the analysis of culture as public which may involve assumptions on the part of anthropologists that can't validly be made, for example, the assumption that cultural ideas shape selves without being shaped and reinterpreted by selves and thus made selves' *own* ideas.

The starting point of Schutz's sociology—Schutz's reworking of Husserl's "phenomenological reduction"—is the subject who experiences the world (Wagner 1970, 5–6). In Schutz's words (from his 1940 essay "Phenomenology and the Social Sciences"),

> This world, built around my own I, presents itself for interpretation to me, a being living naïvely within it. From this standpoint everything has reference to . . . the situation in which I find myself here and now. The place in which I am living has not significance for me as a geographical concept, but as my home. . . . Language is not a substratum of philosophical or grammatical considerations for me, but a means for expressing my intentions or understanding the intentions of Others. My social world . . . is arranged, around me as the centre, into associates . . . contemporaries . . . predecessors . . . and successors. . . . All this is self-evident to me in my naïve life just as it is self-evident to me that the world actually exists and that it is actually *thus,* as I experience it. (Schutz [1940] 1978: 135–36, 137)

These words sound commonsensical, but they carry broad implications. If Schutz's starting point is to be taken seriously, then culture must be investigated in terms of the self's life and relations rather than in terms of larger cultural concepts. Culture can only be investigated "from inside the self out," not "from outside the self in." In the spirit of the above passage, I will begin my analysis of Japanese and

American accounts with the concrete personal worlds they reveal, not with abstractions about Japanese or American culture.[5]

Schutz provides a large part of the analytic foundation I seek; Francis Hsu, in his "The Self in Cross-cultural Perspective" (1985), adds to it. For Hsu, "the meaning of being human is found in interpersonal relationships"; what is needed, he argues, is a "delineation of the individual's relationship with his world of men, gods and things" in terms of "intensity of affective involvement" (27). How does the self, considered cross-culturally, order its affective commitments to its world of others? If from Schutz we take the analysis of the self in its own concrete situation, from Hsu we take the idea of systematically analyzing the self's social commitments—its circles of competing *ikigai,* potential sources of life's worth.

From Walter Goldschmidt's *The Human Career: The Self in the Symbolic World* (1990), we gain two more elements for a theory of *ikigai.* Goldschmidt argues that "the idea of prestige, the recognition of individual merit, is the very soul of the social order" (1990, 31). This assertion touches upon the question, "What do selves seek through *ikigai?*" They seek, as we will see in chapter 6, a sense of personal significance, of *mattering,* of being needed, appreciated, or recognized by someone or something beyond the self. This sense may be seen as the subjective reflection of the social accrual of prestige, broadly defined. Furthermore, selves do not seek significance as culturally molded automatons but as culturally shaped shapers of their lives: "Individuals are not passive actors, but persons with private agendas, with constant concern for their own symbolic meaning which every social encounter has the potential for reshaping" (1990: 202). Selves, Goldschmidt argues, and I argue as well, make strategic use of cultural conceptions and social negotiations to bolster their senses of symbolic worth.

On the basis of these ideas, I offer this cross-cultural theory of *ikigai* in a single sentence: *As the products of culturally and personally shaped fate, selves strategically formulate and interpret their iki-*

---

5. A similar view is taken by Watson and Watson-Franke, whose phenomenological stance in interpreting life histories "refuses to enforce constructs alien to the individual life as it is related" and thus "brings closer an understanding of subjective experience in a culturally defined experiential context" (1985: 13).

gai from an array of cultural conceptions, negotiate these ikigai *within their circles of immediate others, and pursue their* ikigai *as channeled by their society's institutional structures so as to attain and maintain a sense of the personal significance of their lives.*

We examine this theory at length in part 3, but let me now briefly explicate it. A given self is "the product of fate" in that it is shaped by the particular family and larger culture—Japanese culture, American culture—in which it has lived. On the basis of this shaping, the self "strategically formulates its *ikigai*" in that it comprehends what it lives for through its use of cultural conceptions in its social world, including mass media. The self "negotiates its *ikigai* with its immediate others"—spouse, children, coworkers—in terms of how it defines its deepest senses of commitment vis-à-vis those others, which are to some extent in competition to be the object of that deepest commitment. *Ikigai* is "channeled by institutional structures" in that the structural principles organizing Japanese and American societies encourage or necessitate the self's pursuit of its deepest commitment down some paths and not others. Finally, the self "attains personal significance through *ikigai*" in that *ikigai* enables one's life to "make sense" within the cultural frameworks of meaning offered by one's society: *ikigai* is the self's culturally shaped meaning of life.

We can flesh out this theory by looking at some selves, composites of people I interviewed. Consider a woman who has a husband and a small child, lives in a nuclear family, works at a part-time job, and likes television dramas. This woman may feel discontented because she must devote so much of her time to taking care of her husband and child; a part of her longs to make work her *ikigai,* but she also feels a deep sense of responsibility to her family.

This woman may be feeling *ikigai* "pressure" from all of the various others in her life. Her boss says that he will promote her if she will agree to assume more responsibility at work. Her child cries about being taken to a day-care center: "I want to be with Mommy! Mommy doesn't care about me!" Her husband is upset that her work keeps her away from home in the evenings; he's insecure about her devotion to their marriage: "Which is more important to you, work or me?" The television dramas she watches endeavor to "hook" her on their plots, to make them the focus of her daydreams; and her daydreams of a different life indicate to her the inadequacy of her present commitments. She must somehow negotiate her *ikigai* between the circles of others that surround her.

This woman uses an array of cultural conceptions to justify to herself and others her *ikigai*. She may use "self-realization" to justify taking a promotion at work against the wishes of her family, or she may convince herself that her true self-realization lies with her husband and child. She may invoke "commitment to group" to explain the necessity to stay home with her family; or she may use that concept to justify her work: "The boss says that without me, the company would fall apart, so. . . ." If this woman is American, she may formulate her *ikigai* in terms of the gender ideology, held by many Americans, that women have as much right to a career as men. If she is Japanese, she may argue that since her husband is inadequately performing his role of supporting his family on his earnings, she herself is not obligated to play the role of being primarily a housewife.

This woman is subject to institutional channeling. If she is American, she may think more seriously than her Japanese counterpart of getting promoted at work or of getting a divorce, both possibilities being more institutionally ingrained—more objectively likely possibilities, given the structures of society—in the United States than in Japan. If she is Japanese, she may be channeled into devoting herself to family and home, because of fewer opportunities for promotion at work and because of Japanese tax laws discouraging two-income families. American institutional structures will perhaps allow this woman more opportunity to find *ikigai* in work, whereas Japanese institutional structures may channel her *ikigai* into family.

If this woman is fortunate, her sense of significance will come to be aligned with the *ikigai* she is culturally, socially, and institutionally encouraged to hold; for example, she may come to find *ikigai* in being a devoted mother in Japan or the United States or in being a career woman in the United States. If she isn't so fortunate, her *ikigai* and significance may come to lie more in her dreams of a different life, dreams that may make bearable the social reality she must live within but to which she doesn't feel her deepest commitment.

Consider now a Japanese artist, a man in his late thirties with a wife and two children. The happiest time of his life was when he was in art school, in his early twenties. There was no *ikigai* contradiction for him then; he could devote all of himself to his painting and to his dream and *ikigai* of becoming an artist. By his late twenties, he found himself employed by a design company whose work he considered meretricious; his painting remained his *ikigai*, but he felt enormous pressure between the demands of his job and his desire to paint. By his early thirties, he had quit his company to become a freelance designer and had married. He was blissfully happy; he threw himself into both his work, which he saw as being essentially linked to his art, and his relationship with his new wife. His twin *ikigai* of work and home, art and love, were perfectly and harmoniously balanced, he seems to have felt.[6] At the time he was interviewed, however, he had grown weary of the crass demands of his customers, who wanted, he felt, trite, boring designs, and also of what he saw as the increasingly conventional values of his wife, now taking care of his small children. He could paint now for only a few hours each week; that he had so little time to paint, and that his ambition of becoming a great painter seemed less and less likely to be realized, filled him with doubt as to the meaning of his life.

The dominant cultural conception shaping his *ikigai* is that of "art"; his studio contained many folio volumes of the works of great artists, and he would sometimes lovingly leaf through them as we talked. His dream is to become a great artist, like Goya or Picasso,[7] and to express through art, as they did, all he comprehends of life. This is the significance that he seeks in his *ikigai*. But the people around him have different ideas of what he should live for. His wife seems to say to him, "Look, you're not an artist, but a husband and father!" She may dislike the cultural conception of "art," preferring instead commitment to work and family as the value by which a

6. *Ikigai*, as described in chapter 1, is generally a single commitment, and throughout this book, I will analyze it as such. However, as Kamiya maintains (1980a, 88), *ikigai* may involve a balance of commitments. A few people I spoke with, not appearing in this book, told me that they couldn't prioritize between work and family as their *ikigai*: both were essential.

7. American readers may find this man's artistic tastes odd, but there's nothing unusual about a Japanese artist invoking Goya and Picasso, just as there's nothing un- usual about a Japanese music-lover admiring Beethoven. Western art is in general as widely admired by Japanese as it is by Americans.

breadwinner, husband, and father should live. His present customers, too, seem to have little use for "art"; they may see him as a businessman who can make a good living for them and for himself if he will play his work role with the proper commitment, instead of dallying with art. One may imagine the conversations that take place when his customers call ("We're not asking you to paint the *Mona Lisa*. All we want is a sign!"), or when his wife sees his earnings ("You mean, after being at your office sixty hours this week, this is all you've got to show for it? We can't pay the bills with this!").

This man is institutionally channeled in an urgent way: if his customers leave him because of his concern with art, he won't be able to feed his family. He is thus routed to concern about money, having money being a fundamental institutionalized necessity in Japan and the United States, and also to see this as his male role, vis-à-vis the nurturing familial role of his wife. If he lived in a different society, the rules might be different: his art might be subsidized, or respected; his wife might work and leave him to paint while his child was at day care. But he doesn't live in such a society, and so he is paying a steep price for his devotion to art, a price he will continue to pay (unless he is very fortunate) for as long as he makes his art the source of his significance.

The foregoing sketches show how this theory of *ikigai* may be applied to actual lives. Let us now, in part 2, look at length at the lives and accounts of some of the people I interviewed. Then, on that empirical basis, we will return in part 3 to this chapter's theory.

Part Two

Ikigai in Japanese and American Lives

Chapter Four

Ikigai in Work and Family

Miyamoto Ken'ichi (48)

(I had been told that Miyamoto-san[1] had the reputation of being difficult to work for, being furious when work did not go exactly according to plan. I was thus surprised by his demeanor: he was plump and jolly, a bald and beardless Santa Claus. I met him at his company apartment, his wife serving us tea and snacks. After one interview, I showed the two of them the book on *ikigai* that I was reading, indicating that the typical and appropriate *ikigai* of men was work, of women, family. The two of them beamed at this confirmation of their own *ikigai*.)

I work for Asahi Bank; I like my work. I usually get to the bank at seven-thirty in the morning; I try to finish by eight at night, though sometimes it takes until nine. The bank is now telling its employees to leave by eight, but people still stay late. We've got to be more efficient! I can finish by eight if I work more efficiently. If I tried to come home by seven, I'd have to work really hard, but if it were just once a week I could do it easily.

If I had more free time, I don't think I'd know what to do with it.

---

1. The suffix "-san" in Japanese is equivalent to both "Mr." and "Mrs." in English. Once again, all names used in this book's accounts are pseudonyms, and all accounts are in various ways disguised, to protect the identities of those who spoke with me.

If I came home at five every day, I wouldn't know how to spend my time. I like my life the way it is. Since last year, the bank's had a five-day work week. When I first had Saturdays off, well, you get used to it, but at first I didn't know what to do. Now I usually read books or practice golf, but I don't know if they're what you could call hobbies. I am interested in the ancient history of Japan, but. . . .

I don't think it's necessarily good to work until late every night. I don't think it's bad for young people to have hobbies as well as work—cars, English lessons, going out on dates—but young people seem to feel that they're being made to work rather than working because they want to. It wasn't like that before. I get angry at the young workers here: I get angry at them so that they can grow. I tell them that if I stop getting angry, it'll mean I've given up on them!

When I wake up in the morning, I never feel that I don't want to go to work. I feel, "I've got to work hard again today!" Do I feel like a cog in the corporate machine? Well, of course I'm a cog—the bank is a big organization; what I'm doing could be done by others just as well as by me—but while I'm working, I believe that without me the bank couldn't survive. As long as you work, you've got to believe that. I'm now a section chief in my bank branch, third from the top. I have relatively heavy responsibility, but in the end I'm still a cog, a big cog turning little cogs. Each individual is a cog but all cogs have to mesh smoothly in order for the wheel to turn. . . .

What's good for Asahi Bank is good for me. If Asahi Bank has high status compared to other banks, I'll have high status too. If the bank makes a big profit, I'll get a share of it. Since I earn my living from the bank, unless it becomes better, my life won't improve. If the bank stops making profits and can't pay our salaries, it's because we haven't worked hard enough. I can't separate myself from Asahi Bank: I am what I am because of Asahi Bank, Asahi Bank is what it is because of me. I guess I'm a true corporate warrior [*kigyōsenshi*]!

The retirement age here is fifty-five, though we can stay until sixty at reduced pay. I think I'll quit at fifty-five and find another job, but I don't know yet. I'm not too worried about my life after retirement, but if I couldn't work anymore, it would be difficult. If I had no work,

I'd have to spend time on my hobby or doing something I wanted to do. Every day would be a holiday; that would be a problem. My wife always tells me that those who don't have a hobby tend to go senile after they retire. I think I still have enough time to find some kind of hobby before then, but I have to prepare myself. . . .

If I were seventeen again, would I take the same path I've taken in my life? I think so. I like my work, though I don't know if the bank would take me again! But I'd go to college. I wanted to go but couldn't—I joined the bank after high school. My father died when I was eight; he'd been a prisoner of war in Siberia, and died after coming back to Japan. I saw my mother go through a lot of hardship when I was a child. After he died, she started a small store, but life was tough. I'm the oldest son. I lived with my mother until I got married, and since then she's been living alone, in a private old people's home a few hours from here. I think she's happy there. I visit her once every two years or so—I don't go more often because I'm an undutiful son [*oyafukō*] rather than because I'm busy with work! I've asked her to let me know if anything happens; since she hasn't called, I guess she's doing OK. . . .

This is my thirtieth year with the bank. For those thirty years I've never been late for work or taken a sick leave; I've really liked my work. The one thing I haven't liked is the transfers. By the time you get used to a new place, you get transferred again. I couldn't properly do the new work at first, and I felt like I was a burden on others. By now, I've given up on this aspect of work; you just have to live with it. If you refused a transfer, you'd be told to quit the bank.

I got married twenty-two years ago. I met my wife through *omiai*.[2] It's said that with love marriage, your love ends by the time you marry, but with "arranged marriage," love grows after you marry. I guess that for each of us the other is like air; we need each other. I'm happy I married my wife—I was lucky that I met a good woman at a

2. *Omiai* is sometimes glossed as "arranged marriage," but it's more accurately defined as "matchmaking": a man and a woman are introduced through an intermediary for the purpose of marriage, but either one can—and often does—decline, to go on to other *miai* meetings with various people before deciding to marry one of them. Miyamoto-san had several such meetings, he told me, before meeting and marrying his wife. For a discussion of *miai* and *ren'ai* ("love marriage") in contemporary Japan, see Edwards 1989, 53–76.

good time. (No, she doesn't work. She stays home, cooks, does her hobbies. . . .)

My son's a college student. I don't think he'll follow my path; he wants to be a civil servant. I think he likes the idea of leaving the office at five every day. I won't oppose him! If he wanted to quit college, I'd oppose him, but he doesn't have anything else he wants to pursue—he's like me. Maybe it'd be better if he did have something—music, sports, anything. Only a few people can make a living by doing something they really want to do. Most people follow an ordinary path, and become company workers. My son knows that; maybe that's why he wants to become a civil servant, the least risky path of all!

I'm very happy with my life now. It's been good to see the young workers I've trained become full-fledged bank employees. Some have attained a higher position than I have; I feel proud of them. If I lived as I live now until I retired, and died at eighty, would I feel on my deathbed that my life had been good? Well, it's impossible to be completely satisfied; I just hope I can die with only a little regret. Probably I'll feel regret that I wasn't a filial son to my mother. When I was young, I gave her lots of trouble: I was self-centered, and made her worry about me a lot. Since I'm the oldest son, I should have acted as a substitute father for my younger brothers, but I couldn't. I don't know how my mother feels about this. I've never talked about it with her. I don't want her to remember sad things, bring up bad memories. . . . I think it's because I had to go through hardship when I was a child that I could work at the bank for thirty years without feeling that the work was hard. If my father hadn't died, my character might have been very different. Maybe it's been good for me, but even now I wish I had a father.

I'm an ordinary person living an ordinary life. I was happy when my son was born, but there haven't been many ups and downs in my life. Being ordinary is being happy; everybody thinks that way. I don't have any desire for adventure. I grew up watching my mother go through hardship—I can't be adventurous, because the poverty of my childhood is still with me.

The bank has really taken care of me during my life, and I owe the bank for that—it's natural to feel that way. If someone were to quit the bank to do what he himself wanted to do, I'd consider him selfish. But maybe my way of thinking is old-fashioned. Until now, people like me have contributed a lot to Japan's development, but from now on it may be different. Now people are talking about an "age of leisure" [*yoka no jidai*]—times are changing. Maybe that's not bad. If people work less, Japan will be able to join the rest of the world. In the past Japanese people worked twelve hours a day while people in other countries worked eight hours. If we can prove we're still competitive working just eight hours a day, we may really be able to say we're superior as a race [*jinshu*].[3] We'd be able to spend time on leisure; we could recover our humanness [*ningenrashisa*]. Japan's economic power may decline a bit, but that's not bad. What we lose in economic power we'll gain in some other form.... The Pacific War was the turning point for Japan; I remember those days of hardship. My generation wanted to escape that low level of existence— that was the driving force of Japan's development....

I grew up in a Buddhist family, but I have no real interest in religion. Women tend to believe in religion more than men—men have work to give them psychological support, and women usually don't, so they turn to religion. I don't feel scared of death, but maybe I'm still too young. When I die I die, that's all—I don't think there's any life after death. Maybe I'm afraid of death; maybe in twenty years I'll believe in life after death. I say I don't believe in religion, but in the bottom of my heart I may be seeking religion, even if it doesn't appear on the surface; maybe everybody is like that....

What's my *ikigai*? I guess in my daily life it's my work—I'm a workaholic [*waakahorikku*]! I don't think my wife feels lonely—she's used to it. Since I was young I've been called "man of work" [*shigoto ningen*]; I've believed that all my nourishment comes from work— my *ikigai*, my knowledge, the economic base of my life....

When I look at my subordinates, I can tell their *ikigai*. Some work with passion—their *ikigai* is their work. For others, I don't know what their *ikigai* is, but it's not work. Among our new employees,

---

3. By "race" (*jinshu*), Miyamoto-san seems to mean what Americans think of as "nation." Many Japanese think of "Japaneseness" in terms both of race and nation, conceiving of the Japanese "race" and nation of Japan as one and the same.

fewer and fewer seem to hold work as *ikigai.* The sense of oneness with the company is fading. Young people seem to feel that the company is only where they earn money; once they're away, they don't want to think about it. My generation was different. We were always thinking about work, that's all we ever thought about. That sense of oneness with the company is essential! We must create that sense of oneness! Unless there's the sense of oneness among workers, the company won't prosper. We have to educate young workers to become hard-working employees who will be useful for the bank.

Pete Murray (52)

(I met Pete Murray at a local restaurant for three-hour breakfasts on several occasions. He is a young-looking fifty-two, clearly happier talking about flying than about feelings—but the latter came tumbling out despite himself, as his account reveals. At our first interview, he said, "Have you read that book *Passages?* You don't need to interview me, my life is exactly like the book!" When his omelet arrived, he smothered it in salsa, declaring, "All pilots like Mexican food!")

I'm a pilot for Continental Airlines; I like my work, though it has its days. The thing that makes the job most pleasurable is the crew you have. At my age, it's difficult to relate to twenty-year-olds. Some of them are wise beyond their years, but others, you could take their I.Q. with an air gauge! With a crew that's a little older, I don't have to worry about what's going on in back. When a passenger's rude, I hear about it: the crew comes up to vent their spleen. . . . Passengers have changed. Twenty-five years ago, women wore hats and gloves on airplanes; now they wear T-shirts with vulgar sayings on them. Recently, a passenger came on with a large bag, and was told he'd have to stick it down below; he told the stewardess very explicitly where she could stick it. I told him, "If you're going to ride on my airplane, you're going to apologize to her." This absolutely did not happen when I started out with the airline. . . .

As for the technical aspects of flying—well, after thirty years of doing anything, you can make it look easy. But it's fatiguing, because you plug in totally; you become a part of that machine. We talk while we fly, about sports, women, whatever, but you're always listening. If you hear a thump (maybe the flight attendant dropped a Pepsi), everyone makes eye contact, you check everything, scan the instruments; it's instantaneous. In the air, I don't think I've ever been bored. I once saw a video where a psychologist was asking pilots what they liked about flying. The best this one pilot could say was the sunrises. There's just something about it. I have no need to go skydiving on Saturdays for excitement—my work is exciting!

I was on strike for two years. Continental was once a world-class airline; Frank Lorenzo decimated it. He bought Continental in 1981, in a hostile takeover—the previous president of the company allegedly committed suicide. We went on strike in September 1983; it went on until September 1985. I'd been a captain, but after the strike, they used their new hires—I flew second officer. It only hurt them, it didn't affect me. I'm a captain again now. There's only a few of us old-timers left; two-thirds of the airline's been hired since 1983. A couple of years ago, the average age of the mechanics was twenty-three. They had incredible luck, not to have had an accident. . . . This airline is people, us; it's not just an assembly line you can tear all to hell! I don't think Frank Lorenzo ever understood that.

The new guy brought in to head the company is much better, but he's kept the same middle-management people, who we know we can't trust—they're stretching their spots into stripes, leopards trying to look like zebras. Continental went into bankruptcy last year; Frank Lorenzo left us with this huge debt load, and we can't make the payments. These days people find out you're with Continental and they give you a hard time; standing in line at Safeway, if you're in your uniform, people make disparaging comments. It used to be that people would say, "Oh, my aunt flew to Chicago with you once—it was wonderful!" Older airline people will tell you that before 1980, Continental was premier, but then it became an industry joke. Management now can only say, "Hey, we're the best!" You get all the hype, the rah-rah, the little seminars they give on self-esteem. I look at Continental people on the employees' bus, and they look at their feet. Other airline employees, they're peppy, bright-faced. None of the other companies have to give seminars on self-esteem! I really would like Continental to get better. Some of that is selfishness—if they fail, I've failed.

My wife and I are in our second marriages; I have two children by my first marriage. They're now twenty-six and twenty-three. I don't know what they're doing—my son sends me a card every Father's Day and birthday with no return address. Their mother is a very controlling person; I think she manipulated their minds after the divorce. The kids were teenagers then, old enough to know better, but. . . . My marriage had a wonderful facade, but it eroded from the inside. That's probably my fault—we pilots are task-oriented; that's why we make crappy husbands. Being task-oriented eliminates emotion. I was taught that emotions get in the way: you can't be up there with something going wrong saying, "Oh my God!" Be in absolute control of yourself—my military training taught me that, but women hate it!

It's really tough that my kids don't communicate. I don't think I was a bad father to them. I wasn't a drunk, I didn't beat anybody up. It's strange. My daughter would say, "You were never home for the holidays," but I can get out my logbook and see that I was home! My son, when I left, said, "Why did you take all the money?" and here I was paying his mother two thousand dollars a month and I had a thousand dollars to my name when I left! Their mother warped them—don't even get me started on that!—she spread so many lies. You see in the paper where some guy who's blown his former partner away is being dragged away in the police car—I can understand that. . . .

Why did I ever marry such a person? Damned if I know. I basically said, "I've done this and this, it's time to get married." If you'd asked me then if I loved her, would spend the rest of my life with her, I'd have said, "Sure"—that's what you're supposed to do. I was a good Catholic boy; I quit going to mass when I got separated, because the community shunned me. I said, "If this is good-times-only, who wants to belong to that?" It was the women involved, a bunch of screwy women protecting their assets.

I married my second wife in 1983. She carried me for a long time, gave me moral, monetary support while I was on strike. Am I 100 percent sure that my marriage will continue? Well, 90 percent sure. Once you've been there, you realize how fragile it is. . . . What's more important to me, my work or my family? My wife is probably most important to me. And yet, when I strap in to fly, that's what's most important. I can't just kiss my wife in the morning and be back for supper; I'm away twelve, fifteen days a month. Maybe a woman who has to sleep alone half the time doesn't like that. My daughter said that she never knew when I'd be home. I thought she did—maybe that was just my inability to understand children. Now, when I'm away, I talk to my wife every night on the phone. It's good to stay in touch. . . .

Marriage is much more difficult for me than work. I can jump up in my pajamas and fly; I've done that in the military, woken up in the air. Maybe I did my first marriage like that; it was, "You find somebody, have children, bring the money home. . . ." But those are just the mechanical aspects of raising a family, not the emotional things. Now I work on the emotional side. I'd like to hang on to this lady!

In 1941, when I was four, my parents wanted to con me into taking the small bedroom in our house, and said I could have any wallpaper I wanted. I took one that had airplanes all over the walls. Later, I built model planes; that's when I really first dreamed of flying. When I was in ninth grade I wrote in my little school yearbook essay that I wanted to be an airline pilot; I got my own plane when I was in high school. . . .

I don't have a college education. I flunked out of college, took the test to be an air force officer, went in, did pretty well. I joined Continental in 1968. I expected that that was going to be forever, keep moving up until you retire; then here comes a whole new operation, airline managers who are attorneys, MBAs, that just squeezed the guts out of the airline. The loyalty that you once had, you come to feel very careful with; you hold a little tighter to yourself. I saw this wonderful workplace absolutely destroyed by one man's greed. Life isn't fair, but I didn't realize that until I was in my forties, from my marriage, from Frank Lorenzo's buying the airline: he came along the same year my marriage broke up. My wife understood right away—he was what she was. She said, "You're going to lose your job." That's what she was afraid of, losing this lifestyle. She found somebody who made as much as I did, and off she went.

There's tremendous uncertainty in this work. My wife would love not to work, but the day I say, "Go ahead and quit," I might find out on the news that the airline's shut down. You have to go every six months or year to the doctor—he can say, "Uh-oh, you're all done." If I show up with a heart murmur at my next physical, next time we talk I'll say, "Yeah, I've got a glass business." As a pilot, you've got to have a business you can do on the side, to quiet yourself. . . .

In a way I'm afraid of retirement. You think, "Gee, just eight years, what'll I be doing?" But I probably won't retire at sixty—I can fly Second Officer. . . . I'm building my house now myself. I've never been afraid to try something new, so I'm not worried about what I can do, it's what I *want* to do. I don't know. I'd like to visit my friends, travel; I think of the people I'd like to pen a note to but never do, the books I've got stockpiled but never get to. . . .

Do I believe in God? I guess so. I don't know. I've had all the thoughts anybody's had: "If there's a God, why are so many bad things happening?" Somehow I think my belief is in an inner spirit, that you provide lodging. But whatever continues after death, I don't think it's *you*. If there's anything of spirit that runs through us all, it's the thread that runs through life—flowers, animals, any living matter. . . . But damned if I know! How should I know all this?

Is death scary? I've never thought about it seriously, but I've done so many things. I don't know what's ahead, but I've certainly lived more than my share at this point, lived a pretty full life. If I continue with my life as it is and drop dead at eighty, will I be satisfied? Sure. Eighty's a good age! My father died at seventy-nine; my mother's eighty-six. She lives in Florida, drives around in her little red Chevrolet, and plays shuffleboard. Shuffleboard is not my idea of fun. But I don't know—ask me at seventy-nine!

I've had a very fortunate life. Yes, I've had troubles with the company I've worked for, but so have lots of people, people who've worked for Ford and had the plant close, the teamsters who bred horses when the automobile came along. If you slow down, life rolls right over you—you've got to keep moving. The center of my life is probably my work—the flying, doing what I've been trained to do, for thirty-some years. But then, flying is in a way too uncertain to be a center. I could walk away from it; I could do something else.

Miyamoto Ken'ichi and Pete Murray: Analysis

The men portrayed in these accounts are at present quite different. Miyamoto-san feels a deep loyalty to his company, whereas Mr. Murray has been disillusioned by his. Miyamoto-san is the breadwinner for his role-based marriage, while Mr. Murray's similar marriage failed; his second marriage he manages along very different lines. But twenty years ago, these men were apparently quite similar. Indeed, their accounts illustrate some of the cultural changes that have taken place in the United States but not in Japan in recent decades.

Both Miyamoto-san and Mr. Murray seem to have assumed early in their adult lives that work would be their *ikigai* while their wives would find *ikigai* in family. Miyamoto-san's assumptions have gone unchallenged; his life has unfolded with no surprises, except for the affluence he has come to enjoy after the poverty of his youth. Although he doesn't agree with all his company's policies (such as transfers), and although he is no rising corporate star (some of his former subordinates have risen above him), his *ikigai* as found in Asahi Bank seems absolutely steadfast. His wife, judging from my brief talks with her, seems wholly to assent to their familial *ikigai* division.

For Mr. Murray, on the other hand, the basic assumptions about work and family he had held in youth were in the middle of his life proven unwarranted. His first wife apparently challenged the familial *ikigai* division that he took for granted; it wasn't fair, she seems to have held, for him to bring only his salary and not his deepest emotional commitment to his family. At the same time that his marriage was shattered (an event perhaps related to the rising tide of feminism in the 1970s), so too was the company he worked for, decimated in the 1980s corporate takeover binge in the United States: Mr. Murray's *ikigai* as found in flying for Continental Airlines was severely shaken. At present, work and wife seem ambiguously balanced as his *ikigai,* and he realizes the fragility of both commitments.

Miyamoto-san, born in 1941, is younger than the *Shōwa hitoketa* generation discussed in chapter 1, but in his total dedication to his work, he fits the Japanese stereotype of that generation. To younger Japanese, he may seem extreme; as his subordinate told me, "I don't understand my boss. All he ever thinks about is work!" Miyamoto-san explains his dedication to work in terms of the poverty of his childhood, which his company has enabled him to transcend. That young bank employees today view their work only as a job infuriates him. The gratitude toward the bank that he sees as being "natural" they "unnaturally" lack; they are beyond the pale of the "everybody" who live in happy ordinariness.[4]

Mr. Murray too has scornful things to say about young people, but for him they don't represent a threat to the corporate order; that order, he feels, has already been destroyed. His *ikigai* no longer lies in his commitment to his company; nonetheless, his *ikigai,* like Miyamoto-san's, remains bound up in work. If Miyamoto-san's *ikigai* is "working for *Asahi Bank,*" Mr. Murray's *ikigai* is "*flying* for Continental Airlines." Had Miyamoto-san not joined Asahi Bank, he could just as easily have gone to work for an electronics company or an airline and given them the same unstinting devotion he now gives to the bank; his devotion to the bank is thus a "willed" *ikigai.* For Mr. Murray, on the other hand, flying was a calling felt from boyhood; his devotion to flying is a "born" *ikigai.*

It thus seems that Miyamoto-san conceives of his *ikigai* in terms of "commitment to group," while Mr. Murray conceives of his *ikigai* in terms of "self-realization," but we can't say that Miyamoto-san pos-

---

4. Miyamoto-san's views are ambiguous. He says that it's not a bad thing for young people to have hobbies, and for Japanese to have more leisure and become more human, but he also bemoans young people who don't constantly think about the company and feel oneness with it. My sense is that while intellectually he accepts the fact that Japan is changing, that he is becoming a man of Japan's past, emotionally this is unacceptable to him, particularly insofar as young people, in their lack of commitment, threaten the future prosperity of Asahi Bank, his *ikigai.*

sesses "innately" a sense of identity with his company that Mr. Murray "innately" lacks. Mr. Murray, it seems, once had a deep loyalty to Continental Airlines; he lost that loyalty not through his own pursuit of self-realization, but through what he sees as the corporate disloyalty of the airline's owner and management. His "commitment to group" has, he feels, been betrayed, but he still feels that commitment; as he tells us, "if they fail, I've failed."

Miyamoto-san and his wife are "like air" to one another, he tells us: necessary for survival, but taken for granted. Mr. Murray viewed his first marriage in a similar way, but having traumatically lost his family from that marriage, he diligently works "on the emotional side" of his second marriage. Yet for both these men, their *ikigai* seems to be work. At some future point they will have to leave work, to return to their wives and hobbies; what then? Will Miyamoto-san become *sodai gomi* ("oversized garbage"), or will his interest in ancient history sustain him? Mr. Murray seems somewhat better equipped to deal with life after retirement. But flying has been his life; can he so easily "walk away from it" and "do something else"?

It's good for their companies and perhaps for their societies that men such as Miyamoto-san and Mr. Murray find their *ikigai* in work; one would not want to place one's money or one's life in the hands of bankers or airline pilots not deeply committed to their work. Nonetheless, unless one has a lifelong occupation, work alone is insufficient to base a life on: one must retire in Japan and the United States perhaps decades before one dies. Finding new *ikigai* once they retire may be the major life task these men will face in their futures.[5]

These two men can't be viewed as exemplars of Japan and the United States, but only as individual selves making enculturated individual choices. Nonetheless, it seems clear that shifts in the social and cultural "rules" over the past two decades have transformed Mr. Murray's American life and *ikigai*, as they have not transformed Mi-

5. During my fieldwork in Japan, an article in the local city magazine asked, "Are you thinking of your 'second life'?" and advised those soon to retire to find a new *ikigai* to sustain themselves. During my American fieldwork, an opinion column in the local newspaper proclaimed "American retirement—laid off from life." Clearly, these two men's coming *ikigai* transitions involve problems that are not unique to them.

yamoto-san's Japanese life and *ikigai*. Let's now turn to our next pair of accounts, similarly rooted in a shifting American social world and a more stable Japanese social world: two women whose *ikigai* is family.

Wada Masako (40)

(I met Wada Masako at her home, a small rented house. On the living room table lay brochures describing the dream house she aspired to own; upstairs, during one interview, her son practiced out-of-tune chords on his electric guitar. She is a short, lively woman, quick to laugh and to cry. During our first interview, she jokingly accused me of being a private detective. As our interviews proceeded, I sensed more that I was her confidant. Life is tough, she told me: perhaps she felt that it would be a tiny bit less tough if she could tell her worries to someone outside her family and society.)

I do modern dance. My teacher's the head of our troupe, and I'm the assistant teacher. For some people dance is a hobby and for others it's everything, but for me it's in the middle—it's important, but it's not my *ikigai*. If I made it my *ikigai*, I'd have to leave my family, but for me my family is more important than dance. If I made dance the only thing in my life, it'd be awfully hard—I know my abilities.

Now my teacher's sick in the hospital; she's having a hard time psychologically. She's lost confidence; she's uncertain about whether she can continue the dance troupe. She's not married, and supports herself from dance; she must be wondering, "What can I do if I can't dance?" Looking at her, I feel awfully lucky to have a family—she's said that to me too. The only thing she has is dance.

I was born in the country and moved to the city when I was thirteen, after my parents divorced. My mother ran a beauty parlor to support us. I got married at twenty-one. My husband works for a TV station; we have two sons, fifteen and eleven. If I were twenty again, I might not marry—maybe I'd become a female executive!—but then, maybe if I worked for a company all my life, I'd wish I had a family. I think I took the best path; this is the best way for me to live. . . .

It hasn't been easy. My husband's manic-depressive. I couldn't understand what was wrong until six years ago. Before then, I always wondered why he had such mood swings. I was worried that I might be the cause of his depression. When he lay in bed saying that he couldn't go to work, I really didn't know if he *couldn't* go or just didn't *want* to go. I couldn't tell if he was sick, or just lazy—that was the hardest part. Before I understood, I sometimes said to him, "Come on! Get out of bed and go to work!" Mostly, though, I just worried. . . .

Eventually he was hospitalized, and the disease was controlled. Before that, he wouldn't go to work for weeks at a time. One morning he'd feel he couldn't go to work, the next morning the same thing, and the next morning. . . . I felt really sorry for his company. He was in charge of a section, and if he couldn't work, the section as a whole would grind to a halt. For a while it looked like he'd get fired. I sometimes went to his company to talk with his boss; I called in sick for him—I hated it when I had to do that! (The company wasn't at all sympathetic. They really didn't care about my husband; they just said, "Don't take any more days off. If you can't work, we don't want you!" Later, though, the company became more open-minded; now people seem to work in a more relaxed way, my husband too.)

Just after my husband got out of the hospital, my oldest son swung a baseball bat and accidentally hit his friend—his friend lost an eye. We paid compensation; we couldn't give him an eye back, and apologizing wasn't enough. I don't feel resentment toward that family, but I do feel that if our son had been the victim, we wouldn't have asked for money. Our lawyer and their lawyer calculated the amount, based on the child's projected lifetime income. The family wanted more. Why on earth did this happen to us? It could just as easily have been in reverse: my son could have been the victim. We wound up paying a year and a half of my husband's salary. I wanted to move away, since they live close to us, but we didn't. The kids didn't want to change schools, and escaping the situation somehow seemed wrong.

Right now I'm most worried about my older son's college entrance examination. Japan really is a *gakureki shakai* [a society based on school credentials].[6] Maybe that's bad, but that's the trend of Japanese society, and we have to flow with it. My son doesn't have to go to a good college; any college'll do. But he's not even average: I don't know if he can get into *any* college! Yes, when he was born I expected him to work for a good company, like my husband; it disappoints me that he might not be able to. Maybe I made mistakes in raising him. . . . I'm not so concerned with his grades; the problem is that he doesn't try hard. He's more childish than other kids his age. Sure, it's better for him to be childish than to be, say, in a motorcycle gang.[7] But he may get like that later if he doesn't learn good judgment now. If he argued with us, asserted himself more, he'd develop his own judgment, but because he doesn't think for himself yet, I'm worried that he'll fall into a bad crowd. I want him to grow up, but how do you foster that?

My younger son has more confidence than his brother, because he's good at judo and a leader in his class in school. His brother doesn't seem jealous—that's strange. Usually if your younger brother is doing better than you, you feel envious, but he only says, "You can do well because you're my younger brother!" That attitude's sweet, but there's something wrong with it, don't you think? He should feel upset! I'm worried about him. He doesn't have any sense of competition. He's such a sweet kid, but with a character like that, he can't survive in this world. . . .

The happiest thing in my life is that I married my husband. We don't have any *kentaiki* [sense of growing tired of married life]; my friends say that's unusual. The saddest thing is that my older son doesn't study. When my husband and I argue, we always argue over the same thing: our son. My husband thinks I should leave him alone; I tell him to be more strict. . . .

6. In Japan, college entrance examinations form the most important determinant of a youth's future: "an examination winner will be a lifetime winner and a loser will remain a loser" (Lebra 1984, 215). One who passes the examination and attends a top university is virtually guaranteed prestigious employment in the future. One who attends a third-rate university has almost no chance of obtaining such employment.

7. Motorcycle gangs (*bōsōzoku*) are common in Japanese cities, racing and gunning their engines en masse down major thoroughfares late at night. They are made up primarily of teenage school dropouts, and are relatively innocuous, as compared to, say, Hell's Angels. For an ethnography of the *bōsōzoku* subculture, see Sato 1991.

My husband is the center of my life. Because of him I can dance, and because our children are *our* children I look after them until they become independent. In the end it's my husband and me. I don't think he'll ever become *nure ochiba* ["wet fallen leaves": retired husbands who just sit around the house]; he's always interested in learning new things—I'll have to study hard so that I won't get left behind! I'm looking forward to when my kids leave home; I'll be really happy if they both can find their own paths. Since my son's accident, when I hear on the news about some criminal being arrested, I think of how his parents must feel. They must have raised their child as best they possibly could. . . .

Lying in bed at night, I worry about things: "What shall I do if this or that happens?" "How should I behave toward my parents-in-law?" (They live with my husband's older brother.) "Can we get the money to buy a house?" (We have to rent now.) Sometimes I can't sleep. Compared to six years ago, when my husband was sick and my son had his accident, my worries are less intense, but I still worry. I worry about my husband's health; I worry about my sons' future; I worry about my own aging; I worry about my parents and parents-in-law because they're getting old. I cry sometimes when I feel helpless, when there's nothing I can do. I cry when my husband's asleep; he doesn't know, I think. Life's tough, isn't it?

Women are getting stronger in Japan. But some women are still putting up with unhappy marriages, because if they get divorced and go to work, they can't maintain the standard of living they had, especially if they have children. One of my friends stays with her husband only because she needs his salary to support the family. If I got a divorce and tried to raise my kids by myself, it would be impossible. Maybe I could get alimony, but in Japan the court decision on alimony doesn't have much power; there are many cases where husbands simply don't pay.

People often say that women are stronger than men in difficult situations. Women tend to be strong not for themselves but for others, for their children or husbands. Men usually live for their companies more than for their families. What women live for is closer to themselves; it lasts all their lives. But a man's work at his company doesn't last; he'll have to retire. Some men realize that in their work they're just a cog in a machine, but others don't; they believe that they're essential, that without them the company couldn't survive. These men are being fooled, I think. But family is different. It's not like a company: you can't simply exchange one mother for another; a member of a family is not just a replaceable cog. Maybe that's why women are so strong. I think that women tend to be happier than men. Because women bear children, they feel that their children are their own; they have a stronger tie with their children than men can ever have.

I believe 50 percent in life after death, but maybe I'll believe 100 percent when I'm seventy-five! I'm still too young to feel strongly about these things. When I visit the graves of our ancestors, I do sense that they may be watching us. But I've never really thought about it. Instead, I worry about how to look after the family graves. I have to do properly the rites of the different Buddhist sects our ancestors belonged to. I guess it's only a formality, but I have to respect it and convey it to my sons—our older son will have to look after the graves of my husband and me after we die. We don't finally know what'll happen to us after we die—there's no manual telling the truth of all this, after all!—so all we can do is follow the forms handed down to us by our ancestors. (Last June my aunt died suddenly. It gave me a new feeling about death, of death becoming closer. I didn't feel anything about her spirit going to another world, only, "My aunt's gone. I can't see her smile; I can't walk with her, talk with her anymore. . . .")

What's my *ikigai?* Maybe in my heart, my children are my *ikigai,* but I don't want to say it—that would be a real burden on them. I'll have to let my children go some day; if I let them be my *ikigai,* my whole life would be an accessory to them. I do have the responsibility to raise them to become responsible members of society, so as to not trouble others, but not to hold to them as *ikigai*—I've got to grow as an individual! Of course my children are my husband's children too. My husband and children are tied together; since I got married, my *family* has been my *ikigai.* Being for my family is being for myself and being for myself is being for my family. I guess I sound like a very average person!

Men's *ikigai* may appear to be their work, but really they work to support their families. Maybe they don't realize that family is their *ikigai*, but it is. Who'd work, after all, if they didn't get paid the money they need to support their families?

Denise Pratt (41)

(Meeting Denise Pratt at her house, I sensed her resemblance to Wada-san, in appearance and later in character: she seemed to have a similar vitality and emotional warmth. I met her on Saturdays, when her three children were off with their father. In the middle of our first interview, I knocked over the glass of juice she had given me, spilling it over the living room rug. Maybe I only imagined it, but it seemed that after this accident, her thoughts about life also spilled out freely, with only minimal questioning from me.)

My work is to administer continuing adult education programs for the city. I like my work because I can bring a social consciousness to what I'm doing. We have recreation classes, that kind of thing, but also literacy programs and basic math, as well as a course on "divorce and your rights." I really like the work I'm doing, but I also have to be fiscally responsible. The challenge is to see if I can pull off the finances!

I grew up in Maryland; I had a good childhood. My father was an engineer, my mother a housewife; next year, my parents will have been married fifty years. . . . When I got out of college, I ski-bummed for a year. Then I taught mentally retarded kids in Michigan for four years, and got married. Jeff was a ski instructor at a local resort. We moved to Illinois because he wanted to get into the building business with a friend, and I went to graduate school to get a master's in special education. But they did away with the program while I was in it; then I got pregnant and we moved here. I worked as a political activist for a while, with the Democratic Party. Then I got a job directing adult education at a community school. The work was great, but it paid just eight thousand a year. When the divorce happened, I had to find a job that made money. I got a job administering a grant program, but got fired after three months; I don't know why. Jeff wasn't paying any child support, and I had three kids to support; I've never been so scared in my life. But eventually I got this job. That's my history—I've been on survival mode. What runs through everything I've done is a mission orientation, trying to answer some of society's needs. Without that sense of mission, I couldn't get excited about work. (I have three kids I have to educate, collegewise. I have no idea how I'm going to do that! I make about twenty-five thousand dollars a year—I'm still figuring out how to buy the groceries!)

What happened to my marriage? I really haven't sorted it out yet. We were married fifteen years, and there were many things we had in common: a spirit of adventure, a sense of humor. But I take my family responsibilities very seriously, and he's the kind of man who never wants to grow up. He's in real estate development—financially, the big dream was always just around the corner. I was constantly begging them not to turn off our water and electricity. . . .

The divorce process is awful when there are children involved. I've had to fight Jeff in court three or four times. I wanted this man wiped off the face of the earth! He was being obstructionist, and I was fighting for my kids' financial well-being; I didn't know if we were going to have to declare bankruptcy. Jeff now has the kids every other weekend and Wednesday nights. He used to have them Thursday nights too, but he was involved with several women, and had them around when the kids were there; it was causing trauma for my oldest one, so I cut that off. I am basically the solid rock for them. This is their home; they know who they can rely on. . . .

Still, I own, I think, half the reason the marriage failed. I wasn't comfortable with my role as "homemaker." If you've been active in the professional world, you get a lot of strokes; when you're at home and have these little kids who can't even speak English, and the only person there to affirm you is this husband who comes home late, that's not enough. Society doesn't affirm you in that role of mother because you're not making any money. Your husband is only human; it's unfair to ask him to provide all that's missing in your life. . . . Somehow I have a foot in two generations, the fifties and the sixties. And they're at war with each other, though they come to terms as I get older. The fifties: home, family stability; the sixties: political activism, feminism, equality between men and women. . . . I didn't want to be pigeonholed in any kind of role! There's a war that goes on between women and men now. Hopefully it's getting better. I hope my sons, having grown up seeing a mother who works, will realize that everybody does their share and nobody has specifically defined roles; you work it all out much as you'd work out a job-sharing thing, with equal partners.

We're in a chaotic period in America. Families are in transition; the divorced family now is as much a part of the structure of this country as the two-parent family. It's the divorced women who take the responsibility for the kids and go out and work; they do it all. People say that America's falling apart because women are in the work force instead of staying at home. But I say—once I stop foaming at the mouth!—that no, America is falling apart because men have never accepted that it's equally their responsibility to raise children, down to a nitty-gritty thing like, when a child needs something it will call the father as readily as it calls its mother, and Dad will respond.

My kids: Jamie's eight, Eric's eleven, and Victor's fourteen. Victor's really felt the impact of the divorce. I'm worried about his school performance; he's got a few things to learn about hard work and commitment. He's a very bright kid, but he hasn't hit stride at all. I tell him he should be getting better grades; he thinks I put too much pressure on him. I get weekly reports from his school, about his homework and if he did it well. . . . I want my kids to be educated, to go to college, so that they'll have a full range of choices in their future. But I get fearful; Victor is rebellious enough to say, "I won't go to college!" Eric is the peacemaker. He's incredibly loyal to both Jeff and me; he's felt torn by the divorce. If I say something about Jeff, he'll say, "Why do you always say that about Dad?" He does the same with Jeff, I know. He has a learning disability; I had him held back a grade to deal with that—trying to keep that self-esteem intact. He's the best athlete of my kids: such grace, it's a joy to watch him. Jamie is probably the one I will learn the most from—he's had a sense of himself since he was born. Jamie is the straight-A student.

At age four he said, "Mom, can you tell me about infinity?" He's always had that sense of himself, a basic core that never seems threatened. . . .[8]

My kids'll eventually make up their own minds about their values. All you can do as a parent is give them a yardstick. I'd like to follow them around every day, making sure that they're safe and doing the right things. But if you do that, it doesn't allow them to become who they are. So you just try to do the best job you can. . . .

What's most important to me, my work or my children? My kids are. I'm absolutely dedicated to my children. But I need to support them, so my work too is absolutely important. I've been fortunate in that I've been able to work at things that allow me to make a living and still have a mission orientation, letting me help with the problems in the world. But most essential: I want to raise my children to be caring adults who will give back to this world in some form. Whatever I'm doing in the day, if there's a need, I'll be there with my kids. But I'm not a person that's content to stay within the home, that's not me—my kids would really suffer! I'd become so focused on them that it wouldn't be healthy for me or the kids. It's scary too because they're going to leave home at some point. It's critical that I have a life outside my kids. I know it's going to be hard; but I've taken some steps in how to build my life, once I'm alone.

I have to face the possibility that there may never be another man in my life. The loneliness—you've got to learn to deal with it. I've got to have this job, and I've got to take care of my children. Then you have a relationship—of the three of these, what's expendable is the relationship. If you're going to be a responsible parent, you have very little energy left over. I'm incredibly protective of my children. The one thing that I will never get over is the pain they've gone through, because of Jeff and my failure at our marriage. I've created this situation that will affect the rest of their lives, and I will never again put them in that kind of jeopardy.

---

8. Wada-san does not refer to her husband and children by their names, but Ms. Pratt does. This is a general pattern: Japanese tend to refer to family members in terms of their structural position in the family ("husband," "younger child," etc.), and Americans tend to refer to members of their families by their individual names. This may be thought of as both reflecting and constituting "Japanese groupism" and "American individualism."

Yes, getting older is sad for me. Ultimately, when you have a partner in your life, you have this best friend. Now I feel there's a void. You can't rely on that other person to bring you happiness; you've got to create your own. Maybe I'll never meet a person that meshes with me—the opportunities are few. . . . There are scary things out there. How am I going to get my kids through college? And I don't want to be a bag lady! I don't want to be a burden on my kids! Those are my biggest fears. . . .

I think the spirit lives on after you die. There are too many occurrences in this world that we can't explain for me to simply say, "When you're dead, you're dead, that's it." The commonalities of religion throughout the world: there's a reason they're there. I pray a lot. Tevye, in *Fiddler on the Roof,* has these ongoing conversations with God. I have those kinds of conversations, maybe mostly with myself, but there's a part of me that believes absolutely that there's a God, though what form that takes I'm not really sure. . . . I was thinking the other day, what would it be like if there was no starvation, if people didn't go to war but treated each other with kindness, a perfect world, and I thought, we'd never learn anything in such a world. Our basis for learning would be wiped out. We'd have nothing to live for. I think you learn, grow through pain. . . .

I'd say that both children and mission orientation are for me spokes of a wheel; the center of my life is how I am as a human being and how I relate to the world. The journey I take inward is one of seeing all I can see, continuing to evolve. It's sort of "to thine own self be true." I would love to become this wise old woman who had this sense of humor, this depth of compassion that allowed for seeing the injustices of the world without becoming cynical and bitter. Where I've changed over the years is, instead of wanting to set the world on fire, now I take it to a much smaller level. I shouldn't feel that because I haven't saved the world, I haven't helped; if an old woman fell and dropped her groceries and I picked them up, made sure she was OK, maybe that's more important. If you sit there worrying about the global changes you can't affect, you get burned out, cynical; but a thank-you from that old lady keeps you going.

Wada Masako and Denise Pratt: Analysis

These two women are similar in that each seems to live for her children, and each has another focus aside from children: Wada-san her dance, and Ms. Pratt her work and "mission orientation." However, Wada-san is married, Ms. Pratt divorced; Ms. Pratt takes on the responsibilities of both mother and breadwinner that Wada-san and her husband divide between them.

What is these women's *ikigai?* When I asked Ms. Pratt what was most important to her in her life, she insisted that it was herself and her growth, but she also emphatically emphasized her commitment to her children. I interpret her *ikigai* to be her children, but this remains a bit ambiguous. Wada-san's *ikigai* is her family, she tells us, both her husband, the center of her life, and her children, the source of her deepest concern; but she hints at dissatisfaction: "I've got to grow as an individual!" These women seem to seek a balance between self-realization and commitment to family in their interpretations of their lives, but finally family wins out as their *ikigai.*

For both women, there are potential *ikigai* in competition with family. Wada-san refuses to allow dance to become her *ikigai,* seeing in her teacher a cautionary example of the perils of such a path. Ms. Pratt eschews relationships with men because they would interfere with her relationship with her children. Her job lets her "help with the problems in the world," but finally she considers it a means to the end of supporting her children.

But although family and children seem to come first in these women's lives, both feel reluctant to hold their children as *ikigai.* There seem to be two reasons for this. First, both women say that to focus too much upon their children wouldn't allow their children to grow into autonomy; both believe that their children should grow up and become independent as the natural course of things. Wada-san tells us that she looks forward to the time her children leave home, so that she can be with her husband in a happy old age. Whether or not her oldest son can make that transition is the most troubling question she now faces. Ms. Pratt too is worried about her sons' passage to adulthood, especially if they'll attend college and how she will finance it; but once that task is completed, there is no return to marital happiness, but rather the possibility of being alone, and becoming "a burden on my kids" or "a bag lady," her darkest worry.

Second, there is these women's relation to the role of wife and mother. Whether through mass media or dance, Wada-san has been exposed to the idea of self-realization as *ikigai;* she plays with that idea, but finally rejects it: her *ikigai* is commitment to her family as mother and wife, she concludes. Ms. Pratt, although also deeply committed to her children, dislikes the role of traditional mother and homemaker. She sees the ideal society as one in which men and women equally work and share childraising, in which there are no demarcated sex roles of breadwinner and homemaker, no familial *ikigai* division.

Related to these different views of women's roles are different views of men's roles and the world of work. Wada-san holds that women tend to be happier than men, in that what they live for is genuine, not spurious; lifelong, not cut off at retirement. Men's work for their companies is no more than being a cog in a machine, she says. But women's service for their families is different: each mother is uniquely indispensable. In fact, men's real *ikigai* is not work but family, Wada-san tells us, even though they may not realize it.

If Wada-san believes that family is superior to work as one's deepest commitment, Ms. Pratt holds that work is superior to family. She seems to view work not as a commitment to company that is inferior to commitment to family, but as an arena for self-realization that is superior to commitment to family. Ms. Pratt is deeply devoted to her children but can't justify that devotion, given her belief that work in the world is superior to childraising. Wada-san, on the other hand, can justify her deep devotion to her children, given her belief that family is a genuine *ikigai* as compared to the spurious *ikigai* of work.

It's impossible to distinguish the extent to which these differences in *ikigai* stem from larger cultural factors or from personal factors in these women's lives. Wada-san believes that women are happier at home than men are at work, whereas Ms. Pratt believes that men and women should eliminate gender roles; this difference seems in large part due to the impact of feminism in the United States and its absence in Japan. Indeed, Ms. Pratt speaks of having one foot in the domestic fifties and the other in the feminist, activist sixties. On the other hand, Wada-san's mother divorced her husband and supported her three children on her own earnings, while Ms. Pratt's parents have been married almost fifty years, her mother the homemaker, her father the breadwinner. Each woman has followed a path opposite to that of her own mother. Ms. Pratt's greater emphasis on her own growth and Wada-san's greater emphasis on commitment to family correspond to the dominant conceptions of American and Japanese *ikigai* that have been discussed. However, Ms. Pratt is divorced and faces a life alone once her children leave, while Wada-san will presumably be with her husband, and this difference may have much to do with the difference emphases in their accounts: Ms. Pratt doesn't speak in terms of relationships because she lacks what might be the most essential such relationship.

These women are each uniquely themselves, but their senses of *ikigai* are widely shared in their respective societies: in Japan, adherence to a familial division of *ikigai* remains the norm; in the United States this norm of thirty years ago is, for many, the norm no longer. Let's now turn to the accounts of two men who don't fit this norm, men who find *ikigai* not in work, but in other areas of their lives.

Takagi Atsushi (42)

(Takagi-san's house is remarkable. The first floor has a garden and tea room, straight from picture books on "traditional Japan"; the second floor's white surfaces and angular coffee tables look like a spread from an interior design magazine. One might assume that a man living in such a house would be content, but more than anyone else I interviewed, Takagi-san seemed to be ceaselessly questioning and doubting himself. Interviewing him, I heard a man struggling to get to the bottom of himself to behold whatever he might find, however unpleasant.)

When I was a kid, my family was rich; my father was a company president. A huge American car would come by every morning to pick him up. Cars were rare in those days; I remember it well. . . . My father died four years ago. I built this house for my mother: my wife and I and our two kids live on the second floor, and she lives on the first. I had a big fight with her over the house—I didn't want it to be so ostentatious. Even though I'm the youngest child, I inherited the land when my mother decided to live with me after my father died. She can't get along with my older brother's wife, so my brother asked me to live with her. My sisters aren't too happy about this—I inherited this land; I built this big house. I was close to them before, but now we only see each other once a year or so. I can't believe it's come to that. I wish I could throw away the house, the land. . . .

My father didn't really have any consciousness of being high in status, but my mother did; she influenced me a lot. When I was thinking of marrying my wife, what really bothered me was that she was from a farming family; I regarded farming as lower in social status. My mother was against the marriage from the start. Our marriage turned out fine, but I worried about it for years before we finally married, worried that my parents opposed it. . . . When I joined the company I work for, after college, people felt I was different. People knew that my father had been a company president. Younger people now don't know; I feel more at ease.

I work for a financial services company. I don't like being a company worker [*sarariiman*]; I'm always frustrated. You get incredibly concerned with how to sell yourself to your superiors—you want to be valued, promoted—and because of that, you become less frank in your opinions. I hate this work; it could never be my *ikigai*. The toughest thing is that this isn't a path I chose myself. When I graduated from college, I didn't choose this job because I wanted it; I chose this company, to tell the truth, because it looked easy. I thought it would be easier than working for, say, a bank, but the salary was the same. . . .

In the years since I got married, I've been helping my wife's parents on their farm, planting rice in spring and harvesting it in fall. A few years ago, I talked to my wife's parents about quitting my company and farming with them instead. Father seemed happy, but Mother said there wasn't any future in it: Japan will rely more on imported rice in the future, and this area isn't good for growing rice;

it'll decline in rice cultivation. So we couldn't support ourselves on farming alone. . . .

If I were young again, I'd choose a different path. I'd study hard and get a job in a trading firm, or maybe in the United Nations, a job dealing with the world. If my dreams now came true, I wouldn't want to rise in the company; my dreams aren't about the company at all. If I didn't have to worry about my family, maybe I'd go live in a foreign country. I wouldn't quit my work: I'd ask for a long vacation, say, two years. I could do it because I wouldn't care if I got fired. Once I told my boss that I'd be really happy if I could live in a foreign country for a year. He said, "Yes, but Japan's tough, isn't it? . . ."

If I could, I'd quit the company and do something I want to do. But I can't, because I have to support my kids. Actually, though, to be honest, I don't know what I'd do if I could quit—that's sad but true. I've thought about studying history, but I couldn't do that for the next twenty years. . . . Or could I? I'm interested in the age of Genghis Khan. If I were to study, say, fourteenth-century Europe, I'd go there to see the architecture of that time. My interest would grow deeper; my world would expand. . . . If I really wanted, I could start studying now. But I need time—I don't want to be disturbed by work, but just read. I'm waiting for such a time to come.

My wife is a real support to me. One night I looked at her, and at our kids sleeping beside us.[9] She looked so tired from taking care of them—I felt I couldn't quit the company, however much I hated it. Later I did tell her I wanted to quit; she said, "Go ahead." When I asked her how we'd eat, she said we'd go to her parents' farm to live. If we could really do that, it'd be great, but. . . . In Japan, most husbands don't listen to their wives; they just give orders, so their wives become like dolls, deprived of their own feelings. If my wife were a passive woman, like most other wives, she'd only panic if I said I wanted to quit my company: "Oh, no, you can't quit! How could we live?" I'd just feel all the more depressed. I'm lucky she's not like that.

9. It's common for children in Japanese families today to sleep in the same room as their parents, at least until school age. See Caudill and Plath (1966) for a detailed though somewhat dated account of Japanese family sleeping patterns.

I worry about my kids. My daughter's still small, but I tell my son, a second grader, to study hard. I myself went to a fairly good college, but I goofed off in high school, didn't do my best. I feel great regret about that now.... My son's sly [*zurui*]; when he does something wrong, he never admits it. His teacher says that he does well academically, but he has a character problem; he bullies the weak instead of protecting them. Children grow up looking at their parents; I wonder if to his eyes I'm sly too? I have to be careful how I act; I feel tense sometimes around my kids. Maybe we're too concerned about our kids. What I'm worried about these days is that we're making them conform too much. My son doesn't seem to act like a child anymore. But if he stops studying so hard, he'll lose out in his future. So we really don't know....

If ten years ago I knew what I know now, I wouldn't have had kids; I think my wife feels the same way. I don't feel particularly affectionate toward my mother; when my kids grow up, they may feel the same way toward me. Many people want children because they want to rely on their kids when they get old; they don't realize how heavy a burden that is on their kids. I know because I'm experiencing it! Probably my mother felt that of all her children I loved her most, so she wanted to live with me. But this isn't a situation I wanted to be in. I wouldn't want to rely on my children that way. Of course I can say this now: I'm still young. Maybe I'll feel like she does when I get old.

I feel sad when I think about how old I am. I feel a chill when I realize that I haven't done much in my life yet. At forty, you're at the happiest time of your life—you've got a responsible job and lots of confidence. From your forties on, your importance declines. When I see old people, I sense they want to be the center of attention; they're all like that, even those who seem wise. The seventy-year-old feels he could do a better job if only he had the vitality of the forty-year-old, because he has more wisdom, more experience. But he can't keep up; he can't be on center stage any longer; his time is past....

My father died of cancer. For a year every weekend I slept in a bed by his side in the hospital; I even changed his diapers. In his last days he looked like a victim at Auschwitz. I'd never talked much with my father before then, because he was always busy with work; it was only when he was dying that we became close. Since his death, I've come to really feel his presence. When something good happens to my family, I think about how happy my father would be. Every summer we visit his grave. I talk to him: "Dad, how are you doing? Are you OK?" I don't think he's OK—he's dead! But I tell him about the kids, tell him the things I'd tell him if he were alive. . . .

Of course I'm afraid of death. I've been terrified since I was eleven, and my grandmother died. It occurred to me that I would die too, a shocking realization! But now I can accept the fact that after I die, I cease to exist. . . . I don't want to die in the hospital, but in nature. If I were with my family, I'd cling to life, be greedy. It'd be easier to die alone in the mountains. I'd want to freeze to death. When I was a child, I got locked in a storage shed for six hours in winter. My body got cold; my heartbeat got slow. That's how you freeze: your mind is clear, and you only feel the beating of your heart. . . .

If there were life after death, I wouldn't try so hard to live now. I work hard at my company even though I don't like my work; my kids get wisdom, though maybe not much, from my example. I work hard finally for my kids, teaching them how to live. After I retire, I'll study history for my own satisfaction, but my kids will learn from me. When I die I can leave an example of how to live to my children; I'll leave my attitude toward life. . . .

What's my *ikigai?* I want to be able to do what I want to do without worrying about making a living. Now I don't have time to find what I want to do. I can't quit my company because I have to support my kids; I should use the little free time I have for my own study, but that's hard. . . . I guess I don't have any *ikigai.* I love my kids—I want to teach them to be fine human beings. But my kids shouldn't be my *ikigai*—they'll have their own lives to live. My wife can't be my *ikigai* either. *Ikigai* is a matter of living in this world with your own individual purpose. A desire to become a section chief or get married— that's not *ikigai.* I want to live a life with meaning; I want to have an *individual purpose* to my existence! That's the ideal; if I look at my own life, it's far from that ideal. . . .

When I was younger, I never thought about *ikigai.* I thought about it for the first time when my father died. In a way I'm less happy now than I was ten years ago: I didn't doubt things then. But the doubts always come sooner or later. Typically, when a *sarariiman* retires, he doesn't know what to do. He begins asking, "Who am I? All I've done is work from morning to night for my kids. But who in the world am I?" So what I'm going through now would have hit me sooner or later anyway. . . .

My life is relatively happy; I'm well off, I have a nice family. But I don't have a purpose in life. My life is *relatively* happy, but not *absolutely* happy, because I can't find *ikigai*. Most people don't have what I think of as *ikigai*. Probably no more than one in a thousand have *ikigai*, that's my sense of it. Will I find *ikigai* before I die? I don't know; I *want to find ikigai!* But looking at my life now, I'd say that the chance I'll find it is incredibly small.

Jerry Eliot (43)

(The night of my first interview with Jerry Eliot, in his rambling, tree-shaded home, the Gulf War had just broken out. The TV in his living room intoned all the latest news, but it seemed to have no effect on Mr. Eliot. He talked for five hours, then said, "Damn, you've kept me up late! Don't you ever stop talking?" [10] In our concluding interview, he mulled over the word *ikigai* until the early hours of the morning, spinning out what he termed "bullshit" theory after "bullshit" theory as to what life might really mean.) [11]

My dad owned a furniture store. He was an alcoholic, a real mellow alcoholic; my mom nagged the shit out of him to stop drinking, which

10. Mr. Eliot and Takagi-san seem to be equally informal speakers in their respective languages. Mr. Eliot expresses informality by salting his speech with profanities, but Takagi-san, like many Japanese, expresses informality by using plain rather than polite grammatical forms, profanity being all but absent in spoken Japanese today.

11. I told each American at the start of our interviews that I was investigating the Japanese term *ikigai* and its meaning in Japanese lives and equivalents in American lives. For most of the Americans I interviewed, the term *ikigai* never arose in our subsequent conversations; Mr. Eliot was one of the few who insisted on pursuing and mulling over the term.

gave him a good reason to drink more. He died in 1988, of a heart attack. We didn't have any reconciliation; there was a lot left unsaid, a bookfull. We'd started getting some chapters out, but if it was a hundred-chapter book, we had ninety-eight chapters left to go. My father worked seven days a week, twelve hours a day for forty years. That contributed to his death, I'm sure. My mother lives in a retirement community near here; I see her quite a bit. With her it's always, "I don't like this, I don't like that"; she's never happy about anything. No, there's not a chance in hell she's ever going to live here with us! On the other hand, I'd invite my wife's mother here any day; she could live with us as long as she wanted, but by the same token, she'd never ask to move in. . . .

But this isn't a fair assessment of my parents. My dad was a good working man; he was also thoughtful and caring. My mom bitches and moans, but she's a good person too. She'd give you the shirt off her back—not without the third degree, but she'd give it to you. My folks were good people, but the booze screwed them up. . . .

I had an OK childhood. I was lousy at sports as a kid; in high school I'd bury my head in a book because I couldn't get a date, or was afraid to ask for one. High school was bumming around with the guys, having a girlfriend. I missed out on all that. I hated high school. . . . I graduated at sixteen, went to college, then graduate school, studying literature. I was pretty self-centered then; if you hadn't read as much as I had, I didn't want to talk to you. I needed to learn to talk to ordinary people. I'd been teaching as an assistant professor, and also working at a gas station part-time at nights, when one night a buddy of mine came in and said, "Let's go to Las Vegas." The second place we walked into, we were offered jobs. My friend went home after a week, but I stayed. I worked as a blackjack dealer. . . .

One day I met an interesting guy at the tables, and a few weeks later got a call from him—it turned out that he was the president of a large European bank: "I've got an interview set up for you in Los Angeles." I couldn't even balance a checkbook, but I wound up with a job. I worked there four years, doing commercial finance, but then I got laid off, was out of work for a year. I blamed myself—my old man had taught me that if you don't have a job, you're lazy—went through terrible depression. I tried getting a job everywhere, but this was in the mid-seventies recession. Sarah—I'd known her since my student days; we lived together in Las Vegas, and got married after that—was working as a bookkeeper, but she was getting minimum wage, and couldn't support us. I sent out thousands of resumes, went to dozens of interviews. I felt like I was being rejected every time. . . .

Then I found a job at another bank. Then, after I'd given a real estate company a hefty loan, the president offered me a job there. We took $400,000 revenues and parlayed it into $50,000,000 in less than two years. We were constantly working; the adrenaline rush was amazing, and so were the drugs and the booze. Business meetings over meals you drink at, then go to zoning commission meetings, then wine 'em, dine 'em, dump them off at midnight and go back to the office, and there's everyone snorting coke and drinking, so you drink some more while making your game plan for the next day, get home at two, up at seven. It was that way seven goddamn days a week!

I continued that for three years. Finally I said, "Sarah, this isn't doing us any good. I'm not feeling well"—my stomach was starting to bleed—"we got to do something." We moved out here, and I bought a furniture business. I ran that for ten years, but that got to be just as stressful. It wasn't drinking, but the hours: fourteen hours a day. I missed the first ten years of my son Billy's life. Sarah kept saying, "That's no way to live"; I kept saying, "I got to." I guess my priorities were fucked up. I really regretted that I didn't get to know my son, so when my daughter came along, I got rid of the business.

Now I have an office supply company. There are four of us, but I could do it all myself if I chose. I started this business so that I'd be home at five every night, and wouldn't work weekends. It's not a particularly fulfilling job, and I cut my income damn near 90 percent in creating it. If I was smarter, or luckier, I could have a job that was fulfilling and made lots of money, and that I still only had to work at eight hours a day; but. . . .

When Billy was little, Sarah had all the responsibility for taking care of him. I'm doing at least half of raising Jan (she's now three). This life with my family as first priority is without question better than before. I didn't think that was going to be the case, but it is! Sarah and I'd had some big arguments over how hard I worked; probably the biggest thing that's helped us stay together is me not working so much. But I have to put this in: Sarah gave me a hard time for coming home late, but now the shoe's on the other foot. She's head of Volunteer Coalition, an eighty-hour-a-week volunteer job. She yelled at me for ten years; now she says, "I've got meetings; I won't be home till midnight." I'm going, "You gave me shit for years for doing this; now you think it's OK?" But there are days when I know she put aside a ton of things she had to do at her job to be with Jan. She'll balance it; she knows what's needed to bring Jan up right.

I could damn near be a househusband, if I had the money. But both Sarah and I need the fulfillment that can be gotten from a job, paid or volunteer. What we've managed to do with minimum psychic damage (and maximum economic damage) is to share the role at home. During the years I was working all the time, I didn't want to be staying at home with the kid, cleaning house; Sarah did all that. But that's not fair. My dad worked, then came home and sat down in his easy chair with his newspaper. A lot of men are that way; they think they shouldn't share in household tasks. When I first met Sarah, she'd been brought up to play a traditional role, but women like her find they're unhappy just being at home. When they try to express themselves, their husbands don't listen, say, "There's a problem with *you*. . . ." That's a big reason why couples break up. We avoided that. . . .

My kids: Billy's in eighth grade; he's into sports. I'd love to see him go to college, but if he didn't want to, I wouldn't jeopardize our relationship because of that. We worry about his grades. But social development's so important—I'd rather he get Cs and have his act together than get As and be a social idiot. I'm more apprehensive about Jan. Girls are taught to think they're weak; I'm not going to train her that way. But she'll be in school soon; I worry about her succumbing to peer pressure. I want Jan to think she can be a good athlete, or president, to have her own brainpower.

The highlight of my life was getting hooked up with Sarah. Also, when Jan was born, and ever since—when you come home and she says, "Daddy, Daddy," and gloms onto your leg—what an ego trip! My life really has gotten better and better. There are things I wish I'd done differently: I wish I'd been smart enough to spend more time with my son when he was younger. And there's still a certain ego-hunger left, in not making millions, but I'm happy with what's happened. It's taken the last fifteen years to be able to feel that way. My self-confidence has gone up only in the last three or four years; before then, I had confidence in my work, but not in myself. I still have my days, but it was awful. . . . I think I'm becoming more mature as I get older. In a few years, the kids are going to be out on their own; I hope I'll have enough maturity to enjoy the time they give me to its maximum. Maturity'll keep me from fucking it up when Billy gets older, driving him away, saying something that turns him upside down. The same with my wife: maturity will allow me to maximize our relationship. My mom's terribly immature, like a sixteen-year-old. But I think I'll get older and better—that's the way Sarah's mom is. I'm sure she thinks occasionally, "I wish I could do that like I used to"; she's not excited about her physical deterioration. That's what I want to be angry about: "I've got the desire; get these old legs going! . . . I can't do it, but I know my limits, and I'm going to enjoy what I can do!" She's got that kind of attitude in life.

Twenty years ago I was certain that God didn't exist. As the years have gone by, I've become less judgmental, able to accept even the born-again Christians. I don't believe in God at this point, but that's an area where I'd say I need more maturity. I used to think it was a weakness to take comfort in a deity, but I don't feel that way now: yeah, there's a good chance I'll come to believe. But if I were to die now, my soul would go nowhere. When you're dead, you're dead. That's the biggest hurdle I'll have to get over to accept faith. . . .

I don't think death's scary. I'm afraid of dying painfully, but dying itself? No. Probably my biggest fear is that I'll die without leaving Sarah and the family comfortable financially; otherwise, I'm not afraid. I'm pragmatic. Hey, I'm gonna die. So I'll make the best of it while I'm here. I haven't thought much about death. My brain's too filled with what I'll do tomorrow! Even when my dad died, my own dying never entered my mind. . . .

The center of my life is my relation to Sarah. Everything I think about and do revolves around her; if I were ever to fear death, it would be hers more than my own. I count my blessings every day: the things that Sarah has taught me, the experiences I've had with her. Ten years ago, if I'd had to choose between my wife and my work, I wouldn't have said work was most important, but that's the way I lived. Culture leads many men to think that work is most important, but what's really most important to them is their families. It's an animal instinct to have your deepest commitment to your family. There are many people who think that they live for work, but the reality is that it can't be a true commitment. Culture—American culture, anyway—gives people a false sense of what's really most important to them in life.

Takagi Atsushi and Jerry Eliot: Analysis

These two men are similar in that they have both sought something beyond work to live for, but their differences seem more striking. Mr. Eliot is an optimist, Takagi-san a doubter, a pessimist, a man preoccupied with death. Mr. Eliot has had a kaleidoscopic work history; Takagi-san has worked for one company all his life. Mr. Eliot believes that family is the only true commitment; Takagi-san believes that family can't be a true *ikigai*. Mr. Eliot's *ikigai* has shifted from work to family (he wishes he had spent more time with his children), while Takagi-san's *ikigai* is neither work nor family, but pursuing his individual purpose in life (he wishes he had not had children).

From these men's accounts, we gain a rough idea of the personal shaping of their *ikigai*. Takagi-san's father was immersed in work, his mother, apparently, in social status. Nursing his father in his last days, Takagi-san perhaps saw the futility of living as his father had; thus, he doesn't hold work as his *ikigai*. Living with his mother, and feeling a lack of affection for her, he realizes the fragility of the parent-child bond and will not consider his children his *ikigai*. Spurning family as *ikigai*, Takagi-san holds to his distant dream of self-realization, a dream he knows he will probably never attain.

Mr. Eliot's father, like Takagi-san's father, was immersed in work, his mother unhappy. He followed in his father's footsteps in finding his deepest commitment in work, even owning, as had his father, a furniture store. He shifted that commitment at his wife's urgings and in recent years has devoted himself to his children. Indeed, if Takagi-san *works* for the sake of his children, Mr. Eliot *does not work* (does not work hard) for the sake of his. Like Takagi-san, Mr. Eliot has a deep commitment to his wife; unlike Takagi-san, he considers that commitment the center of his life.

These men's personal cultures have thus clearly shaped their *ikigai*, but their relations to their larger cultures seem more ambiguous. In his belief in gender equality, Mr. Eliot adheres to an emerging cultural ideal in the United States; in unreflectively adhering to the division of "men at work, women at home," as well as in refusing to hold his wife as his *ikigai* (to do so would be viewed by many Japanese men as *memeshii,* unmanly), Takagi-san holds to attitudes widespread in Japan today. In crucial respects, however, these men may be seen as anomalies in their larger cultures. Takagi-san is an anomaly in Japan in that he refuses to accept a role definition of the self. He isn't content to find his identity in being a company worker, or in being breadwinner and father; he seeks a self beyond such roles, and it is his sorrow in life that he can find no such self. Takagi-san's misfortune is that he seeks self-realization in a society that, in its dominant emphasis on making one's social role the essence of one's self, discourages that pursuit.

Mr. Eliot is an anomaly not simply in choosing commitment over self-realization as his deepest value, but also in that he makes family and not work his deepest commitment. As writers such as Faludi (1991, 60) and Hochschild (1989, 20) note, middle-class American men may claim to value family over work and to agree that men should participate as much as women in childrearing and housekeeping, but few live this way. Mr. Eliot, by his account, does indeed live this way (as confirmed to me by his wife). American culture gives its members false values, he tells us; he invokes nature to justify his lived commitment to family because American culture, as he sees it, doesn't accept that commitment.

Looking at these men's accounts, it is in a sense Takagi-san, in his emphasis on self-realization, who sounds stereotypically American, Mr. Eliot, in his emphasis on happiness in relations with others, who sounds stereotypically Japanese. Despite this, however, Takagi-san seems to have been shaped by cultural conceptions of commitment to group, Mr. Eliot by cultural conceptions of self-realization. Mr. Eliot has been in his life a college professor, a gas-station attendant, a Las Vegas blackjack dealer, a bank employee, an unemployed job-seeker, a high-rolling real-estate developer, a furniture-store owner, and the owner of his present small company. It's perhaps because he has experienced so many different worlds of work that he now can deemphasize his commitment to work and make his family his primary commitment in life. Takagi-san, on the other hand, has held only one job in his adult life, a job he hates. It's as if his single occupational choice at age twenty-two foreclosed all future choice: his die is cast, his fate sealed.

These two men may be extreme examples and don't fully reflect the occupational structures of their societies—I know younger Japanese men who have job-hopped with abandon and older Americans who have stayed with one company all their lives—and yet, in general, American occupational structures make more allowance for changing jobs and careers than do Japanese. (The same may hold true for schooling. It may be more than just personal happenstance that Mr. Eliot should make no use of his status as Ph.D. in his current life, while Takagi-san continues to regret not working harder in high school and thus going to a better college and attaining a job in a company of higher prestige.) This difference in occupational structure seems at least partly due to the American emphasis on pursuing one's own well-being and growth without encumbrances of corporate loyalty, as opposed to the Japanese emphasis on the individual's being a part of his corporate group rather than a free agent out to better himself. Thus, despite Takagi-san's "un-Japanese" pursuit of self-realization, and Mr. Eliot's "un-American" (for men) emphasis on family harmony over self, these men's lives have been shaped by their societies' dominant cultural conceptions of self-in-world. Though they don't adhere to these conceptions, they cannot escape them.

Let us now consider in a more general sense the relation of *ikigai* to gender and gender roles.

Ikigai and Gender

Gender in Japanese and American Accounts

Ideas about gender and gender roles are central to understanding this chapter's account of *ikigai*. Miyamoto-san's *ikigai* of commitment to company he sees as being primarily for men (as he conde-scendingly comments, "Men have work to give them psychological support, and women usually don't, so they turn to religion"). Wada-san views men's *ikigai* of commitment to company as less genuine than women's *ikigai* of commitment to family ("Family is . . . not like a company: you can't simply exchange one mother for another; a member of a family is not just a replaceable cog"). Takagi-san's *ikigai* of self-realization he sees as one that very few men or women can enjoy, but like Miyamoto-san and Wada-san, he seems to take for granted that men work to support their families and women stay home to nurture their families.

All three American accounts reject the familial division of *ikigai* so apparent in our Japanese accounts, to hold instead that husbands and wives should not have separate *ikigai* by gender role but should each find their *ikigai* primarily in family and secondarily in work. Mr. Mur-ray once found his deepest commitment in work rather than family, and he may have been divorced because of that. Ms. Pratt's marriage dissolved in part because "I wasn't comfortable with my role as 'homemaker.' . . . I didn't want to be pigeonholed in any kind of role!" Mr. Eliot's marriage survived because he was able to discard the role division of husband at work, wife at home: "Probably the biggest thing that's helped us stay together is me not working so much," but instead helping to raise his children.

This acceptance in our Japanese accounts and rejection in our American accounts of a familial division of *ikigai* seems to reflect larger cultural currents in the two societies. A recent survey (cited by Amaki 1989, 179) asked American and Japanese women if they agreed with the statement "Men should work and women should stay home." In Japan, 71.1 percent of respondents agreed, 23.7 percent disagreed; in the United States, 34 percent of respondents agreed, and 65.1 percent disagreed. A 1974 Louis Harris poll in the United States showed that men and women favored (49 percent to 45 per-cent) a marriage with the husband working and the wife minding the home (Harris 1987, 87). It thus may be that a generation ago Ameri-can women were closer to contemporary Japanese women in their acceptance of gender-specific roles, but that there has been a shift in many American women's views on gender roles—although gender remains a source of deep conflict in America today (Ginsburg 1989; Traube 1992).

The Japanese accounts in this chapter cannot be understood without considering Japanese conceptions of gender roles; but the most basic issue of *ikigai* in these accounts is that of whether it is to be found within one's social role or beyond one's role, an issue that to some extent cuts across gender lines. Is *ikigai* to be found through total immersion in the roles of man as employee and breadwinner, woman as housewife and mother? This is the view held by Miyamoto-san, and to some extent by Wada-san. Or is *ikigai* to be found not through one's total commitment to one's allotted role, but by finding one's own individual purpose in life? This is the view of Takagi-san, a view apparently considered but rejected by Wada-san.

In the American accounts, the dominant issue is not self-realization and commitment to group apart from gender, but in terms of gender. Women should have as much opportunity as men to find self-realization in work, and men should have as much commitment to their families as do their wives, both Ms. Pratt and Mr. Eliot tell us. Why this difference in emphasis? Why are the American accounts so much more concerned with escaping from gender roles than are the Japanese accounts? The answer involves the different conceptions of "self-realization" in American and Japanese societies.

Gender and Self-realization

This chapter's American accounts show more transient commitments to work and family—more divorce, more job changes—than the Japanese accounts. American institutional structures enable relatively easy divorce and job change, as Japanese institutional structures do not. In this sense, "self-realization" may be easier to pursue in the United States; one can more easily "change one's life" and follow a new path.

In Japan, although writers such as Kobayashi (1989) extol the pursuit of "self-realization," to follow one's own personal dream remains the exception, a path alluring but chimerical for most people, men and women, who find themselves within their social roles. In the United States, on the other hand, people may readily discard social roles in pursuit of a self that transcends such roles. The frequency of role change in the United States carries a social and personal cost; for example, a spouse who leaves a marriage in search of something better may leave behind a partner with dreams awry and children to support. But despite this, it seems that the freedom to change roles in the United States helps create opportunities for fulfillment apart from adherence to role, opportunities that remain comparatively rare in Japan.

But there remains a gap in opportunities for attaining such fulfillment between men and women in the United States. "One reason that half the lawyers, doctors, business people are not women is because *men do not share the raising of their children and the caring of their homes,*" writes Arlie Hochschild (1989, x; italics in original). Indeed, American cultural conceptions and institutional structures may be amenable to the pursuit of "self-realization," but men seem to have greater opportunities than women to pursue it; this imbalance is the major reason for the emphasis on gender in our American accounts. "There's a war that goes on between women and men now," Ms. Pratt tells us, in that "men have never accepted that it's equally their responsibility to raise children." "During the years I was working all the time, I didn't want to be staying at home with the kid, cleaning house; Sarah did all that. But that's not fair," Mr. Eliot tells us. This gender-role tension was apparent in the words of most of the American women I interviewed. "My dependency on my husband for almost everything was really starting to eat at me," stated one American woman in her fifties, who eventually began working outside the home. A thirty-year-old woman with a career in real estate said of her former husband, "I became resentful . . . because he didn't carry his weight around the house. I'll fully expect my next husband to carry his load." As for her own career, "If I didn't work, that would be very difficult for me. I really want to work, that's how I was taught." American survey results support these sentiments: "When working mothers are asked what they would do if family finances were not an issue . . . 82% say they would work anyway. Among nonworking women . . . 71% say they would prefer to be working" (Harris 1987, 92).

Indeed, Ms. Pratt, as we have seen, seems to view her work as an arena for self-realization, and thus as superior to the commitment of family. But Wada-san does not share this view. For her, both men's work and women's family involve not self-realization, but commitment, but men's commitment to company is false in that men are not truly indispensable for their companies as woman are indispensable for their children. In this difference, whereby work in the world is seen by Wada-san not as self-realization superior to commitment to family but as a form of commitment inferior to commitment to family, we have an answer to why our Japanese accounts are so little concerned with escaping from gender roles. But let me begin by discussing Japanese gender roles in more general terms.

The Role of Wife and Mother

In a society in which separate gender-specific roles—men at work, women at home—remain generally accepted, there is less cause for the kind of gender friction that exists in the United States, a friction resulting from gender roles that a majority say they have rejected but that apparently have not yet been transcended. More women seek to become *sengyō shufu* (full-time housewives) in Japan than can attain that status, holds a comprehensive study of Japanese housewives (Kokusai Josei Gakkai, 1980: 207). At present, women make up 40 percent of Japan's labor force (Ono 1991), as opposed to 45 percent of the United States' labor force, but more than in America, Japanese married women's employment tends to be part-time, so as to not conflict with duties at home. "The middle-class ideal," writes Ueno Chizuko, "is still the woman as mistress [of the house] without a job" (Ueno 1987, 80).

In Japanese newspapers and magazines I've read a number of accounts expressing Japanese women's dissatisfactions. For example, an anonymous women's magazine article entitled *"Tsumatachi no hontō no honne"* (The true feelings of wives) quotes scores of wives speaking of their husbands in such terms as, "I don't understand my husband at all. I've given up on him; I just ignore him," and "The ideal family for my husband is one that doesn't bother him, that leaves him alone" (*Kurowassan* 1990). In a more ironic vein, Amano Yūkichi (1990) reports in *Asahi Shinbun* on the many women who convey their husbands' dirty underwear to the washing machine with chopsticks because they can't bear to touch the intimate clothing of men they detest. For the most part, however, these articles illustrate women's dissatisfactions with their husbands rather than with their roles as housewives and mothers. The *Kurowassan* article may be compared to a recent American woman's magazine article (Tevlin 1992) on "Why women are mad as hell": not only because they tend to see their husbands as "selfish, self-centered and not interested in . . . home life," but also because, in a larger sense, "social and domestic realities have not kept up with demands for equality," demands Japanese women generally do not feel compelled to make.

There is a minority of Japanese women who do seek careers on an equal footing with men. I interviewed a young executive-in-training who waxed long and indignant about the corporate discrimination she has had to suffer: "I give presentations to our large customers. It's good for the company's image that a woman is representing it, but that corporate image is a fake. The company . . . doesn't give women any substantial role to play. I'm really just a show window." There may also be broad changes taking place in the ways Japanese women view their lot.[12] I interviewed several young Japanese women who said they would not want to lead the kind of lives their mothers led. Generally, however, it seems that many Japanese woman—the large majority of those I interviewed—are content with their domestic role in life.

One reason why the Japanese women I interviewed seemed more satisfied with their lot than their American counterparts may be that Japanese *sengyō shufu* continue to enjoy more social respect for their roles than American wives staying at home; the American phrase "just a housewife" has no Japanese parallel. A second reason involves economic pressures. In the United States, real family income has stagnated over the past two decades, but in Japan—at least until the

12. In English, Iwao (1993) sets forth a comprehensive (though perhaps overly sanguine) view of today's Japanese women. In Japanese, *Asahi Shinbun* (1990c) reports on the one-third of women who don't want to follow tradition and share the grave with husband and his ancestors, and Yoshihiro 1991 discusses "The reasons why women don't want children"; her book offers women-centered explanations for Japan's alarmingly low birth rate.

recession of the past few years—it has risen. Although economic pressures do cause many Japanese women to work part-time to supplement their husbands' incomes, in general Japanese women may feel less compelled to work outside the home than their American counterparts. Furthermore, Japanese women make, on average, far less money compared to men than do American women; thus Japanese women may be less motivated than American women to enter the work force.[13]

A third reason may be fear of divorce. Because of high American divorce rates, many American women feel that they "cannot rely absolutely on marriage as a means of support for themselves or their children" (Hochschild 1989, 140). As Wada-san tells us, divorce in Japan is economically threatening to women, but because divorce is less frequent in Japan (1.4 per thousand people in Japan in 1991, as opposed to 4.7 per thousand in the United States in 1993) it may be less feared. Many of the American women I interviewed felt the need to work in order to protect themselves from reliance upon their husbands' incomes, as the Japanese married women I spoke with did not.

There is still an additional explanation for Japanese women's frequent acceptance of the domestic role and American women's frequent rejection of that role, a difference in perspective seen in Wada-san's and Ms. Pratt's accounts. It seems that many Japanese women, seeing the difficult lives their husbands lead, tend to be content with their lot, whereas many American women, seeing the difficult lives they themselves lead in comparison to their husbands', tend not to be content.

"To be a woman in America at the close of the twentieth century—what good fortune. That's what we keep hearing, anyway" (Faludi 1991, ix). As a number of American feminist writers (Faludi 1991; Hochschild 1989; Hewlett 1986; Ehrenreich 1983) have demonstrated, this "good fortune" is illusory: American women tend to hold unremunerative and unfulfilling jobs compared to American men and

13. On the basis of figures in the *Japan Statistical Yearbook* (1991, 94) and the *Statistical Abstract of the United States* (1992, 412), I calculate that Japanese women receive on average 50 percent of the wages of their male counterparts; American women receive on average 74 percent of the wages of their male counterparts.

to shoulder most housekeeping and childrearing tasks at home. The same may be said of most Japanese women. Even more than their American counterparts, *their* jobs are unremunerative and unfulfilling, housekeeping and childrearing *their* tasks, with no aid from their husbands. (Takayama 1990, 11 cites surveys showing that Japanese men do an average of just eight minutes of housework a day. As one young wife and mother said to me, "My husband never does anything for himself in the house. He leaves his clothes lying on the floor; at mealtimes, he won't even take out his own chopsticks, even when I'm busy with the children.") The difference, however, is that many Japanese women (most of the married Japanese women I interviewed, including the women cited in the preceding sentence) find their identities in being housewives and mothers and their *ikigai* in their commitment to family. They are content to do housework and childrearing because this is their *ikigai;* they may accept unfulfilling jobs because work is *not* their *ikigai.*

Although many of the American women I interviewed, including Ms. Pratt, seemed to view the role of housewife and mother as unappealing, many of the Japanese women I interviewed, including Wada-san, seemed to find it very appealing compared to the lives their husbands must lead. Japanese company employees, aside from having far longer working hours than their American and European counterparts (Nagashima 1989; Lummis and Saitō 1991), may also feel compelled to drink with coworkers or entertain customers at night, and go on company outings on weekends. As Iwao tells us, "Men's lives in Japan today are confined and regimented by their jobs to an extreme" (1993, 15). Their wives, on the other hand, may enjoy considerable freedom. It is they who take classes in "culture schools," who learn dance, tea ceremony, and English, and who, increasingly, travel abroad; although they may have little power in the world, it is they who wield the power at home, generally controlling all family finances.

Indeed, as the social critic Asada Akira argues, "In many ways, it is really the [Japanese] men who need to be liberated. . . . Most of them identify with their companies and nothing else" (quoted in Takayama 1990, 15). As Iwao maintains, "Today it is, in a sense, the husbands who are being controlled and the ones to be pitied" (1993,

7); according to Takayama, Japanese women "have no intention of accepting lives as dull and unrewarding as their wage-slave husbands' " (1990, 14). Of the three Japanese in this chapter, only Wada-san has any sustaining activity apart from work and family; she has dance, but both Miyamoto-san and Takagi-san seem chained to their companies.

Many middle-class American wives of the 1950s may have led lives not dissimilar to those of many Japanese wives today.[14] "In the 1950s," writes Ehrenreich, "there was a firm expectation . . . that required men to grow up, marry and support their wives. . . . But by the end of the 1970s and the beginning of the 1980s, adult manhood was no longer burdened with the automatic expectation of marriage and breadwinning" (1983, 11–12). What the 1950s editors of *Playboy* advocated—that men avoid entrapment in marriage and the financial support of their wives—was advocated in later decades by the woman's movement: Betty Friedan envisioned an America where "women carry more of the burden of the battle with the world, instead of being a burden themselves" (Ehrenreich 1983, 102); Gloria Steinem proclaimed that "men will have to give up ruling-class privileges, but in return they will no longer be the only ones to support the family" (Ehrenreich 1983, 116).

In today's America, although perhaps not tomorrow's America, *Playboy* would seem to have been more prescient than Friedan or Steinem. Many of the women in Hochschild's ethnography are afraid to protest too vociferously to their husbands about the inequities of their relationship for fear that their husbands will leave (1989, 251–53). Newman discusses the drastic economic "downward mobility" experienced by many divorced middle-class American women (1989, 202–28).

This apparent shift in American gender relations, this diminution

14. The demarcated gender roles of "husband at work, wife at home," are the products of recent history in Japan and the United States. Japanese *sengyō shufu* (full-time housewives) became widespread only in the Taisho era (1912–26), with the emergence of *sarariiman bunka* (company employee culture) (Kokusai Josei Gakkai 1980, 206). In the United States, the full-time housewife was the product of an historical aberration in American family structure in the first two decades after World War II (Stacey 1990, 6–12).

of the role of full-time housewife and mother in many American circles, may be due to a shift in moral values over the past forty years among men, from an ethic of responsibility to family to an ethic of self-fulfillment over all else (Ehrenreich 1983, 169). It may also be due to economics, to the decline of the family wage system, making it increasingly difficult for a lone wage-earner to support a family (174). It may be the result, as well, of a gender revolution not yet completed: "The old way of being a woman in a patriarchal but stable family system is fading. . . . But a new equal relationship with men at work and at home is not yet in reach" (Hochschild 1989, 264). It may be that at some future point, a society based in true gender equality will emerge in the United States, a society in which men and women share responsibility equally in both workplace and home. But this has not yet happened.

Ikigai and Gender

The *ikigai* ideal held by American feminists, men and women alike, and by Ms. Pratt and Mr. Eliot, is of *ikigai* equality rather than a familial division of *ikigai*. Both men and women, by this ideal, should be committed to their families first, but to their work as well, as a means of supporting the family and of attaining self-realization and contributing to the world. *Ikigai* and gender should thus bear no relation; *ikigai* should be gender-free. The social transformation potentially bringing about this ideal is being led by women. "The 'female culture,' " writes Hochschild, "has shifted more rapidly than the 'male culture.' . . . Over the last thirty years, men's underlying feelings about taking responsibility at home have changed much less than women's feelings have changed about forging some kind of identity at work" (1989, 205). If millions of American men were to follow Mr. Eliot's example, men might "catch up" with women, to create a society based in gender equality and genderless *ikigai*. If, however, men continue to hold back at home as women devote themselves to work (whether out of personal preference or economic necessity)—if both men's and women's *ikigai* become work rather than family—the American family may all the more wither away.

Today, some 40 percent of American children live with a divorced parent. Often these are families in which the absent father does not pay court-ordered child support. If men thus give up their families so readily (Hochschild 1989, 250 cites research showing that 43 percent of divorced fathers have had no contact with their children during the previous year), can women be far behind? "Society cannot afford for people to start deciding, several years into parenthood, that they do not want to be burdened with their children anymore" (Baumeister 1991, 175). If family is not the major component of either men's or women's *ikigai*, then American society may lose the capacity to reproduce itself. (This potential problem is apparent in Ms. Pratt's account. Her love for her children overrides her belief that, as a woman, she should be deeply committed to work and to changing the world. But if the balance in her life were tipped, her children might be in a family where neither mother nor father hold family as their *ikigai*.)

In Japan the major potential social shift is from role to self, from *ikigai* as commitment to group to *ikigai* as self-realization, a shift that may be occurring across gender lines. This shift could enable Japanese men and women to lead more personally fulfilling lives; through such a shift, Japanese people could perhaps, in Miyamoto-san's words, "recover our humanness." But this shift may also bring social problems.

If men such as Takagi-san find *ikigai* in their own pursuits rather than in their companies, what will become of their companies, and of Japanese production? Miyamoto-san's worries about his subordinates are not his worries alone. Surveys (for example, *Hokkaidō Shinbun* 1989a) show that young people now seek their *ikigai* outside work—not in work but in leisure, not in commitment to company but in the self and its pursuits. If women come to find their *ikigai* in their own pursuits rather than in their families, what will become of their families, and of Japanese reproduction? Japan now has one of the world's lowest birth rates: an estimated 1.45 children are born to a woman in her lifetime (*Japan Times* 1994), far lower than the 2.08 natural replacement level. The Japanese government has debated offering monthly allowances of five thousand yen (approximately fifty dollars) to women who bear children, but many young women seem merely to scoff at this (Weisman 1991), being more interested in their personal freedom than in the commitment and confinement brought by children.

It seems that the current transformations in gender roles and *ikigai* apparently taking place in Japan and the United States can make the two societies more humane places in which to live, if Japanese roles become less rigidly circumscribing of the selves who occupy them and if American gender relations become based on true equality at both work and home. On the other hand, these transformations may perhaps serve to erode the two societies: if most of a society's members are deeply committed to neither work nor family, then that society's ongoing prosperity and survival may be in jeopardy.

The philosophical question raised by these issues is this: Is individual freedom to pursue one's own *ikigai,* an *ikigai* found in self rather then in social role, a necessity for any truly just society, or is it an individual luxury that no society can for long afford? The ways in which Japanese and American societies answer this question will very much shape their futures.

Meanwhile, the Japanese and Americans whose accounts we have examined in this chapter all seem to some degree to struggle with the question of self and role in their conceptions of gender and in their formulations of their lives. "Who am I? A unique self, or a role played to perfection? How does this relate to my being a man / a woman?" These questions, whether directly asked or not, resonate through each of their portrayals of their lives.

And so too do they resonate in those portrayed in the next chapter: not those in the prime of life, but rather those at either end of the lifecourse, finding *ikigai* in future dreams or in past roles and relations continuing into the present and future.

Chapter Five

Ikigai in Past and Future

Nakajima Yuri (21)

(Near the end of my research in Japan, I realized that I hadn't interviewed any young people like the wealthy young consumers described in recent books [for example, Ōhira 1990]. I asked my friends if they knew anyone who might fit that description and was given Nakajima Yuri's name. I met Nakajima-san at several trendy coffee shops for our interviews. I was immediately struck by her clothing: I felt I was conversing with a fashion model. Initially, what she told me seemed so innocent in its calculations that I had trouble believing her; eventually I realized that this was who she was, in all sincerity.)

I started working for this company last April. At first it was fun, because there was lots to learn: how to receive guests, how to answer the phone. But it's boring now; there's no challenge anymore. Before I started work, I went to a Catholic junior college, noted for its education in good manners for women. I wanted to become a stewardess after college; I applied but failed. Now I think that marriage is better for me.

I've traveled a lot. I've been to America, Europe, Singapore, Hong Kong, Hawaii; I go abroad twice a year. I love traveling: going to dinner in a nice dress, watching a nice show, going shopping—I can feel rich! I'd like to live in a foreign country, study overseas for a year instead of just going for a week, but my parents would never let me.

My parents say it's OK for me to do whatever I want once I'm married, because then they'll leave everything to my husband, but until I marry, they're responsible for my well-being. I don't want to be unfilial [*oyafukō*], doing things they don't want me to. When I go abroad, my parents aren't watching me; I'm free, but I don't do bad things. I have a curfew now, but even if I didn't, I wouldn't want to stay out late. It would be bad for my skin: I'd be too tired to wash my face when I got home; I'd sleep with my makeup on. I'd rather come home early and take a bath.

I can't endure hardship. My father's generation grew up during the war, and suffered a lot. He doesn't want his daughters to have to experience that. I grew up protected from life's hardships. Because I'm a girl [*onna no ko*], I don't want to make my parents worry about me; I want to walk the path they want me to take. If they think a certain person is best for me, I'll marry him. I always think that I'll be happiest if, when I bring my future husband to my grandparents and relatives, they'll bless our marriage. That would be the greatest thing I could do for my parents. In junior high school I rebelled a bit, but no more. I don't feel rebellious toward my parents because what they want me to do and what I want to do are exactly the same.

I don't have a boyfriend now. Today young women get involved with men pretty easily, but I keep my distance. Men sense that, and don't try anything—sometimes they'll try to hold hands, but nothing more. Mostly I date someone two or three times and that's the end of it. I feel bad when they give me presents, because I'm not interested; I stop seeing them, tell them I'm too busy. . . .

Actually, I did have a boyfriend, but I broke up with him; I know he wanted to marry me, but I wasn't interested. I don't especially want to marry a rich man, but I do want to marry someone who can preserve the lifestyle I have now. But I'll choose my husband not on the basis of income, but by the company he works for: he must be someone working for a first-rate company everybody knows, or else a medical doctor. The company my boyfriend worked for isn't first-rate; it used to be, but not anymore. My grandfather always told me when I was small that I should choose my husband not by his face but by his occupation; I resisted, but now I agree. At my wedding, my relatives will talk about my husband; I feel restricted by that, but I'm not a child anymore. It's better to win favor in others' eyes, so I think I should find someone my relatives consider perfect.

I don't know what love really means; I've never experienced the feeling that I'd die without this person or that. People say you can marry someone who's poor as long as there's love between you, but I couldn't; most girls my age couldn't. If you don't have money, your love will go sour; only when you have money and can enjoy life together can your love grow. I don't mean that money's *more* important than love, but it's *as* important! My father always says that money can solve 80 percent of the problems you face in this world. . . . (I don't have any savings. I spend my income on clothes and travel; my parents pay for my lessons: jazz dance, English conversation, flower arranging, tea ceremony. They also help me out on clothes and travel when I need extra money. I really couldn't live on my own income.)

The reason my mother wanted me to take lots of lessons and go to a good school is that she wants me to marry into a good family; if I'd gone to a better college, a four-year college instead of a two-year college, I'd have a better chance of finding a good husband. I lived with my parents when I was in college because I wanted to learn cooking, but also because someone from a good family would rather marry a woman living with her family than a woman who lives alone and maybe leads an immoral life. I may be old-fashioned, but that's why I live with my parents.

I want to marry by the time I'm twenty-three. I've never had *omiai.* I want to marry someone who I come to love naturally. Last weekend I went to a resort with some other young men and women—the men were doctors in their late twenties. Since all of us are single, we talked about marriage. The men said they didn't expect their wives to be home all day. When a friend and I said that women's happiness is to be found in marriage—women are much happier with a good husband than with a good job—they said that women like us are rare in this day and age. For me, my husband will come first. If I work, I'll find a job that enables me to leave home after him and come home before him; that way I can prepare dinner for him. . . .

No matter how much you love the person you marry, you'll get bored, just as you get tired of hamburger if you eat it every day. But if the husband and wife are mature, they can work it out. The husband will be busy with work and the wife can have her hobbies; when they feel tired, they can refresh themselves by taking a trip together. To solve their marital problems, the wife must be very wise. Just getting married doesn't make a man and a woman husband and wife [*fūfu*]; it's a long process—it'll take until they die and are buried in the same grave. You can't avoid small frictions no matter who you marry, but I can't imagine ever getting a divorce because of them.

I'm certain that I'll have a child; before, I thought I didn't want one, but I changed my mind after I saw the movie *Baby Talk*. A child is the clamp that binds together husband and wife; I can entrust to my children my dreams, the things I wanted to do but couldn't. Only after you have a child can you mature as a woman. Because I was born a woman, I want to bear a child.

My father always says that women should be beautiful. Every morning my mother puts on a new outfit and ties a matching ribbon in her hair. After I get married, I'll wear a cute apron; I can't become sloppy. Men don't have to worry about their appearance as long as they wear clean clothes—they have work to do—but it's better for women to be beautiful: soft and delicate. We talk about equality between men and women, but men and women are fundamentally different: men have men's roles to play and women women's roles. I think that women should rely on men rather than be independent.

I love to dress up; my friends say I'm a clothes horse [*oshare*]. I used to wear only brand-name clothing, but now I don't care so much about brand names. If you only shop at brand-name boutiques, you'll look the same as everyone else. I go abroad to shop; that way, I can find clothes other Japanese people don't have. In Hong Kong I bought a lovely lace dress, very cheap; it doesn't matter if it's inexpensive as long as I like it. When I was in junior college, I had a dozen Louis Vuitton handbags: I gave them all away or sold them. I get tired of things easily; when I was in junior college, I usually gave away my clothes after wearing them for a year, to my sister or my cousins.

When I have a date, I spend hours choosing my clothes. When I went to that resort, I had to choose clothes for the trip there, tennis wear for the first day, clothes for after tennis, tennis wear for the second day, and clothes for the trip home.... Appearance is important: men prefer women who may be a little stupid but are beautiful to look at to those who are smart but not concerned about appearance. I want to wear what looks good on me.

Our family doesn't have any religion; my grandparents were Buddhist, and I went to Catholic schools. I think there are many gods; each person has their own god, but there's also a God in the sky. I believe that after a person dies, they watch over their children and grandchildren; when I pray, I call on God and Great-Grandma and Grandpa to help me. When I get old and die, I'll see my parents, who will have died already. I think that heaven is in the sky, above where airplanes fly: people dressed in white, watching their children in this world. When something bad happens to their families, they'll come down and help. They don't help too much, though, because it wouldn't be good for their families, who need to learn the lessons of life....

There are tragedies like wars in this world, but I don't know why they happen. I'm living in a peaceful and happy country now; people who lived in those bad old days were unlucky. I think that everybody, even those who did wrong, will go to heaven. If you send a bad person to hell, he'll repeat bad things in his next life, but a bad person can become good in a good environment—that's why everyone goes to heaven.... You often hear that some people's spirits can't go to the other world. Some spirits return to this world because they bear a grudge; they come back to take revenge on someone who made them suffer.... But I really don't want to talk about spirits! I'm scared! [Cries.]

My *ikigai?* I want to meet a nice person and marry, but it's only natural for people to marry, so that can't be my *ikigai.* Work now can't be *ikigai;* it's a means of making money and killing time. My *ikigai* is travel. When I travel, I can get dressed up and go to fancy restaurants and eat good food; I can go shopping, and I can take pictures of myself in nice clothes, and the pictures will remain with me forever. After I marry, my husband will be my *ikigai.* Later, my child will be my *ikigai;* but the center of my life now is travel.

Kirsten Peters (19)

(I met Kirsten Peters in an empty classroom at her school. She is tall, attractive, and matter-of-fact, even jaded in the way she presents herself. Because I knew one of her teachers, I worried that I represented the "adult world" for her—indeed, she made a face behind my back after our first interview, for the benefit of her friends. But the feeling of our interviews later shifted; her talk became a matter of sorting out her feelings to herself about entering an adult world that she finds alluring but is not at all sure she wants to enter.)

I graduate from high school next week; next year I'll go to community college. I'll take some computer classes, I think, but I'm not sure what I'll do with the rest of my life! Everything today has to do with computers; my dad says that if I learn how to use one, he'll buy me one. (He's a doctor. My mother used to be a nurse. I live at home with my parents and my older sister.)

I used to go to a public high school, but I was getting straight Fs. My parents switched me to a private school; I get As and Bs now. The school's helped me a lot: the teachers led me to believe in myself. In public school, I was going nowhere; ever since seventh grade, I'd gotten in with the wrong group of kids. I put my parents through hell. I'd get in arguments with them, yell and scream, and then leave; my boyfriend would come and pick me up. I feel bad about it now; I think that's why me and my parents have a good relationship now. They were good parents; it was me that was bad. I felt that my parents loved my sister more than me. "Why can't you be like your sister?" My dad must have said that to me a million times. I adore my sister, but I just hated being compared to her. That might have been why I got into drugs: I didn't want to be like her; it seemed like she was always so happy. I wanted to be happy in my own way. . . .

I got high on pot for the first time in eighth grade; then I started doing acid because my boyfriend was doing a lot, and cocaine too. I had bad experiences on everything—a bad acid trip, a seizure on cocaine—so finally I just quit; people say I have a will of iron. My mom knows I did drugs, but I'd never tell my dad. My mother's lenient, but my dad's like totally strict: if you don't obey the rules, he can be hard to live with. But I don't have that many rules. He bought me my car, pays for the insurance, the gas. I have a one o'clock curfew. I'm nineteen, so some people say I shouldn't have a curfew; but it's his house, so I abide by his rules. My dad doesn't know anything about me; I'm sure he thinks I'm still a virgin. My mother knows, but my dad would flip out!

Yes, I worry about getting pregnant, about disease. Once I got pregnant—I didn't know it until I had a miscarriage at work. I would have had to either get an abortion or give it up for adoption, and I couldn't have done either; I adore children. . . . I'm pretty responsible when it comes to diseases; I say, "If we're going to do this, we're not going to do it with any other people." The boy I'm dating now is very honest; we've only been dating three weeks, but I can trust him. The boyfriend before him, our relationship lasted two years. I've had three relationships, long-term, but I've dated lots of boys, from eighth grade on. (I wish I'd waited when I lost my virginity; the boy was a jerk.)

I buy lots of clothes, jewelry, makeup. In junior high school, it was brand names; now I get what looks good, and that's usually expensive! My closet's packed, and I'm like, "I need new clothes," because I get sick of old clothes; I give them to my cousins. . . . I've worked at various places, fast-food restaurants, over the past few years. My parents say I have to. They say that if I don't get a job this summer, they'll take the car away. I'd like to work at something where I could sit there and the money would come in. Work is boring; I can think of a million things I'd rather do. My father loves his job; if I had a job I loved, I'd do it, but. I don't want to work in the future; I'd rather inherit some money from an uncle. I want to be rich! There's just so much out there to buy. I want to go to Rome, get an apartment, go shopping. I daydream about that; I plan on going someday. It's my parents I have to convince—they're very protective.

To be happy, you need money. Love doesn't make the world go round, it's cash. You've gotta have money; there's so much stuff I want, and the only way to get it is to have money. I'd marry a rich man I didn't love over a poor man I did. I'm into money, not love. Some people say that money can't make you happy; well, it can definitely make me happy! If I didn't like the guy, hey, I could divorce him, take him for every cent he's got. That's a terrible thing to say, but I could do it. If there was another guy I liked who didn't have money, I could date him on the side. If my husband were making lots of money, he'd be busy; he wouldn't know. . . .

Love? I see so many families that get divorced. My parents are still together, but most of my friends' parents are divorced. I'd have affairs, maybe. I'd keep quiet about it to my husband; if you tell your husband, it's not a challenge! Most guys know that I'm a challenge; if they get old, I'll go out for someone else. It's a challenge being with someone behind a person's back—a rush, a natural high. Yes, it's wrong, but not in the sense that I'm sinning, that I'm going to hell for it. It's my life; I can do what I want!

I do think it's possible to marry someone and stay in love with him, if he treats you good. I'd choose money over love if today I had that choice, but ten years from now I might be different. I'm nineteen— I guess to every nineteen-year-old, money's real important! (I was in love once, with that guy I went out with for a long time, but I broke up with him: he was on a road to nowhere. He dropped out of college, quit his job; the only thing for him was partying and drugs. I still love him, but I don't like him. I think he's a jerk.)

What's most important to me, future career, relationships, or shopping? At the moment, shopping and boys, they're most important, because I'm so scared to go out and get on with my life. I'm frightened about graduating from high school; I wish I could start over. A year from now I'm going off to college. I'm not going this year because I don't think I'd be able to make myself study. I'd think, "I don't have to be home tonight. I can do anything I want!" Going off to college and being hit with no parents, no curfew—I'd get in that rut, get in so deep I couldn't get out. . . .

My mother and father don't give me advice about who I should marry; they just want me to be happy, able to take care of myself in the future, live on my own without being scared. I think I'll be able to do that; it'll take about ten years, but. . . . Maybe I'll be at home after college; I'd want to be with my mom and dad for a little bit longer. You feel safe there, protected; that's how everybody feels. My parents really want me to stay at home; in the world's eyes I'm an adult right now, but in my parents' eyes I'm still their little daughter. In my own eyes? I'm right in-between being a child and an adult. I already feel old. I wish I could be ten again. I've never wanted to go to college; my sister said it's like paid vacation, but it doesn't sound like much fun to me, just a lot of work! I want to take a long vacation! Of course nowadays you've got to have a college degree; I'll probably go to some college or to some kind of school, like travel school, to get into the airline business. . . .

My life ten years from now, if my dreams come true? I'll have a house with a white picket fence; I'll have money and be happy; I'll have children and a career. I'd like to do something with animals: an animal psychologist; I could get an advanced degree to do that, if I really wanted to. I'm good with animals—you should see my dog! I'd like to be married to a rich man with a good job, maybe a lawyer, a very distinguished man, and up-to-date, knowing all the fashions, into nice cars, vacations, and good-looking, a good father and good husband. I'd like two kids. My mother would take care of my kids when I was gone, she's said she'd be glad to. If I had children, I wouldn't have affairs. But I hope I get married once and am happy. I think babies make you happy; they just kind of bring that joy in. If I had a child, he'd be the most important thing to me in the world. . . .

When I date a guy, I think about marriage. The boy I went out with for two years—we got engaged; he gave me a rock of a diamond ring. I broke it off, because it was big pressure for an eighteen-year-old to handle: "I'm engaged to be married? My life hasn't even started!" It still hasn't started. . . . I've always wanted to get married at twenty-two, be a young mother. I'd be happy just staying home taking care of my kids. But I've got to have some career skills, because if the marriage didn't work out, I'd be left high and dry; my husband would have his business, but I'd just have my kids. I'd never want to be stuck with kids after a divorce and not have the education to get a job.

Do I believe in God? My parents and sister believe, but I'm not really into it. I used to not believe at all, because I felt He'd done nothing for me; but now my life is so much better than it was that I can maybe start believing. But I don't know; I have a hard time with Adam and Eve, heaven and hell. I think of heaven and see space and stars; I think of hell and when I look down, there's dirt. It's hard to imagine, you know? If I died now, there's maybe a fifty-fifty chance my spirit would continue. If there was a heaven, I'd go there—I'm a good person; I've never killed anybody. I think of heaven as having lots of clouds, and misty; that's the way I've seen it on TV. . . .

I don't want to get older; I'd like to stay nineteen for the rest of my life. If I had wrinkles, it'd be like immediate facelift, or a gun to my head! Yes, my parents are happy, but they can't do all the things they used to do; they have arthritis, grey hair. It's like you're getting to that point where you're soon going to die. I'd rather be at this point, where I'm just about to start my life. I'm scared of death; sometimes I worry if I've got an incurable disease. To get sick and know you're going to die—that would be terrible, I'd be so frightened! I try not to think about it. . . .

The most important thing in my life is myself, getting myself taken care of; I come before anything else. I don't like to think about the future—I try to take everything day to day—but sometimes it just pops into my head. It kind of depresses me to think about it. I hope I'll have a good life. It's pretty scary. My life now is most important, just being happy, not letting things stress me out, get me down. . . .

Nakajima Yuri and Kirsten Peters:
Analysis

Nakajima-san and Ms. Peters are both young, have wealthy parents, and are appreciative of fashion and enamored of money. They are both immersed in present pleasures and in dreams of future marriage and motherhood. But Nakajima-san (if her attestations are to be believed, as perhaps they should be)[1] has led a sheltered life, while Ms.

---

1. There is a term in Japanese, *burikko,* which refers to the feigned innocence of young women who have had more worldly experience than they let on. Nakajima-san's claim of keeping those who date her at arm's length, and her tears of fright during our talk of spirits, might indicate such feigned innocence; but those who know her have told me that her expressions of innocence accurately reflect the way she thinks and lives.

Peters has apparently been involved in drugs and sex throughout her teenage years. On the other hand, Nakajima-san plots out her future in a calculating way, whereas Ms. Peters seems to seek to avoid her future.

Nakajima-san's *ikigai* is travel, she tells us. But her travel seems not only a matter of present pleasures, but of future plans as well: in going abroad to shop, she can find clothes that will make her look beautiful and thereby better her odds of finding a husband of high status. Nakajima-san and her family have sought to maximize her chances of marrying such a man, through the advice given to her from her grandfather's knee on, through her Catholic girls-school education and her lessons in *hanayome shugyō* ("bridal training": "English conversation, flower arranging, tea ceremony," that which a cultivated young woman is expected to have studied), through the fervent attention she gives to looking attractive and, not least, through her "feminine" attitudes. Nakajima-san says that "it's only natural for people to marry, so that can't be my *ikigai*." Marrying a man of high status isn't an effortless act of nature, however, but the result of intense effort, an effort that seems key to Nakajima-san's life. Her past and present efforts and future dreams are centered in marrying a man of high status; this dream of marriage, rather than travel, I interpret as her *ikigai*.

When I asked Ms. Peters to choose between future career, relationships, or shopping as to which was most important to her, "shopping and boys" was her response. "Shopping and boys" could conceivably serve Ms. Peters too as a preparation for the future; but these seem, from her account, to be her means not of investing in her future but of avoiding it. *Ikigai* as we have defined it involves "one's deepest sense of social commitment," and commitment entails the future as well as the present. In this sense, "shopping and boys" seem to represent not Ms. Peters' *ikigai*, but rather her efforts to avoid having an *ikigai*.

Nakajima-san has an *ikigai*, and she looks forward to her future, as Ms. Peters does not. Why? The two women's accounts reveal a clear difference in self-confidence. Nakajima-san believes that her aim of marrying a high-status man has a good chance of success; Ms.

Peters believes that she could not succeed were she to leave home. This difference seems largely due to their personal backgrounds. Ms. Peters felt unloved as a child compared to her sister, as Nakajima-san did not; and Nakajima-san is two years older than Ms. Peters and more sure of herself on the path to adulthood. Most important, Nakajima-san has internalized her parents' values ("I don't do bad things," she tells us, even when abroad and unwatched), as Ms. Peters has not: she wants to live with her parents and their rules because she can't trust herself apart from those rules.

There are also larger cultural factors contributing to this difference. Nakajima-san feels no need to become independent, but will, with marriage, simply shift her reliance from parents to husband.[2] She lived at home during college and will continue to live at home until marriage. She need not prove herself at work, for like many Japanese "office ladies," she will probably quit work upon marriage. She need only find a high-status man to marry (although this in itself is no small task) and then play fully her future role as devoted wife and mother.

Ms. Peters has high-flying personal dreams, of becoming an animal psychologist and marrying "a rich man with a good job . . . a very distinguished man . . . knowing all the fashions . . . and good-looking." But apart from such dreams (and apart too from the dream of getting rich off divorce), she realizes that her future reality may be less glamorous: she must get some kind of career training to survive. Ms. Peters doesn't want to become independent of her parents because her future career and academic path seem less than promising, and future marriage, she realizes, may not bring her a husband who will reliably take care of her and her children, given the prevalence of divorce. Her parents, she feels, are the only people on whom she can rely, and so she will rely on them for as long as possible. "That's how everybody feels," she tells us—as if to justify what some Ameri-

2. It may seem that in seeking to become a stewardess, Nakajima-san was seeking independence but, having been stymied, gave up that desire. However, from all that she told me, I interpret her desire less as an effort to attain personal independence than to experience the company-chaperoned pleasures of travel and consumption for several years before subsequent marriage.

cans might see as a shameful lack of independence, but which she sees as a personal necessity.

In analyzing the accounts of Takagi-san and Mr. Eliot, I argued that the freedom allowed the individual by American institutional structures helped Mr. Eliot to change employment and shift *ikigai*, something that Takagi-san, within his more restrictive Japanese world, has felt to be impossible. But freedom is a mixed blessing. Ms. Peters seems a victim of the American cultural emphasis on individual freedom. Having been a teenager in a world of indulgence, she now doubts she has the personal discipline required for successful American adulthood. Nakajima-san seems a beneficiary of the Japanese cultural emphasis on commitment to group. Having grown up in a sheltered environment, now preparing to transfer her dependence from parents to future husband, she seems confident that she can make the transition to Japanese adulthood.

These women's lives may yet move in unforeseeable directions, but by their present accounts, their self-assessments seem well founded. Nakajima-san seems to have a good command of the game of cultural success she is playing; Ms. Peters seems not to. Given the different rules of their societies' games of success and their own culturally shaped characters, their personal choices of *ikigai* seem to represent their accurate gauging of their odds of attaining success in their different adult worlds.

These two women are at the cusp between childhood and adulthood, preparing for or avoiding adulthood. Let's now turn to two men who, half-a-dozen years into adulthood, have dreams of a perhaps unrealizable alternative life for themselves.

Kinoshita Toshiyuki (30)

(I first met Kinoshita-san in a cafe in Delhi, India, in 1984; I was amazed to discover that he lived just a few blocks from where I had lived in Japan. I interviewed him six years later on a bench by a pond on several summer nights. He is a short, talkative, intense man, whom I have always admired for his spunk and his rebelliousness. I saw him through more conventional eyes at his wedding, when a young woman exclaimed to me, "Now that he's married and will have to support a family, maybe he'll stop being such a child, with all his silly dreams!")

I got married last week. We'd been living together for six months before then. Now I can answer the phone myself instead of having her answer it (I didn't want people to think that she was loose, that she had a man hanging around! For a woman in her thirties, as she is, rumors spread easily), and when I fill out paperwork, I mark that I have a dependent. These little things make me realize I'm married! My mother wasn't against my living with her. My mother and I were living with my sister's family; it was crowded; I wanted to get out. I looked for an apartment of my own too, but economically it wasn't feasible.

I graduated from college four years ago. I went to college for three years, then took a year off and went to India; then I went back to college and intently studied law. After I graduated, I worked in the personnel office of a large department store—I thought I could study law while I worked there. The examination to become a lawyer is incredibly hard, so I planned on spending seven or so years to study for it; but I've given up on that. . . .

I quit the department store after three years; then I worked at my friend's clothing store, and then I became a *juku* [private "cram" school] teacher: I taught English and math to kids from preschool up to ninth grade. I didn't like the idea of putting students under my thumb, so I let them be free, but they got out of hand. I quit because my boss was strange and the pay was low. Then I got the job I have now, driving a delivery truck. I'm alone in my work. I feel relaxed; because my body knows what I'm supposed to do, I don't have to think about it. . . .

What I'm doing now isn't what I really want to do. In Japan, even now, people generally don't quit jobs as I have; but from the start I'd decided to quit the department store after three years, because there were other things I wanted to do. While I was at the department store, I began to think about becoming a doctor; I still haven't given up that dream. If I studied hard to pass the exam for medical college, I could do it.

Maybe people think my dreams are impossible to realize, but I think they're quite possible. Some of my friends seem envious because I still have a dream, but my mother and other older people say, "What kind of crazy things are you thinking of! Get serious!" Last January I took the exam to get into medical college. I failed. I'll try again in two or three years. I also want to be a school teacher. If I were a teacher, I could earn what I earn now, but still have time to study for the exam. I'd be very happy if I were a doctor in twenty years, but probably not if I were a teacher. As for my work now—I don't want to think about the possibility of doing it all my life! I'll quit this job by next spring at the earliest, or in three years at the latest. Then I'll try to get into medical college, or get a license to be a teacher. I still have time: the age limit for the licensing exam to be a teacher is thirty-seven; for medical school, there's no age limit. Three years ago, a thirty-three-year-old woman passed the entrance exam at a top medical college—I read about her in the newspaper.[3] I could do it, too. . . . I feel frustrated because what I'm doing now isn't what I want to do. But I won't give up! If I try hard, I can do what I dream of doing. . . .

I've talked with my wife about my dreams; she doesn't like them. She'd prefer the stable life of a *sarariiman*'s wife. She asks me not even to joke about quitting my job! I want children. My wife is thirty-four now, and if I went to medical college, we'd be poor for the next eight years. She works as a photographer's assistant, but would quit if we had kids. I'm saving money now; in college, maybe I could get scholarships. . . . (If I can't become a doctor? There are other interesting things I could do. The good thing about Japan now is that you have the freedom to choose jobs—any job will give you enough money to live on. . . .)

Last year, when I was thinking about marriage, my mother was against it. She'd been upset because I didn't stick to one job like most people, and now I wanted to marry a woman older than me. I told

3. Her achievement was newsworthy not because she was a woman—there are many woman doctors in Japan in such fields as pediatrics—but because of her "advanced" age.

her that even though she was my mother, I had my own life to live: "If you gave me two lives, then I could follow your advice this time, and live my own life next time. But I have only one life to live, and I don't want it to be crushed by other people." Of course I feel grateful to my mother—she raised me by herself. But as far as my job and marriage are concerned, I'll decide them for myself. They're something other people, even my mother, shouldn't interfere with.

My father died in a coal-mining accident when I was six. I remember laughing with my friends at his funeral. I didn't understand what it meant to die; probably I saw him so little when he was alive that his presence wasn't very big for me. After he died, my mother went to work at the coal mine—if you worked there, you didn't have to pay rent. Later, she worked in a factory; now she's a cook in a company cafeteria. My mother was really strict when I was little: when I was noisy at other people's houses, she made me keep quiet; when I cried, she pinched me. Because of that, I later felt enormous constraint when I tried to do anything. So I tried to change myself. Maybe that's why I went to India. If my mother hadn't pinched me, maybe I would have become a *sarariiman*; maybe I wouldn't have wanted to try so many things different from other people. . . .

When I was in grade school, I was a little bully [*gakidaishō*] and bossed around even older kids. By the time I got to junior high, those kids wanted to get even, and they beat me up. For the first time, I learned how difficult human relations could be. Their bullying didn't last long, but because of it I stopped talking, and shut myself off. Eventually I learned to be more considerate; I wasn't so smart-assed [*namaiki*] anymore, like I'd been. . . .

India influenced me more than anything else in my life. Japanese people work and work, but we don't follow our dreams. People get so caught up in their daily lives that they give up. If I hadn't gone to India, I might have had that kind of attitude. . . . After India, any idea I'd had of suicide disappeared. In India lots of people live on the streets. Seeing them, I realized that suicide was a luxury. As long as you can eat, there's no need to die. I'd thought about suicide because human relations were hard, society wasn't as I'd hoped. But after

India I saw that it was a waste of time to worry; I had to *live* before worrying about such things. . . .

Which is better, my life or that of a *sarariiman?* My life's better—living as I do, I won't feel regret when I die. To experience as much as possible before you die is a good way to live. So far in my life, I've done and seen a lot. People say lots of things about me. My mother opposed our marriage because she was ashamed in front of her relatives that my wife was older than me. I told her, "Let them talk! I don't care!" Maybe I'm not a typical Japanese. Maybe if I'd had a father, I'd have become a typical *sarariiman.* Maybe it was good that I didn't have a father. It seems to me that as long as you don't give trouble to others you should be free to do what you want. Japanese people aren't free; the eyes of your relatives and of society are always watching you. When I see company employees in their suits and ties downtown at lunch time, I feel disgusted. Companies take priority over everything else in Japan, and people working at such places are just cogs. They don't have selves. They don't know what freedom is; they don't know their own identities.

I don't study much these days, I'm just too tired. I have lots of dreams, but if I don't study, I can't realize them. This is my biggest worry in my life. Time passes too quickly. . . .

I've thought a lot about death. Once you're born, you're bound to die. Basically I don't believe in life after death, but I guess I do believe, like a child, when I see TV programs about psychic phenomena. . . . But something can't exist just because human beings dream of it. I don't believe in gods or Buddhas; religion is something human beings have created. Everybody wants to be healthy and happy, but we get sick and unhappy. We need some power to pray to; we want to rely on something.

There's no reason why human beings live: we're just alive. I believe human beings will become extinct, like dinosaurs. When I think about that, I feel relaxed—I can do what I want instead of following others! If in two hundred years human beings will die out, then what I'm doing now will mean nothing. When I'm worried about something, I solve it by thinking this way. "Why do I have to worry about such trivial things?" Human beings don't amount to much anyway: it wouldn't be any big deal if we became extinct. Sometimes I wonder how much value the ability to think really has. Spiders spreading their webs may be better than human beings. Sure, humans can feel *ikigai,* but maybe spiders feel *ikigai* when they're eating their prey. . . .

My *ikigai?* Work can't be my *ikigai.* If I became a doctor, work would be my *ikigai,* but then I wouldn't feel that it was work; it'd be my mission [*shimei*]. My *ikigai* now is to move closer to my dream. I'll try to make time to study, to go to medical college, or become a teacher and then go to medical college—that's what I think about all the time now. I'd like to join the Red Cross and go to places in the world that need doctors. I also want a family, but it would be OK to live apart from them for a while. My mission will be more important to me than my family; I think my wife will understand. Well, I'm not sure. I wonder what her *ikigai* is? Maybe she doesn't know now. Raising a family with me may be her *ikigai.*

I don't know what my friends' *ikigai* is. Maybe they've never thought about it—if they started thinking about it, maybe they'd have to quit their work. I have a friend who works until midnight every night. His work doesn't seem like *ikigai,* but he can't quit; he lives only looking forward to playing golf a few times a month. . . . People are deceived, exploited; people spend a large portion of their precious time for their company regardless of their own will. The capitalist system requires that workers be cogs of the machine. Nobody wants to be a cog, but it's necessary for the system, and probably can't be changed.

Sam Isaacs (30)

(I met Mr. Isaacs at his company; we talked before the flickering patterns on his computer screens. He is a handsome young man, appearing a quintessential yuppie, but his words soon show the depths beneath that appearance. I sent his account to him after our interviews, and later met his wife, who told me that he had given it to her to read. I froze; but she said that they had talked about it, and it had made their marriage stronger. They indeed appeared happy together, when I last saw them.)

I work for a large computer company; I've been here two years. Before that, I was working back east, but then I made a lot of life changes: got married, quit my job—I couldn't see spending my life helping rich people get richer. Here I'm not doing that. I help design future computer software; it's something I can get excited about.

My first job out of college was working for a software company. After that, I worked on a defense project; from there I went back to grad school. I've held four different jobs. I got something out of all of them, but then they started to lose their challenge. When I left my first job, people were saying, "It's the right time to go. You've seen what's around here." That's the norm. They treat us well here, good salaries, good benefits, but we're not expected to be loyal to the corporation. We're expected to help the company survive, but nobody tries to represent it as being a benevolent entity: it's business! In the companies I've worked for, since we're in R and D, there's a lot of pride. I feel like I'm good at what I do, and I work hard to do it well. . . .

Is this my life's work? That's a problem; I believe that people have callings, but I don't believe this is mine. Well, it might be, but I'm not sure I'm not fooling myself. Software engineering is very lucrative; you get a lot of perks, people stroking you because you're valuable for the corporation. But I'm not sure my calling might not be psychotherapy, for example. I'm fascinated by the human mind; my wife's a therapist, and I love talking to her about what she's doing. But it's difficult for me to look at that clearly because of the fear involved in taking a 50 percent cut in pay, and not being valued. So I'm not sure. Making money for a corporation would not give my life meaning. Designing good software—that's a worthy goal, but it may not be enough to be a life's calling. If any of the stuff I'm working on gets out, it'll make people's lives better in some way. But whether I can make an even greater contribution in different, less technological ways, I'm not sure. I think about my purpose in life on a frequent basis because we don't get any younger. If you're going to make a contribution, you want to have as much time as possible to do it; you don't want to dick around, waste time. I struggle with that.

Until about five years ago, I was very much a part of mainstream culture. You grow up, go to college, get a job, work hard, get ahead— I never really questioned that, until my brother died. The two of us were hiking: it was wet—he slipped, fell off a rock ledge. I was the older brother—I felt I should have done something. . . . After that, I dropped out: quit the prestigious company I was at and worked at a bicycle shop. Then I went back to graduate school, where I took a personal development course. At the end of this course, I had this clear sense of what I wanted to do with my life: become a trainer, where I'd be opening people up to their full potential. I've gotten away from that, but it's still a dream, to be able to teach people to live their dreams: doing what they want to do, making the contribution they want to make, being happy with themselves and the people around them. I think that if people respected one another, we could have a society much better than the one we have now, where people treat other people as objects, as work units. There was a wide variety of people in the course, and you came to respect them; only later did you find out that this person's a janitor, that person's a college president. It was irrelevant by then because you knew these people as human beings.

What I've been doing in personal development worries my parents: the courses I was taking they saw as a kind of cult, like brainwashing. But I'm getting to the point where I don't care as much what they think. They live their lives, I live mine. It helps to be a thousand miles away! I remember telling my father I was taking a personal development course and he exploded: "You're spending $1800 on what?" I said, "Look, if you want me to share my life with you, you have to accept what I'm doing." They did. They can't affect it, so they may as well accept it!

If all young engineers had ideals like mine, would America go down the drain economically? I don't know. If America changes radically enough so that success has little to do with material goods, then if people feel fulfilled, they won't care if they have the latest car. I used to be very materialistic; I've toned that down a bit. There was a big fire a few weeks ago; if the wind had pushed it in our direction, we'd have lost our house. It was kind of funny. We packed the car—the cats, a few photo albums. I said to my wife, "Look, there's nothing in the house that means anything to us. It's all stuff, that's all."

My wife has a degenerative muscle disease, and it's really acting up now; she's in constant pain. I knew when I married her that she might become wheelchair-bound. Before we got married my father said, "Life's hard enough as it is. Why would you want to make it harder by marrying somebody with a problem like this?" I said, "Yeah, but if you or mother came down with cancer or something five years after you got married, would you run away? No. You make a commitment and stick to it. . . ."

I do get twinges now and then, when Rhonda and I have arguments, or when she's feeling really bad. We can't do things together—bicycling, windsurfing—that I really want to share with her but can't. Her flare-ups come and go, but the deterioration is constant. If I knew what I know now, would I still have married her? I'm not sure. She's very angry. I know she's in incredible pain, but it's hard to live with. Sometimes I think, "Am I just being a masochist?" But I've never met anybody I care about as much as her. Yes, it's a burden, her being sick, but you take it a day at a time. Rhonda feels bad about it; she says sometimes, "I don't know why you're here. I should probably just go off and kill myself. . . ." It's tough, but I also know that if the situation were reversed, she'd take care of me. The depth of her caring is at least equal to mine.

If my dreams came true, we'd have two or three kids; we'd be living in some small, pretty community, or maybe on a cliff over the Pacific. Rhonda would be well, a successful psychotherapist; I would have my own business doing self-realization work, running seminars around the country. I'd say there's a better than 50 percent chance that this will come true. But it's hard to say; maybe my priorities will shift; maybe family security will seem most important five years from now. But it's unlikely that I'd give up my dream. I could put it off for a while, as I'm doing now, but not indefinitely.

I had a good family environment as a child, very traditional; my father's a lawyer, my mother a housewife. At an early age, I started reading science fiction. My impression was that the world was a neat place; people could go to Mars and travel through time. All through school, I'd finish my homework in an hour and spend the rest of the night reading science fiction. In college, I studied astrophysics—I wanted to be an astronaut—then switched to computers. In a way I was searching for what I wanted to do through science fiction themes: one was space travel; another was artificial intelligence, the idea of a created intelligence. . . .

My goal before my brother died was to make lots of money. If he hadn't died, I wouldn't have taken the personal development courses, married Rhonda, moved out here. I wouldn't have been able to take that distance from my family. My brother's death really was generative, in an indirect sense. After his death, I kept feeling that I was a lousy human being: "What kind of person lets their brother die?" I didn't consciously hear that question until I did the course and finally came to believe that I wasn't a bad person. I thank God I did that course: I was heading down a path that was dark, closed-in, fearful. . . .

Where is my brother now? Rationally I have no idea, but emotionally I do sometimes sense that he's near. . . . What will happen to me after I die? I'm not sure. In college, I took the rationalist view. I resolved to become a famous scientist, like Einstein or Galileo, so that people would remember me. After my brother died, I amended that, to think that it's the people who know you as a human being that matter. As for whether I'll have an independent existence after I die—I kind of think not. This doesn't jibe with my idea of Bill being out there somewhere; it may well be that when I stand by the ocean talking to him, I'm talking to myself, to the memories I have of him. . . .

I went to church as a child, but I don't go now. I don't believe in a God who cares about our prayers; I don't think that human beings have any divine purpose. I just want to be the best human being I can be, and help other human beings to be the best they can be, given the constraints of their physical beings. . . .

Yes, Rhonda's disease has been tough. We've both started facing the fact that this disease doesn't get cured. I'm worried about what will happen when we have kids; I don't think Rhonda's up to it. . . . If she doesn't get better, I'm not sure what'll happen to my dream— it'd be difficult. With Rhonda's medical bills paid for by our insurance, and by being more frugal, moving into a cheaper place, we could do it. It would put a crimp in my plans, but I don't think it would kill them. . . .

Of the three aspects of my life, work, marriage, or the dream of becoming a trainer, which is most important to me? Definitely the career track I'm on now would be last. As for the other two, if I had nothing but my relation with Rhonda, I'm not sure my life would be fulfilling. If I had to pick one thing, I might pick working as a trainer; but I'm not sure that that alone would keep me completely happy— I also need my relationship. The dream comes first, the relationship second, though it's still necessary. But my priorities may change as I have kids. If you came back in five years, I might give you different answers. Maybe my center will become working with my kids, to make them the happiest human beings they can be.

Kinoshita Toshiyuki and Sam Isaacs: Analysis

These two men have much in common. Both recently married. Both have changed jobs frequently, now work at jobs for which they don't feel *ikigai,* and dream of a future work that will be their *ikigai.* Both now feel apart from the mainstream of their societies and feel pressure to live within that mainstream. Both also feel the pressure of time in attempting to make their dreams reality. However, Kinoshita-san is now a dropout from Japanese middle-class norms, while Mr. Isaacs only contemplates dropping out; and Kinoshita-san seems under more pressure to "be like normal people" than is Mr. Isaacs.

These men's *ikigai* is their dreams: Mr. Isaacs's dream of becoming a trainer and Kinoshita-san's dream of becoming a doctor. Why do these men, at age thirty, still make their dreams their *ikigai?* The answer may lie in loss: Kinoshita-san's loss of his father, Mr. Isaacs's of his brother. Kinoshita-san tells us that "maybe if I'd had a father, I'd have become a typical *sarariiman.*" His mother constrained him excessively when he was little, he says; his lifelong struggle against constraint is what has made him so different from others. Mr. Isaacs was a part of mainstream culture, he tells us, until his brother died. The guilt he felt led him to question his life's goals, a questioning that brought him to the personal development courses that seem to have "saved" him. In the years since, he's married, moved out of his parents' orbit, and changed jobs, to a research position that seems in many respects fulfilling. But he remains unconvinced that this is his "calling"; his transformed values call him elsewhere, although he has yet to act on that call.

Kinoshita-san's equivalent "personal development course" was India. Like Mr. Isaacs, he had been profoundly unhappy, even contemplating suicide, but India taught him to rise above his difficulties with others. Mr. Isaacs's personal development courses and Kinoshita-san's India revealed to the men valuations of life different from the mainstream of their societies.

Kinoshita-san more than Mr. Isaacs seems vociferously to battle *sekentei,* "what other people think";[4] but both men feel pressure from others over their values, and feel compelled to defend their *ikigai* against those others. Kinoshita-san tells us that his mother admonishes him to "get serious" about life; Mr. Isaacs's parents saw his personal development courses as "a kind of cult, like brainwashing." Both men resist parental pressures, saying, "I have my own life to live," but they perhaps can't so easily resist pressure from their wives. Kinoshita-san's wife doesn't understand his dream, he tells us, a lack of understanding he seems prepared to live with, his "mission" being most important to him. He does, however, want children. His wife,

---

4. Kinoshita-san and Nakajima-san both discussed with me *sekentei* as a powerful force, particularly, for these two, in terms of what one's relatives think of one's marriage. But this force is one that Nakajima-san is most concerned with mollifying through impeccable behavior, Kinoshita-san with resisting. Although Mr. Isaacs discussed parental opposition to his dream, no American I interviewed spoke directly of feeling pressure from "relatives and society."

given her age, must bear children within the next six to eight years, during which Kinoshita-san hopes to be in medical school; he speaks of getting scholarships, but supporting both his family and his dream will be extremely difficult.

Mr. Isaacs's wife does seem to understand his dream. If he and his wife have children, his dream may be less threatened by having to support them than supplanted by his love for them; he may turn his children into his life's dream. The greatest obstacle to his dream is his wife's illness. He believes he can pursue his dream even if his wife's condition worsens (although he wonders if his wife will be able to take care of children); but like Kinoshita-san (albeit with better odds), he faces a difficult path ahead.

Aside from these personal obstacles, the two men face institutional obstacles, obstacles that make Kinoshita-san's dream in particular seem all but unattainable. The examination he must pass to go to medical college requires years of intensive study. Almost invariably, only students or recent graduates studying at exam preparation schools have the training and leisure for such study. Kinoshita-san tells us of a woman in her thirties who passed the entrance exam for medical college, and if he manages to pass, he too may appear in newspaper articles marveling at his achievement. Meanwhile, it's perhaps not only chance, given the "commitment to group" orientation of Japanese institutional structures, that his job-hopping has brought him work that is progressively lower in social status. (Kinoshita-san became upset when I mentioned this, insisting that "I don't care about status!")

The institutional obstacles faced by Mr. Isaacs seem more benign but may be just as threatening to his dream. His work offers him such remuneration and prestige that he may be reluctant to leave it; the security of his present position may take precedence over his dream. American institutions tend to be structured in terms of "self-realization." Indeed, Mr. Isaacs has changed jobs (although not careers), dropped out and then gone back to graduate school (albeit in his established field of expertise), and unlike Kinoshita-san, he has gained in social status and salary in this process. But if he throws away his professional progress for his dream, society might not be so forgiving, the institutional bottom line in both Japan and the United States being that if you don't make money, you can't live well; his realization of this is at the root of his hesitation to follow his dream.

These two men dream of culturally atypical forms of "self-realization," dreams that require intense negotiation within their immediate social worlds and that require them to swim against the current of their societies' institutional channeling. In their dreams, these men seek not merely self-realization, but "societal realization" as well: Mr. Isaacs seeks an America in which people define success not in terms of how much they possess, but of who they are as human beings; Kinoshita-san seeks a Japan in which people are free rather than coerced by social pressure. If they succeed in realizing their dreams, they will serve, in a sense, as agents for social change, exemplars to those around them of alternative paths to fulfillment. If they fail, they will serve as exemplars of the dangers of following such alternative paths. Their dreams, fulfilled, failed, or compromised, carry implications beyond themselves.

Let's now turn to the other end of the life course, to two women not far from death, assessing their lives and their lives' coming ends.

Murakami Mitsuko (68)

(An unfolded *futon* lay on the living room floor of Murakami-san's large house, a rare sight in daytime Japan and a sign of her illness. She appears aged and stooped but has a spark in her eyes. The interaction between her and her husband was something to behold. During her husband's interviews (chapter 6), she occasionally interrupted with wry comments—"I can't die on him! What would he do without me?"—as he interrupted hers: when she said that her life would make a good movie, he arched his eyebrows from the adjacent room and said, "That's narcissism!" Such comments attest, I think, to the closeness of their relationship.)

I was born in 1922; my father was a storekeeper. As a child I was always busy helping my parents. I had to babysit and do all the housekeeping, cooking, and cleaning. There were five kids in my family; when I played, I had to carry a baby on my back. I envied kids who could play alone! . . . In those days, most girls didn't go on to high school; I had to work in my father's store. During those years, men were being sent off to fight, and women were mobilized to polish guns and mend uniforms. I hated the war because in place of my mother, who was working, I had to go send off the soldiers. We were taught the emperor was a god; I knew he was a human being, but I thought that maybe he was like a god—I didn't know anything in those days! I was told never to say anything about the emperor; I might be arrested by the military police. . . .

When the war ended I was twenty-three; I got married a year later. I was educated in the old way, that I'm to be "the soles of my husband's feet." He was a nice person, but he had affairs—women fell in love with him. While he was having his affairs I was really mad at him, but after he died I realized that it was the women who clung to him. He died after seven years; half that time he was sick in the hospital. I didn't feel like I'd gotten married; it was like I went to work—I was always tired. We were running a laundry; we made a lot of money. While he was sick, I managed the business alone.

My husband's younger brother tried to drive me away after he died, so that he could take over the business. He said I spent too much money even though I was just a woman, and that I bought *tabi* [socks worn with *kimono*] without permission. It was none of his business! I left and went to Tokyo, where I met my present husband. I remarried when I was thirty-six, in 1957. He was twenty-nine. Because I'd been married before and was older than he was, my parents were opposed; they thought he'd have affairs and leave me; but he's never done that. I've been sick for a long time now, and feel sorry because I can't help my husband. I've been living my life always thinking that I have to do all I can for him. That's been my *ikigai.*

My husband was working in Tokyo as a *sarariiman,* but then he decided to quit. I couldn't stand Tokyo's summers; I said, "Why don't we move up north. It's cooler there!" He said, "Let's go!" He'd been studying calligraphy. I told him, "I'll go to work. Take your time; maybe you can become a teacher." I didn't worry; I knew we could eat somehow. I could start up the laundry business again. He asked me to wait ten years during which he'd study hard and become a master of calligraphy. I said fine—I never wished that he'd hurry up and start work, because I liked to work myself!

I was thirty-eight when I had my child. When I got pregnant, my husband told me that we didn't have to have a child—my health was most important—but I wanted to try. Just as we feared, I got sick: my kidneys went bad when my daughter was two. I was in the hospital for a year. I don't know how my husband managed to survive—my medical costs were high; in those days there wasn't any national health insurance—but somehow he eked out a living. . . . In the hospital, it was painful when people walked near my bed; even the heartbeat of a person touching my bed caused me pain. I nearly died twice, but I was determined to live no matter what. I felt that I couldn't die, leaving my husband and child behind—they were my *ikigai*.

I've been living with this disease for thirty years now. I've been on a strict diet all these years as to what I can eat and drink. For kidney patients, if you eat and drink what you like, you'll soon die. I started working again right after I left the hospital. I'd collapse if I worked too much, so sometimes I'd stay in bed all morning, but I had to work. I had to help my husband! I told him, "We don't have any money, but you just study hard, so that you can do calligraphy that nobody can match!" He said, "I will!" He studied until two or three in the morning every night. He promised he'd be able to support the family in ten years, and he really did it! Since he was trying so hard, I felt I had to do all I could to help. My husband was serious-minded; he studied, he didn't play around. I really respect him. If he went out drinking with women, my attitude would be different, but he's not like that. Of course he goes drinking when he has a meeting, comes home at three, but he can't avoid that, it's a social obligation.

Before I went to the hospital, I'd started selling cosmetics. I carried my daughter on my back and knocked on doors as a saleswoman. In the hospital I kept at it by telephone; my mother-in-law would go pick up the order and deliver it to the customer. By now, I've been selling door-to-door for many years; I haven't earned that much, but enough to support us when we needed it. Now I'm supported by my husband and his calligraphy; I've used my money for *kimono*. But I don't need *kimono* anymore. I don't need anything anymore!

I've had to be hospitalized again many times, about twice a year for many years. I began dialysis five years ago; since then I've been hospitalized only once. I hate dialysis, though, because it's so painful. After dialysis I can't do anything—my husband has to cook his own dinner—though I feel better the next day. I'm amazed at how I could have lived for thirty years with this. I think it's because I've been fighting so hard. I've kept telling myself I couldn't die. I still can't die—my grandchildren are small; until they reach school age, my daughter has her hands full, and so I have to help. My daughter says I can't die until my granddaughters get married, but I don't think I can live that long. I wonder how many more years I can live? If you're well today, you may die tomorrow—that's the way dialysis is. I feel scared of death, but there's nothing I can do about it; when you die you die. But I can't die for at least five or six more years.

My daughter, her husband, and their two children live on the second floor here, my husband and I on the first floor.[5] My daughter's husband's company wanted to transfer him, but because he felt my daughter had to stay with me, he quit and found a position in a new company—he's great! I never asked him to do that, but he quit his job so that he could stay with us!

I don't have many friends. I worked hard; whenever I had time, I went out selling door-to-door. When I was invited somewhere, I couldn't go. I had to cook for my husband; he'll eat only the food I cook. I don't regret not having friends; my family's the best thing for me. I don't want to cause hardship for my husband; if he was worried about money, he couldn't do good calligraphy. Thirty years ago I didn't know if he could make it, but now he's regarded as a great calligrapher. I feel that my assistance in those years has been rewarded.

I feel really happy right now; I don't have to worry about anything.

5. This is the same household arrangement that Takagi-san's family has: parent(s) on the first floor, child and spouse and their children on the second, in separate residences. This seems to be an increasingly common alternative, among Japanese who can afford it, to the traditional three-generation household.

My daughter's married, my husband's doing fine. Of course I don't want to die yet, but if I had to die, I could die with peace of mind. One worry is that my husband drinks a bit too much. I'd feel sorry if he got sick after I died. But basically, if I died now everything would be all right.

In my sixty-eight years, a lot has happened to me. Sometimes I think that if a movie were made of my life, it'd be very interesting. The main theme would be my disease. I've overcome it in a way; I've been doing what I wanted to do in life—I've been lucky. . . . I don't have any dreams anymore; I can't do anything! I'm looking forward to seeing my grandchildren grow up, and to seeing what my husband's going to do with his calligraphy; but I can't do anything myself. If my legs were OK, I'd work; I wish I could. My daughter says I should live on even if I'm bedridden.

I can't say for sure that there's no life after death, but I've never heard of anyone who went to that world and returned. If I knew someone like that, maybe I could believe in it, but. . . . I don't believe a lot of what the Buddhist priests say. Priests are only human. They've never been to the other world; what they preach they've only learned from books! . . . I often think about how my parents are Buddhas [*hotokesama*] now. I speak to my parents at the altar [*butsudan*], and offer them rice, but I still can't believe in that stuff.[6] It's better to believe, but I can't. . . . I'm not afraid of death, but sometimes I feel I'll be lonely because I have to go alone, leaving my family behind. Last night in a dream I saw my grandmother. I was wearing her *kimono*. I told her it was too small for me, and then she disappeared. I wonder if she wants to tell me something?

For the past thirty years my *ikigai* has been my husband, to help and support him. My daughter's married and has a good husband; of course I think of her too, but I'm most concerned with my husband.

6. When Murakami-san speaks of parents, she means her husband's parents, it being her duty as wife to look after them at the *butsudan* (Buddhist altar). *Hotokesama* means "Buddha" but also "departed soul"; the cognitive content of the term is vague for many Japanese.

My husband's *ikigai* is his calligraphy; as a calligrapher, he's invited to lots of places. This year he'll go to Europe. I'm very happy when he travels—I feel as if I were making those trips myself! My *ikigai* has been my husband since I married him, and will be until I die. . . . I just don't want to die, that's my *ikigai!* Life is good! It's joyful to be alive; I want to live as long as possible. I'm very greedy!

Life is never free from worries, but if you remember that there are people suffering much more than you are, you can see that your life isn't so bad. Though my legs hurt, I go to the market and cook meals for my husband; I feel *ikigai* in that. We get lots of deliveries for my husband, so someone has to be home all the time; my husband needs me for that too. I'm really happy I'm needed. Also, I can go to a hot springs resort once a month with my sisters, and my husband doesn't complain. My daughter drives me there and back; I feel grateful. Still, sometimes I wish I were ten years younger. I don't want to live five hundred more years, but I wish I could live a little longer.

Sally Tucker (60)

(Ms. Tucker's house is low-slung and sagging, a cowboy's house in an area enveloped by the compounds of well-to-do suburbanites. We held our interviews by the stove, a wood fire burning through its window. She is a grandmotherly woman, speaking with great concision; I asked her no more than twenty questions in all. She cried not while discussing her illness, but in recounting how her mother had thought she had gotten married decades earlier because she was pregnant rather than out of love.)

I was born in Texas in 1930; I had ten brothers and sisters. My father was a sharecropper, until he was able to buy his own place. Then he lost everything in the Depression. I really didn't have a childhood; from the time we could walk, we were in the fields working. September meant picking cotton, gathering corn; we never started school until about mid-November. When we came home from school, we'd work in the fields until dark. Then we'd put supper on the table, heat water and wash the dishes, wash whatever clothes we needed the next day for school, then do homework, and lamps out until 4:30 the next morning. On Sundays, my father wouldn't mind us walking five miles up the railroad tracks to go to church. I understand why we had to work so hard—there was so little money—but we overdid it. My father was so scared of not having money that he was the hardest taskmaster I ever saw, and he worked just as hard himself.

When it came time for my senior trip in high school, my mother said, "You can't go." I said, "Mother, I've earned the right to go!" "Your daddy won't let you!" "I'm not going to ask my daddy, I'm going!" I was scared the whole trip of what he was going to do to me. When I got back, I walked home nine miles up the railroad track, got into my work clothes, went to the fields. My father never said a word. . . .

I eloped when I was eighteen. Mel, who's thirteen years older than me, managed a nearby ranch. We started going together in September 1948, and in November, Mel asked me to marry him. My mother said, "Over my dead body!" My parents wanted to keep me on the farm, working. We couldn't see each other after that; through one of my brothers, we exchanged letters. Mel decided that we'd get married in January, on my birthday. My girlfriend, who was in on the plan, came and said, "We're giving Sally a birthday party." She talked my mother into letting me go for an hour. I had butterflies in my stomach, because I was going to disobey my parents. When my father found out we'd gotten married, he got his gun and went looking for us. That passed; but later, if we saw my parents on the road, they'd look away. I'd never been alone in my life until I got married; it was frightening. . . .

When I got married, I didn't know anything about Mel. I didn't know he was color-blind; he shows up to get married in black pants, a green shirt, a grey tie with yellow flowers. . . . When we went to his house, this house I'd never been in before, the wallpaper was peeling off. He and my brother had turned the water hose on the kitchen walls to try to clean them. . . .

After we were married, I got pregnant and had a child. When she was eight months old, Mel announced, "We're going to your mom's and dad's tonight." He'd talked with my father over the fence, said, "Hasn't this gone on long enough?" and my father'd agreed, but hadn't told my mother. I cried all afternoon; I knew he was going to kill us! We came to the door; my mother sees who it is and falls into a dead faint. My father says, "Come in," and that was that—it was never mentioned again, that there'd ever been a problem. . . .

I don't think I even knew that it took nine months to have a baby; I needed three days to be married nine months when I went into labor. Many years later, when our own daughter was pregnant without being married, my mother said, "First you and now your daughter!" All those years she'd suspected that I'd been pregnant, that that's why I'd gotten married! I still can't talk about it without it really hurting. . . . I'm sure my father went to his grave thinking, "She was pregnant, that's why she got married!" But it wasn't that at all! I was in love!

We had a daughter, then a son, and much later, another son. Mel managed the ranch for several years, then started horseshoeing. We moved here in 1967. This county had seventy-five thousand horses; by Mel's second day here, he had all the work he could do! . . . Mel's just turned seventy-three; he broke his back last summer, and two years before that, his neck. I'm not sure he'll be able to shoe anymore. (There aren't many horses here now. For years, this house of ours was the only house here. But no more) . . . As for me, I've done some part-time work, but mostly I've been at home. While our youngest was in grade school, I was a teacher aide for six years. But I wanted to make more money, because I thought I'd like to go to college; I took a job at a store and worked a year before I became ill.

It turned out to be a tumor on my spinal cord. We did surgery fourteen years ago; it can't be done again. The tumor's terribly painful; even with the medicine I take, it only cuts the sharp edge off for a few hours. My doctor said, "I hope you've enjoyed the fourteen years that you've had, because I'm not saying that you're not going to have fourteen more, but they're going to be rough." From the pain I'm having now, we suspect that the tumor's growing upwards; in that case, it'll eventually paralyze my breathing. Still, when I have a bad day, I think, "tomorrow's gonna be better." And it usually is.

I don't think about my tumor much; I've had fourteen years to come to terms with it. There was a period when I was resentful. Our youngest son was still at home, and every morning I had to get up with a smile on my face. I resented the fact that I was the one that had to make everything all right. But then one day I wrote down all the things I was upset about and all the things that were good in my life. The column of good things was so much longer—that was the end of that!

I have no medical insurance—five years ago my insurance went to $428 a month, and I couldn't pay it. Maybe I'll go into a hospice. A hospice will take you regardless of how much money you have, and they don't hook you up to a life-saving machine. I don't fear death; I fear what's between here and death, the pain that's going to come. . . . I guess I've always thought that Mel would go first. If there's any fear, it's that I'll be left alone without enough money to survive on. Our daughter in Texas would like us to live with her. But I'd like to stay here so that I could go to a hospice—there's a good one near here.

The most important source of happiness in my life has been the love that Mel and I have found together. We love our children dearly, but Mel was first, because once they were grown, Mel would be the only one I'd have left. We brought them up to go out and make their own lives. I had many friends who put their children first; when their children were gone, they looked at their husbands as if they were strangers. . . .

Our daughter in Texas is a nurse; she got remarried and has a child. Our older son's married, has two children, and is a welder. Jerry, our youngest, is single; he's a carpenter. All three were stubborn, determined to do things their way, but all three have come back to the values we brought them up on. If I had one wish, it'd be to see Jerry married, with a home. The others are married, have homes, children, careers: they're doing all right.

When I was little, I wanted to be a nurse or a schoolteacher. But if I'd gone to college, I would have outgrown Mel. Mel is one of the few people in the world who is comfortable with who he is; I'd have left him standing in the middle of the road. I did the very best I could at being a mother and a wife; I'm proud of what I've accomplished. The key was marrying Mel; if I hadn't done that, I'd still be on the farm. Marrying Mel was the best thing that ever happened to me.

Yes, it'd be ideal if Mel and I could live together many more years without pain. I've had fourteen years because God intended it. It's a test of faith, of how much you want to live. I very much want to live! In the morning you get up and say, "Thank God the sun's shining." You go forth and make the best of it.

I've never prayed to God to take this tumor away. What I've prayed for is the strength to endure the bad times, and the thankfulness for the good times. God has not failed me; I've failed Him, but He's letting me live on in spite of that. I've had days where I've forgotten to say, "God, this was a wonderful day, thank You," and He's forgiven me. I know that I'm not as strong a Christian as I should be, but I'm comfortable with the fact that I'm on a first-name basis with God. . . . I'd like to think that my son Jerry, who's not a Christian, is going to heaven, but I don't know. I'd feel much better if he had God in his life, but you can just do so much with bringing a child up. After they're on their own, you encourage them, you hope you've lived a life that's an example. His girlfriend told me that Jerry said that he never got in the car and started to work that he knew I wasn't praying for him. He's just about right. . . .

I've often asked myself, what lesson was I to learn from being ill? I think God's given me a chance to appreciate what I have and reach out to others. Jerry was thirteen when I was diagnosed; God gave me the chance to see him grown. God doesn't cause people to suffer for no reason. It's been a hard lesson to learn, but I think I've grown more in the last fourteen years than I did in the forty-five before. . . . If I died right now, I don't think I'd have regrets over my family, but there might be doubt over whether I'm truly ready to go to heaven. I'd like to think I'm ready. But we sin daily; if we haven't asked for forgiveness on that day, does that leave us wide open to not go to heaven? I think there's more sins than the Ten Commandments. I think that when we don't show our Christian faith with a kindness to a neighbor or to a stranger, I think we've failed that day.

I never go to sleep at night that I don't pray; I know completely that God and Christ are real. If my illness did anything for me, it made me stop just saying I believed, but live it. I was so busy in my younger years with my children that it was lip service; I thought I believed, but it isn't until you're put to the test that you see whether your faith is truly strong.

In this world I live for Mel. Mel can't do anything about the pain, but he understands. You want to be as kind and gentle and strong for him as he has been for you. Still, in the end religious faith is all we're left with. As much as I love Mel, that last walk is by ourselves. Mel can't go with me; it's something I do alone.

Murakami Mitsuko and Sally Tucker: Analysis

Both these women, after childhoods filled with toil, have enjoyed long and happy married lives; both have suffered for many years from diseases that may kill them; and both have continued to live vital lives despite their illnesses. However, Murakami-san is an agnostic, while Ms. Tucker is a committed Christian; Ms. Tucker is focused on her future in the next world, while Murakami-san remains focused on her family in this one.

These women's *ikigai* has been their relation with their husbands. Neither made children her *ikigai;* neither made her own career her *ikigai.* The dominant factor shaping these women's lives has been their illnesses. Murakami-san was stricken with kidney disease during the years her husband was studying calligraphy. It is a testament to her belief in him that despite almost dying, she continued to work while in the hospital and to make her sales rounds after leaving the hospital; she apparently never pressured her husband to abandon calligraphy. Her personal incantation seems to have been "I can't die yet!" because her husband and child depended on her. With her daughter now married and her husband successful, she can say, "If I died now, everything would be all right," but still she feels needed: to receive her husband's packages and prepare his meals, and help care for the grandchildren. It's because she feels needed that she can live so happily; her only wish now is to "live a little longer."

Murakami-san's disease seems to have strengthened her *ikigai* as family; Ms. Tucker's tumor (although interrupting her plans for college, and in that sense bringing her back to family) seems to have led to a shifting of *ikigai* from family to God. Her earlier faith, she tells us, was "lip service"; she was so immersed in raising her children that she didn't devote herself to her faith. It was, she says, her tumor that put her faith to the test, from which that faith seems to have emerged triumphant. Faith would not have to be in competition with family as her deepest commitment. Her husband and she could perhaps find their *ikigai* in family and work under the guidance of God. But Ms. Tucker is slowly dying, her pain inexorably increasing. She very much wants to live, she tells us, but her awareness of dying seems to lead her increasingly to think not of this world but of the next.

In our earlier accounts, those I interviewed discuss their religious beliefs, but only in this pair of accounts is religious belief linked to *ikigai*—perhaps because of these women's proximity to death. Murakami-san is skeptical about life after death; yet, after seeing her grandmother in a dream, she wonders, maybe not just whimsically, if her grandmother is trying to tell her something. She speaks with her parents-in-law at the *butsudan,* and although she can't believe in their continuing existence, she seems to yearn to believe. Ms. Tucker feels no such skepticism; she prays to a God she believes in completely. Her doubts concern not the existence of God, but her own readiness to go to God: does her sinning leave her "wide open to not go to heaven?" This question may be at the heart of her increasing concern with religion; her family in this world is secure, but her place in heaven, she feels, is not.

Murakami-san is a religious skeptic, while Ms. Tucker is a religious believer; this is the clearest reason for their difference in *ikigai*. Murakami-san holds to family as her *ikigai* because she believes that after this life there is no other; Ms. Tucker is apparently shifting her *ikigai* from family to God because she believes that after this life there is indeed another, looming ever larger as death grows ever closer. But aside from this obvious difference of religious skepticism on the one hand and religious belief on the other, differences within both Japan and the United States, there also seem to be some key differences between Japanese Buddhist practices and American Protestant faith contributing to Murakami-san's ongoing *ikigai* as family and Ms. Tucker's apparent shift in *ikigai* from family to God.

As David Plath has pointed out in his essay, "Where the Family of God Is the Family" (1964), the Japanese household includes the dead as well as the living; departed parents or grandparents will regularly be spoken to and given offerings. Murakami-san may be skeptical about a world beyond the grave, but in that she practices ancestor worship and thinks of the familial ancestors, the disjunction between this world and the next isn't absolute. At present she performs rituals for the departed, whereas in the future she will have those rituals performed for her; she will continue to be a valued member of her family.

For Ms. Tucker, on the other hand, the disjunction between this world and the next does seem absolute, unbridgeable by love of family. As Jesus warns in the Bible, "I have come to set a man at odds with his father, a daughter with her mother ... to make a man's enemies those of his own household. Whoever loves father or mother, son or daughter, more than me is not worthy of me" (Matthew 10:35–37). Ms. Tucker tells us that her son's fate in heaven or hell lies beyond her ken; heaven may be entered only on the basis of individual faith. It is as if, to ensure entrance to heaven as she conceives of it, Ms. Tucker *must* shift her *ikigai* from family to God; otherwise she may be deemed insufficient in faith and denied salvation.

Many American Christians don't have as draconian a view of heaven as Ms. Tucker. Indeed, a number of Christians I spoke with felt that there was no conflict at all between family and God as one's deepest commitment; the two are in intrinsic harmony. Many Japanese, including several I interviewed, seem to shift their *ikigai* from family to religion as they grow older and closer to death. Nonetheless, this apparent difference in these two women's ongoing *ikigai* at least partially reflects the cultural patternings of religion in their two societies—patternings of American individualism and Japanese groupism—as used by these women in making sense of their lives and coming deaths.

For the younger people we've considered in this chapter, their dreams are of the future. For these two women, on the other hand, their dreams on this earth are almost done. Yet their dreams continue: where, they wonder, might they go once they die? Let us now consider the relation of *ikigai* to dreams.

Ikigai and Dreams

Dreams, Culture, and Gender

The accounts over the past two chapters illustrate what may be a broad patterning of *ikigai* over the life course in Japan and the United States: young people finding *ikigai* in dreams of the future, those in the middle of their lives finding *ikigai* in present commitments to work or family, and old people finding *ikigai* in past pursuits and relationships continuing into the present. These patterns show *ikigai* shifting from future to present to past as the self grows older, but in another, more fundamental sense, all *ikigai* are located in the future. *Ikigai* is not only "that which most makes one's life seem worth living," but also "that which evokes one's deepest sense of social commitment." Commitment is not fleeting but enduring, an endurance that bridges present and future. *Ikigai* thus involves both the reality of one's present and the dream of one's future. These dreams may be of a future *ikigai* not yet experienced as reality, or of sustaining one's present *ikigai* into the future, but all *ikigai* are in part the stuff of dreams—dreams internal to the self, but culturally, socially, and institutionally shaped.

The shaping of dreams can be seen in all the accounts we've examined. Miyamoto-san thinks of his occupational *ikigai* dreams in terms of his company's success, something Mr. Murray hesitates to do, given his sense of corporate betrayal. Wada-san mostly identifies with the role of wife and mother in her *ikigai* dreams, whereas Ms. Pratt distrusts such roles, dreaming of personal wisdom as well as of future happiness for her children. Takagi-san's dream of self-realization must remain a dream, he believes; Mr. Eliot has been able to live out his chosen dream of commitment to family. Nakajima-san's *ikigai* dreams are of marriage to a man of high status, a dream Ms. Peters dare not hold too strongly, given the prevalence of divorce in America. Mr. Isaacs's *ikigai* dream is to become a psychological trainer, enabling selves to become fulfilled, an occupation nonexistent and a dream all but undreamable in Japan. Murakami-san's *iki-gai* dream is in terms of her continuing commitment to her family; Ms. Tucker's dream is of her own salvation.

In these pairs of dreams, we see various individualized versions of the Japanese cultural principle of commitment to group, and the American cultural principle of individual-centeredness and self-realization. These Japanese and American *ikigai* dreams seem self-evident to many of those who hold them, just as the objective institutional structures of their different worlds seem self-evident—both are shaped through a dialectic of self and world, ever recreating "Japanese groupism" and "American individualism."

In his study of maturity in modern Japan, Plath discusses Japanese as opposed to American conceptions of maturity: "[The American] cultural nightmare is that the individual throb of growth will be sucked dry in slavish social conformity. . . . The Japanese cultural nightmare is to be excluded from others. . . . The American archetype . . . seems more attuned to cultivating a self that knows it is unique in the cosmos, the Japanese archetype to a self that can feel human in the company of others" (1980, 216–18).

A single concept of maturity can't do justice to Japanese and American selves in all their diversity. Kinoshita-san and Takagi-san seem, by Plath's characterization, attuned more to an American than to a Japanese concept of maturity, just as Mr. Eliot seems oriented more to Japanese than to American maturity. Still, these contrasting conceptions clearly dovetail with the different kinds of American and Japanese dreams we've just outlined.

Dreams are thus shaped by culture, but they also are shaped by gender. Plath's concept of Japanese maturity fits many Japanese women, but many American women as well; Plath's concept of American maturity fits many American men, but many Japanese men as well. In his study of the American male life cycle, Daniel Levinson writes of "the Dream": the youth's sense of the future life he seeks to live. "My life is enriched to the extent that I have a Dream. . . . If I have no Dream or can find no way to live it out, my life lacks genuine purpose or meaning" (1978, 246; see generally 90–93, 245–51). Levinson seems to suggest that having such a Dream is universal (322); but as Carol Gilligan points out, the Dream's "vision of glorious achievement" may describe American men's more than American women's conceptions of their lives (1982, 152; see 151–74). In the male lives Levinson describes, Gilligan notes, "relationships are subordinated to the ongoing process of individuation and achievement" (154); in the female lives she describes, on the other hand, "identity is defined in a context of relationship and judged by a standard of responsibility and care" (160). To these women, it is not individuation and achievement but "ongoing attachment as the path that leads to maturity" (170).

These different paths to maturity are reflected in the accounts we've looked at. Mr. Isaacs, as well as Kinoshita-san, values his dream of alternative occupational success over all else (although his priorities may change in the future, he tells us). Mr. Murray—as well as, in a different sense, Takagi-san—reflects on how his occupational dream has and has not come to fruition in his life. Ms. Pratt, on the other hand, as well as Wada-san, seems finally to value familial relationships over her own achievements. Even Ms. Tucker, apparently locating her *ikigai* dreams not in family but in God (which too is a relationship) still devoted her adult life to nurturing her family, as did Murakami-san, and even Mr. Eliot, locating his *ikigai* dreams in family relationships, nonetheless spent twenty years of his adult life pursuing occupational achievement.

There is a remarkable similarity between Plath's formulation of Japanese as opposed to American maturity and Gilligan's formulation of female as opposed to male maturity in the United States. In both, relationships with others are valued over personal achievement, the growth of self as a part of others over self apart from others. Gilligan's formulations seem to apply to Japanese as well as American gender differences apparent in our accounts: generally (although Miyamoto-san may be an exception), Japanese and American men's *ikigai* dreams seem focused more on personal achievement, Japanese and American women's *ikigai* dreams more on personal relationships. There is of course an obvious link between *ikigai* as rooted in family and *ikigai* dreams conceived in terms of relationships, as opposed to *ikigai* as rooted in work and *ikigai* dreams of achievement.

Extrapolating from our accounts, it may be that Japanese and American societies' apparent difference in orientation, toward the group and the individual respectively, is overridden by their similarity: both are oriented toward men's achievement and women's nurturance. It may be that this shaping of dreams by gender leads many Japanese and American women to resemble one another in their *ikigai* dreams more than they might resemble their own husbands, and many Japanese and American men to resemble one another more than they might resemble their own wives. As we saw in the previous chapter, however, it seems easier for individuals to resist this shaping of dreams in the United States than in Japan. The shaping of dreams by gender seems both more powerful and more taken-for-granted in Japan than in the United States.

Dreams and History

Ikigai dreams are shaped by culture and by gender, but also by history, as experienced by those I interviewed. The historical baseline of many middle-aged and older Japanese was World War II and its aftermath. Murakami-san tells of being sent to see off the soldiers as they left for war and of being warned to say nothing about the emperor for fear of the police; Miyamoto-san speaks of the poverty of his postwar childhood after losing his father and of how it has shaped his outlook on life ever since. A women in her fifties said, "I remember as a little child wishing that my school were closer to my house, because then I could go back to my mother when the air-raid sirens went off instead of staying at school—I was terrified that she would die without me." A man in his sixties told of seeing the factories in his city come crashing to the ground before the bombardment of the American battleships. A man in his seventies described being a prisoner of war in a Russian hospital: "About seventy people died every day, of dysentery. Every day I had to bury the bodies. It was like hell." A man in his fifties told of his shock when, after Japan's defeat, the American soldiers did not kill Japanese children but handed them candy bars instead: "Even now I feel grateful."

Many particular events have colored Japanese life in the decades since World War II: the Korean War, the advent of television in the late 1950s, the protests against the U.S.-Japan Security Treaty in 1960, the Tokyo Olympics of 1964, the student activism of the late

1960s, the oil shocks of the 1970s, the "bubble economy" of the late 1980s, and the economic recession and fundamental shifts in Japanese politics in the early 1990s. But all of these events pale in significance before the growth of the Japanese economy in these decades from ashes to dynamo. There are exceptions, such as Takagi-san, but generally, their place on the trajectory of Japanese economic growth has been the major historical factor shaping the lives and *ikigai* of those I interviewed: from Miyamoto-san's hectoring the affluent young for their lack of commitment to the company to Kinoshita-san's comment that "the good thing about Japan now is that you have the freedom to choose jobs—any job will give you enough money to live on," and from Murakami-san's grueling childhood to Nakajima-san's family's wealth, protecting her "from life's hardships."

As we saw in chapter 1, Japan's transition from devastation to affluence has led to Japanese soul-searching. Is "a life worth living" to be found through living for one's role in the company or family (Miyamoto-san, Wada-san, Murakami-san), or for the hope of one's own eventual self-fulfillment (Takagi-san)? Is such a life to be found through following one's parents' rules and roles (Nakajima-san) or through rejecting those roles, to live a life by one's own lights (Kinoshita-san)? These different ways of conceiving the meaning of one's life reflect what may be the key cultural dilemma in Japan today.

The baseline for many of the older Americans I interviewed was the Great Depression. Ms. Tucker's father lost everything in the Depression, and her childhood of toil was shaped by that loss. Others I interviewed described the loss even of the will to live: as one man told me, "My father was never the same after he lost his business in the Depression—it killed him. Being in business was all he lived for." If the postwar period in Japan represents a time of poverty in contrast to today's affluence, the postwar period in the United States (1946–63) represents, for many of the Americans I interviewed, a time of familial stability as opposed to today's instability. Mr. Eliot tells us that he grew up in a family ruined by alcohol, while Ms. Pratt and Mr. Isaacs describe their upbringings in more positive terms, but all three had families in which the father worked and the mother stayed home. In the 1950s in the United States, some 55 percent of families conformed to this pattern, whereas today only 30 percent do (Louv

1992, 43–44); and this pattern is what many of those I interviewed apparently meant when they spoke of the "stability" of that age.

World War II didn't affect the Americans I interviewed as much as it affected the Japanese; by the same token, the cultural upheavals of the 1960s didn't affect the Japanese as much as they affected the Americans. Those upheavals directly affected Ms. Pratt, she tells us, in her advocacy of activism and of gender equality, but indirectly they seem to have affected Mr. Murray in the breakup of his marriage, Mr. Eliot in the renegotiation of his marriage, and Mr. Isaacs in his search for psychological fulfillment. Even Ms. Peters, in her fear of future divorce and her desire for a career, reflects American social trends emerging in the 1960s and 1970s: the drive for women's equality as a major social force, the emergence of psychological growth as an ideal of how to live, and the widespread fracturing of the family.

As I noted in chapter 2, the United States between the end of World War II and the 1960s bears a certain resemblance to Japan over the past twenty-five years. In both societies, unprecedented prosperity eventually led many to question the values of self-denial and commitment to group, to instead seek to live lives on the basis of personal happiness and self-realization. Since the 1980s, however, there has been a growing chorus of voices advocating the return to a sense of commitment in the United States; Mr. Eliot's account, in particular, echoes those voices. The historical question facing the Americans I spoke with is not different from that of their Japanese counterparts, albeit coming from a different pole of emphasis. Should one live for one's own self and its growth, or for something larger than the self? Many of the Americans whose accounts we've examined are attempting to shape their lives through the ways in which they hear and answer this question.

The shapings of recent history can be seen through the comparison of different generations in our accounts, for example, Nakajima-san and Ms. Peters in contrast to Murakami-san and Ms. Tucker. Murakami-san spent her childhood working to help support her family; Nakajima-san has spent her childhood in training to be a graceful wife. Ms. Tucker labored through her childhood; Ms. Peters has played much and worked little through hers. The two older women produced in their childhoods, while the two younger women consumed; the two older women were raised to be puritans, the two younger women to be hedonists. Of course these women can't be said to represent their respective generations; but compared to the American Depression or the postwar poverty of Japan, the two societies now enjoy remarkable affluence, an affluence that seems to have shaped the two younger women's *ikigai* dreams just as poverty shaped the dreams of their elders.

We can also see history's shapings in the contrast between Miyamoto-san and Mr. Murray versus Kinoshita-san and Mr. Isaacs. Miyamoto-san has devoted his life to his company, seeing it as his lifeline out of his childhood poverty; Kinoshita-san, growing up in a more affluent Japan, refuses to devote his life to any company but only to his own dream. Mr. Murray too has devoted his life to his company, to which he remains loyal despite his sense of betrayal; Mr. Isaacs easily shifts companies and plans to leave the corporate world to pursue his dream. These men too can't be said to represent their respective generations, but the older men seem to value security, the younger men dreams. Again, it may be that a childhood sense of scarcity breeds the adult longing for risk-free security; a childhood sense of affluence breeds the longing for risk-filled fulfillment.

If this is the case, then it may be that the arrival of widespread affluence in the United States and particularly in Japan has created a historically new generation of young people (termed in the 1980s *shinjinrui*, "the new breed," in Japanese) less concerned about security and more concerned with self-realization than their elders. But this is debatable. Edwin Seidensticker has commented that when the current younger generation of Japanese reaches forty, they'll "act just like everyone else at forty" (Tergesen 1990); their current self-oriented attitudes are due simply to the fact that they're young, rather than to a historical shift in Japanese values. Minami makes a similar argument. Using statistically measured attitudes toward work and leisure among Japanese generational cohorts, he claim that stages in life course are the primary factor shaping attitudinal changes between generations, that the attitudes of today's young basically resemble those of their parents at a similar age (1989, 113).

On the other hand, Sengoku (1991) maintains that today's gap in values between old and young is not recurrent with each generation but unprecedented: the question "Why work so hard?", the question so frequently asked by today's young (152), is absolutely new, he argues, the result of Japan's shift from premodern to postmodern values in the 1970s and 1980s without the intervening modern values of individual responsibility ever taking root. Sakurai (1985) and Narita (1986) make similar arguments about the unprecedented values of today's Japanese young, as did most Japanese I interviewed over age forty-five. As one man in his late fifties said, "Probably it's better for Japanese to work less now, but I feel upset when I see a young man with dyed hair driving around in a fancy car with a pretty girl. Forty years ago, people his age all died in the war; they didn't have the chance to enjoy their youth! I want to drag that guy out of his car and put a *judō* hold on him, teach him a lesson!"

In the United States, the generation gap was widely discussed twenty-five years ago (as in, for example, Reich's extravagant claims in *The Greening of America*). In *Culture and Commitment* (1970), Margaret Mead distinguished between "postfigurative" cultures, "in which children learn primarily from their forebears," "cofigurative" cultures, "in which both children and adults learn from their peers," and "prefigurative" cultures, "in which adults learn also from their children" (1970, 1). She argued that the United States and the world were emerging into prefiguration, in which children, the youngest generation, serve as their societies' pathfinders into the future. In a narrow sense Mead was wrong—the youth revolts of the 1960s have become the nostalgic memories of the middle-aged—but in a broader sense her point may be valid. Today's American and Japanese youth are experiencing influences such as video games and computers that no previous generation has experienced. The historically new conditions of childhood—conditions that, because of rapid advances in technology, may continue to be new with each succeeding generation—will perhaps create new sites for the *ikigai* dreams of adulthood.

But the effects of new technology and mass media in the accounts of this chapter seem more conservative than revolutionary. It was not her mother but a movie that convinced Nakajima-san to want chil-

dren, not priests but television that influenced Ms. Peters and Kinoshita-san to imagine heaven and believe in life after death (thus legiti-
mating life in this world)—choices supporting the social status quo.
The influence of the media on those I interviewed was not always
toward preserving the status quo; two young men I spoke with, one
Japanese, one American, immersed themselves in rock music to express their alienation from their societies. But for the young people
in this chapter, new media serve more as new channels for old *ikigai*
dreams than as sources of new ones.

If technological developments reshape the limits of each new generation's imagination, social and economic change reshape the odds
that what is imagined may become reality. Young Americans today
can't assume that they will remain married all their lives and can't
expect to raise a family on a single wage; young Americans and Japanese can't expect to find a well-paying job with a high-school education and can't expect to enter the professions of their grandparents.
These observations are commonplace, but indicate how each new
generation faces historical circumstances different from generations
past, circumstances that shape dreams. Each new Japanese and
American generation has in at least some respects no precursors.

Dreams, Aging, and Death

Dreams are shaped in history, but also by one's own history: one's
place in the life course from youth, to middle age, to old age, to
death. For many of the old people I interviewed, the dominant issue
of their lives at present seems to be the fact of being elderly. Murakami-san and Ms. Tucker seem to view their lives very much in terms
of their diminishing life expectancy in this world; it has been a struggle for them to come to terms with age and illness. Indeed, almost
all the Japanese and American elderly I interviewed were experiencing some degree of physical and social diminishment: a sense of less-
ening physical capacity, a sense of having little useful to do with
themselves, a loss of spouse and of friends, and a sense of death as
ever nearer.

Some of these diminishments are inevitable, but others are created
by society. "Whatever intrinsic value older people might have, there

is comparatively little *market* for them—either economic or social," writes an American authority on aging. "Aging involves the movement toward rolelessness" (Rosow 1982, 47, 48). "America . . . is a country in which the only value of a human being is the ability to produce" (Gornick 1978, 29); "What we call retirement is in fact compulsory unemployment" (Comfort 1978, 81). "Personal ability and performance are our gods," writes Endō Shūsaku of contemporary Japan (1989). "Unable to work like younger people, the aged are deemed worthless." In capitalist, technologically driven societies such as Japan and the United States, these writers indicate, what is valued is the young and the new, not the old and the "obsolete."[7] Although in the United States the elderly are on average financially better off than their juniors, the elderly in both Japan and the United States are often removed from social productivity long before their abilities have seriously declined.

Despite the societally generated push toward rolelessness, most of the elderly I interviewed continued to have *ikigai* dreams. Of our two old people in this chapter, Murakami-san continues to find her *ikigai* in "being needed" by her husband and family, and she dreams of "being needed" for years to come; Ms. Tucker remains deeply involved with her family, praying for the well-being of her children. Yet there is a melancholy in these women's accounts, and in the accounts of all the old people I interviewed: as Murakami-san tells us, "I don't want to live five hundred more years, but I wish I could live a little longer."

In youth, any or all of the self's dreams may come true. One may become a famous athlete, novelist, or company president; one may marry an ideal spouse and have ideal children. By old age, these dreams, whether realized or unrealized, are past. The novelist James Baldwin has written that "though we would like to live without regrets, and sometimes proudly insist that we have none, this is not

7. The rolelessness of the elderly is a problem born of the increase in life expectancy in the United States and particularly in Japan, as discussed in chapter 1. When people die on average two or three rather than twenty or thirty years after retirement or the completion of childrearing, as was the case until recent decades in the United States and Japan, the problem does not appear, because death precedes social obsolescence.

really possible, if only because we are mortal" (quoted in Levinson 1978, 250, and Plath 1980, 13). The multitude of potential paths of our future progressively become the single actual path we have taken. There is a narrowing of future possibilities in this world, a narrowing that ends in death.

But for many of those I interviewed, there's another world beyond this one. For Ms. Tucker, her this-world possibilities have progressively narrowed, but her next-world possibilities seem absolutely real and compelling. Even Murakami-san, not completely certain that there is no life after death, still continues to dream of a world beyond. To the extent that one believes in life after death, one's personal dreams don't end as death approaches; to the extent that one doesn't believe in life after death, one's dreams do end, but for the hope of being remembered and of the future happiness, unbeknownst to oneself, of one's family and descendants.

And this leads us to the subject of much of the rest of this book. Given the fact of death, awaiting each of us and coming progressively closer with each passing instant of our lives, how do Japanese and Americans find the significance, the meaning of their—our—lives?

Chapter Six

Ikigai in Creation and Religion

Murakami Junji (61)

(Murakami-sensei[1] is a round man, fitting the image of the eccentric artist. He is an extraordinary raconteur and a lover of *sake;* by our interviews' close, we were quite drunk. His most enlightening conversation always came when the interview was over and the tape recorder turned off—he wouldn't let me turn it on again. I last saw him months after our interviews, when I accompanied him to a class he gave for the deaf, with whom he seemed to fit right in as, in a sense, a fellow outsider.)

I teach *shodō* [calligraphy]; I have about a hundred students. For financial reasons it's better to have more, but for teaching well, it's better to have fewer. A hundred's about right. . . . You learn *shodō* through the calligraphy of ancient Chinese texts; you try to master them, but it's also important to create something new from them. The problem with students is that they try to imitate me. I tell them, "First imitate me, but then go beyond that." They can imitate the character forms, but they have to create their own way of writing, their own line. What divides good calligraphy from bad is line, how

1. The husband of Murakami Mitsuko, in chapter 5. *Sensei* means "teacher" in Japanese, an honorific term applied to, among others, schoolteachers, teachers of arts, and doctors.

much feeling you can put into line. . . . When you look at calligraphy, you don't have to read it. Reading is for literature; you can look at *shodō* the way you look at an abstract painting, appreciating the beauty of its line. In spring, wildflowers bloom. Even though you don't know their names, you can feel their beauty! It's the same with *shodō*. . . .

Yes, I want to become wise through *shodō*. But what prevents people from becoming wise through art is the lure of money and fame. In the early nineteenth century, there was a man who called himself *Rokumusai* ["Six Nothingnesses"]: he had no parents, no wife, no children, no money. . . . It's impossible to have that kind of mentality in today's world: human beings have lost their instincts. You can't hoard food; it'll go bad. But you can hoard money and fame indefinitely. Ever since human beings created money, things have gotten strange! A few years ago, the newspapers ran a lot of articles about the Vietnamese boat people, and why Japan wouldn't accept them. My thought was that if they settled in Japan, they wouldn't be able to keep up with the way of life of "economic animals"; they wouldn't fit in, since they're happy if they can just live each day. We, on the other hand, are busy hoarding: we take out loans to build our houses, and work hard all our lives to pay back the loans. All we ever do is save. . . .

Anyway, I think I was wiser when I was younger. Until I was forty, I never argued, never offended anyone. When I was forty, I decided that I'd speak my mind, since Confucius said, "At forty a man knows what to do." So I guess I was wiser in the past! In calligraphy, though, as in all art, you've got to have something you want to express. To express myself in art, I had to express my opinions. Of course you have to be responsible for what you say, but by binding myself to that responsibility, acting out what I believed, I could create something new. My frankness caused lots of trouble with my teachers and other calligraphers, but I survived all that. I've been really lucky.

I grew up in Tokyo. My grandfather made a fortune from a brush he'd invented to clean pots and pans. But his sons squandered his fortune, and my family was poor. My father made wooden clogs [*geta*]. His drinking gave my mother lots of trouble, so I vowed I'd never drink. But one day there was a farewell party for a friend going off to military training; they made me drink a cup of *sake*. With that, I realized I'd made a terrible mistake. I thought, "Why didn't I start drinking such delicious stuff long ago?" . . . When I was in junior high school, I was teased because I was fat and couldn't play sports. The guy sitting next to me in class was two years older than me; he said all kinds of big-sounding [*erasō*] things, but was a nice guy pretending to be bad. He took me to *rakugo* theater, where entertainers told funny stories. In those days, in wartime, if students went to restaurants or movies, they'd be caught and punished. But *rakugo* theaters—probably they thought no student would go there![2] I never got caught. Listening to *rakugo*, I thought, "I shouldn't be teased all the time. I should start teasing people myself!" After that I changed completely. . . .

Late in the war, I was in school and also working in a factory with my class, making airplane parts. Our factory was bombed. Since my classmates and I went through such hardship together, we've always had a strong bond between us. . . . I worked my way through college after the war, running a bookshop. Usually people read while standing if they don't want to buy anything. But I read while sitting down, and the old woman who owned the place was always scolding me, telling me not to read but to manage the store! Then, after college, I went to work for an electrical appliance company.

Everybody in the office played mahjong after work. I wasn't much good at it; one day I suggested we form a *shodō* club, and the company union got us a teacher. I'd read Okakura Tenshin's *The Book of Tea*—he writes that "tea is a way of comprehending just a bit the mystery of life"—and I wanted to learn tea ceremony, too: we got a teacher for that. Later, because people were smoking too much, I decided to start a chorus. Most companies have clubs, so it wasn't so unusual; still, in the six months since I'd started work, I'd help set up three of them. One day my boss said, "Just why exactly did you join this company?" I worked hard, too, but. . . .

My boss once told me that a client had said that he'd never before met a salesman like me; he was amazed that I'd never once asked

2. *Rakugo* is (and was then) a traditional form of entertainment most often enjoyed by older people.

him to buy our products. I talked with him about lots of things, but not about that; I figured I didn't need to—why else would a salesman visit a potential customer? If I hadn't married my wife, I might still be there, a low-level *sarariiman*. When I told my wife I wanted to quit, she told me, with no hesitation, to go ahead. Even now, once a year or so, I have nightmares of being shouted at by my boss because the papers I was supposed to finish weren't done. I quit thirty years ago, but I wonder if I'm not still working for that company!

During those six years as a *sarariiman*, I studied calligraphy in my lunch breaks. After I quit, we lived in my wife's aunt's apartment. I wanted to relax, but a month after we'd moved, ten kids barged in one Sunday morning, saying, "You're a *shodō* teacher, aren't you? Teach us!" I hadn't known, but my aunt had advertised. . . . I didn't have any plans, when I quit the company, as to how we'd eat. A large part of me thinks like a Southeast Asian. Even if I'm not sure I can eat tomorrow, I don't worry. My family's maybe suffered! [Mura-kami-san: "One day I gave him twenty thousand yen to pay for some-thing, but he dropped it in the street somewhere. In those days, that was a lot of money—we could have eaten for months off that!"] She's not the type to nag, but that time she kept at it for a whole month!

After I quit the company, I studied *shodō* really hard for ten years. Back then, I didn't know anything about *shodō*, but acted as if I were an expert. Probably I'll feel the same way about today ten years from now. . . . When my wife got sick, a friend who was worried about us advised me to cancel my entry to a *shodō* exhibit (which costs a lot of money), but I told him that I wasn't about to do that; it was an important way of expressing myself. Now, my work is shown at most big exhibits, so I feel secure; but I used to worry about how my work might be evaluated. But I'm over sixty now; all the work I can do is on the basis of what I've done in the past. From that root I hope to produce lots more work. When I do my work, I don't think about other people; if you think about what others might think, you can't do your own real work.

My stomach's felt funny lately, so I went to see the doctor; he said I have a polyp. I thought about how my body was starting to break down. I'd better hurry up and do the things I want to do! If the polyp is malignant, I might not live long. But in the time before I die, I've got to do some work. I've got to do all I possibly can while I'm alive. Why? Because I *want* to, that's why! . . . I'm very happy when I'm drinking *sake,* but when I pick up my brush, that's the happiest and the most painful time for me. If I had a year to live, maybe I'd drink a little, but I'd do a lot of *shodō!* The other day I thought about what I'd do if I had cancer; all that came to mind was *shodō.* . . .

I've thought a bit about posterity, about leaving something behind after I'm dead. A calligrapher friend once told me, "You should write calligraphy for history"—he believed he'd left such work himself. I said, "All I can write is what satisfies me now. It's nobody's business whether my work will remain in history or not!" I think it's better to leave your work without leaving your name. Through *shodō* I want to leave proof of my existence: not my name, but my work. . . .

Life after death? I have the feeling that death isn't the end. Maybe when you're about to die, though, you only feel that you're leaving this world, your family and friends. When Natsume Sōseki died, he was finishing the novel *Kokoro;* he died saying, "I shouldn't die yet!" He didn't think about the other world; he just felt that he wasn't ready to die, because his work wasn't done. (Am I afraid of death? Not now. You feel scared of death when it's next to you, not if it's still a bit away. But death is something you can't avoid. . . .)

I feel *ikigai* when I'm doing *shodō.* For me, *ikigai* is what I feel when I'm using my body, in calligraphy. But if I went blind, say, I think I could find something new. Some people are flexible in their *ikigai,* but others lose that flexibility. . . . Finally, though, humans can't live without *ikigai.* Maybe heaven's a boring place because there's no *ikigai.* If you asked people in heaven, they might say, "I can eat delicious food all the time. But *ikigai?* Well. . . ." In a world where people don't have to die, there's no need to think about *ikigai.* . . .

Of course there are things in life that make you sad, but being alive itself—that I can think, work, have friends—that's true happiness. Human beings are made to forget; to forget is a privilege. I do think of my parents. When my daughter had a baby, I thought, "My mother would be so happy to see her great-grandchild!" But if that's sad, then life is nothing but sadness. . . .

If all my dreams came true, I'd like for all the people in Japan, all

the people in the world, to see the work on which I've spent my life.
I don't care if they like it; I just want them to *see* it! After you die,
you don't know anything—heaven's another world. But who knows,
maybe I'll see this world from afar and think, "Damn, I should've
done *that* kind of work!" Or maybe I'll go to a museum and think,
"Why's *that* guy's work here, but not mine?" For now, though, I'll do
my *shodō* with all my might, without worrying about what others
might think.

Louise Weiss (59)

(I met Louise Weiss at her home, separated from the city by a thick
pine forest. She is a sturdy, friendly woman, with a sense of humor
equal to Murakami-sensei's: when I asked her about disguises for her
account, she spun tales of being a champion skier and a spy whose
cover is blown by her extraordinary beauty. During our first interview, I pressed the wrong button and erased half of my recording;
she kindly assented to saying the same things all over again in our
second interview.)

I'm a writer. I write in the morning, two hours each day. If you do
that times fifty years you get eleven books! Everything I'm interested
in I write about: Judaism, history, music. . . . I don't use my family in
my fiction—God made those people already—I use my imagination.
But my plots do reflect my life. You can't help leaving your goddamn
fingerprints over what you write!

My earliest books were quite successful; the books since then
haven't been. Occasionally—when I read the *New York Times Book
Review* and they say that nothing good's come out this year, when
something you've written has come out—I feel put upon. But if you
give it any more than four minutes! For famous people, there's a
separation between them and other people; but I have this face that
nobody knows, I can go wherever I want. I'm not saying there aren't
moments, but. . . . There's an inside and an outside as a writer. The
outside is the fame, the reviews—the less you think about them, the
better. The inside is the thing you do. The outer and inner have to

be completely separate. . . . I'd like to get better as a writer; if I had a wish, that would be it. I've spent my life pounding on the walls of my limitations! You never get perfection. As close as I've come is a good paragraph. Twenty years later I read it and think, "This thing's built like a brick shithouse. It resonates!" And then the next paragraph, you say, "What is this mess!" . . .

Most of the writers I know who are in a mess have identified themselves as writers only. I was at a writer's conference and this lady said, "But writing is my *life!*" Someone said to her, "I'd hurry up and get some life if I were you!" You'd better: the art's marvelous but the trade stinks. You're bound up with what someone thinks a readership would want, which will make them a profit for publishing it. . . . Writing is a game—it's so much fun to write! It's like the natural, free sport of a good skier. What'll happen if I lose my gift? You know, God once said to me, "You're going to get old and stupid anyway, what are you worrying about?" There's the desire to cling, but if you do, the fun's gone out of it.

From when I was small, I knew that something was wrong with me. I heard voices. The first time was in a storm; a voice said, "Your life is going to be like this." It kept getting worse: life didn't seem good to live. When I was thirteen, the faucet ran blood. I was hospitalized when I was sixteen, tied up in wet canvas sheets to restrain me. It was terrific, because there was no place to go but in. In that state, I saw for the first time what sanity feels like. The yammer stops; you can look into your mind and see what you think. Wow! Later you try to reach that state outside of a coldpack, and soon, like any habit, sanity takes over. (The way to that craziness is wide open. Even now, hell yes, I could get back there, though it's what I would want to do least!)

I was hospitalized for three years. The big diamond-encrusted medal for my parents is that they didn't take me out of the hospital early; they waited. Not just until I stopped blowing square bubbles, but until everybody, me included, said that I was all right. Most people thought that what I had wasn't curable—you're just in remission. Remission for me means you're OK unless someone mentions shoelaces or Thursday! I had lots of people staring at me and wondering, even relatives. When I'd come back, they'd be waiting for something. . . .

I was nineteen when I left the hospital. I'd quit the world when I was seven; I'd never been on a date, never had friendships. The doctor told my parents, "Don't make an invalid out of her. Let her go!" So I went to college, lived by myself: I got engaged and jilted, worked on a Navaho reservation and in a five-and-dime. . . . I was writing all this time too. It wasn't very good, but I kept writing. I met William when I was twenty-two, married him and had my two children (he's an accountant). My first novel was published when I was twenty-eight. Those years and all that happened to me—hearing it from you it sounds remarkable, but it didn't feel remarkable at the time!

I taught elementary school from when I was thirty, team-taught sixth-graders for thirty years. The first ten years were an absolute joy, the second ten less of a joy, the third not so joyful at all: kids and schools are changing. The last few years the kids were saying, "You're teaching beyond us," and I'd say, "That's what I'm here for! How high can you jump?" I teach English in college now. I did other stuff, too. I was on the fire department—there was a big fight over having women on the department. And I was on the ambulance team for a number of years. The neighbor situation was different then; I left the kids with the neighbors while I did my things. I said to the lady I left them with, "Can I pay you?" She said, "You teach my kids." My bridge in my mouth was a "Latin" bridge, because I taught Latin to the dentist's kids. That was the great joy of living in this part of the country then—everything you did was flexible.

My daughter Janice and I have always had good communication, but my son Adam I never really understood. He ran away when he was fifteen; we thought, "Six nights out in the cold, he'll be back." And then he and a friend robbed an A&W; he was in the slammer six months. I have a lot more respect for him now than I've had. He was goofing up his life, and that's hard, because I love him a lot. There's a funny deal mothers make. Because I bear so fast—in my family, babies are born within half an hour of the onset—there's a possibility of getting ripped up. When you consent to that, you say,

"If it means the difference between me and him, let him live." That's an interesting thought for a self-centered person like me! . . .

What would I wish for at this point in my life? That I'd die first! I wouldn't want to be left alone without William. It would be more selfish to die first, but there you go! You want to leave before the party's over. Most of us in my family died of renal failure; now you're not allowed to do that, but I don't know if I'd want to do what you have to do to stay alive. I think I'll die of orneriness! . . . Aging is melancholy because you crumble to bits: things fall off you. Your teeth—the fake stuff—fall out when you're eating; your body doesn't metabolize the way it should; you have a growing feeling of ricketiness. I put in the patio for my nephew's wedding here and have tendinitis from that; he'll be divorced or have ten children by the time this goddamn tendinitis is over! But there are plusses: stuff you took for granted years ago you no longer take for granted. Friendships mean more. Now, as people pop off around me, it's going to be harder—one man told me, "If I wanted to hang out with my friends, I'd have to go to the cemetery"—but I'm not there yet. Sabbath means more. I always did it before, but now it's like water in the desert.

After I die, what's going to happen? Work: Writing! . . . Without mortality, though, we wouldn't have anything. As a violinist says, in a story I know well, "The reason we play so good is that we're mortal; we live and die, and lose what we love. . . ." Probably after I die, there'll be nothing. And that's fine. When my father died, my sister and I had dreams. My sister saw Dad eating and eating. He'd had an ulcer and a heart attack; she said, "Dad, please don't!" He said, "Don't you know that I don't have to worry about that anymore?" In my dream, my father greeted me the way he often did in life: "What are you crying for, schlemiel?" I said, "I'm crying because you're dead!" He said, "Don't you know I'm genetic in you? I'm in your plasm, and the plasm of your children. Wipe your nose!"

Is there a God I communicate with? Certainly, continually. He-She is not up there, but is resident in people, and in the miraculousness of life. To be permitted to see the blue of the sky—the beauty of things makes God completely apparent. Rabbis say that the Holocaust means that the idea of a personal God is dead. But the beauty of things. . . . In Menotti's opera *The Saint of Bleecker Street*, the heroine's brother says, "You speak of God, love God as though he were human." She says, "How else can I love Him, since I'm human?"

Ten percent of my relationship with God is a wrangle. When Martin Luther King got it, I wrangled: "Why do you take from the edges? Isn't there enough slime for You to take?" The 90 percent is love letters: Who do I thank? Yes, there are horrors in life; and we are responsible for that, according to Judaism, because we are cocreators, unequal but cocreators. Well, we've done a shockingly bad job! But it's forgivable, because what do you expect of somebody who doesn't know where he's going to be next Tuesday?

Leaving my writing for posterity? No, I don't think about it. It's unlikely that I'll endure any longer than it takes to keep me out of print for thirty years. Yes, it'd be nice for someone in the future to be able to read my books, but don't hold your breath! When I think of the congeries of people around Shakespeare, Pope, Milton. . . . I read a terrific manuscript, and think that someday I'll be a footnote: "She's of interest because she saw the gifts in this man. . . ." Yes, it's highly unlikely that I'll be known five hundred years from now: (a) I'll be dead, and (b) you know, God has funnier jokes, but that would be a very, very funny one! But I'm not doing it for that anyway. . . .

What's most important to me, my family, my writing, or my religious belief? I can't say: it's a kit. If part of the kit falls off, that's the most important part. When Adam ran away, the Vietnam War ended; they were still fighting, but I didn't give a damn. If one of us has a stroke, that'll be the main thing. But I wouldn't want to be out of harmony with God. Am I certain that God exists? I have no evidence except all my senses and understanding. To lose that thankfulness, that'd be the worst. That means that the universe has no purpose. God gives the universe purpose. . . .

Writing is incredible fun; as long as I'm on this earth, that's what I'd be wanting to do. But the basis of that is my religious faith. I never knew I'd be saying that. . . . It's a kit. I like living where it's green, I like being with William and I'd like him to be whole, though we're both kind of rickety. I'm really fortunate to have such a kit. Absolute, 100 percent dumb luck!

Murakami Junji and Louise Weiss:
Analysis

Murakami-sensei and Ms. Weiss are similar in that both make their art a central pursuit of their lives. Both were on different paths in earlier years: Ms. Weiss suffered from insanity in her youth, and Murakami-sensei was a *sarariiman* in his twenties, an occupation for which he seems to have been spectacularly unsuited. Both enjoy close relations with their spouses, and both sense deeply the joy of being alive. They are dissimilar in gender and the gender roles they have lived or resisted: Ms. Weiss raised her children in the course of her writing career; Murakami-sensei opted out of his breadwinner role to pursue his calligraphy. They are also dissimilar in that Ms. Weiss is religious, as Murakami-sensei is not.

Murakami-sensei's *ikigai* is *shodō*, he tells us; *shodō* is how he "leaves proof of his existence" on this earth. Ms. Weiss, when asked to choose between family, writing, or religious belief, says "It's a kit," with her faith at the kit's core, but let us here emphasize her writing, her joyous pursuit on this earth, so as to compare her account to that of Murakami-sensei.

In holding their creative pursuits central to their lives, these two differ from the people whose accounts we examined earlier. Miyamoto-san can't imagine what he'd do without his job; Takagi-san hates his work, but is afraid that without work he'd be lost. Murakami-sensei, on the other hand, quit his job to pursue *shodō*, starting as a hobbyist and becoming, eventually, a master. Wada-san and Ms. Pratt make their families and children their core, relegating dance and "mission orientation" to second in their lives. But Ms. Weiss, after leaving the hospital, had her first novel published within a decade, while raising her children; she's been writing ever since. How and why did these two pursue *ikigai* paths so different from other people?

In part, these two were able to pursue their paths because of their "gifts." Japanese society can support only a small number of calligraphers, American society a very few novelists. If Ms. Weiss didn't have a remarkable storytelling ability, she might now be a housewife with manuscripts gathering dust in closets; if Murakami-sensei's *shodō* were mediocre, he might be a salesman once again. But these two also possessed the confidence to develop those gifts. Murakami-sensei's coworkers must have thought him mad to quit a corporate career for a dream of art; Ms. Weiss's relatives perhaps saw her pursuit of writing as proof of her madness. For both, a decade passed before they attained success; had they less self-confidence, they would almost certainly have given up their creative pursuits.

Their self-confidence may be thought of as selfishness. When Murakami-sensei's wife became ill, he didn't cancel his *shodō* exhibit entry; he didn't quit *shodō* to take a regular job and pay the bills, but continued to practice his art. As for Ms. Weiss, although she doesn't discuss the practice of art over care for family, it's clear from our interviews that her two hours of writing each day have been sacrosanct, to be disturbed neither by screaming children nor ringing telephones. In those two hours, writing is her single inviolable commitment.

This shows *how* these two pursued their paths; but *why?* Both say that the pursuit of recognition isn't their motivation. Murakami-sensei tells us that he seeks to become wise through his art, but what blocks wisdom "is the lure of money and fame." He resists that lure, he tells us, and resists thought of posterity, though he can't help but wonder whimsically about his reputation after he is dead. Ms. Weiss says that "the fame, the reviews—the less you think about them the better," but she can't help but feel "put upon" when the journals don't mention her work. Both seek a wide audience, but this seems due less to their pursuit of fame than to their desire that their work be seen. As Murakami-sensei tells us, his name need not be attached to his work; his work should stand on its own.

Rather than fame, both emphasize the joy of their paths; both say their arts are what they most want to do on this earth. These two are blessed in that they not only experience life, but transmute that experience into art, which they give back in a dialectic of creation (as mothers too give back, in a very different way). This shouldn't be romanticized—there are many miserable artists in the world, and perhaps not a few joyful housewives and businessmen—but it does explain the joy of these two. Both are experiencing bodily decline, and seek to create works transcending the walls of their limitations, as Ms. Weiss put it, before they die or lose their abilities. But although Murakami-sensei believes in life after death as Ms. Weiss does not— as Ms. Weiss believes in God as Murakami-sensei does not—both hold mortality as being at the heart of their work. Loss and life's brevity is what pushes them to create all they can in their lives.

These two make their creative activities a key to their *ikigai,* both because it is for them a joy to create, and because their creation enables them to express their sense of what life is about. Murakami-sensei emphasizes that his work is expression and proof of his individual existence, and this may be true for Ms. Weiss as well. No one else has ever done calligraphy exactly like that of Murakami-sensei; no one else has ever written novels exactly like those of Ms. Weiss. Both have other sources of significance—their families, and for Ms. Weiss, her faith—but this creation of personal significance through their creation of art seems central to their lives.[3]

Creation may serve as a powerful assertion of one's personal significance, but significance through creation is self-created, and can't fully transcend the self. Ms. Weiss indicates this when she says that she doesn't use her family in her fiction because "God made those people already"; they transcend her fiction. As she implies in her account, it is religion that takes the search for significance beyond one's fleeting, finite self. This is the theme of our next pair of accounts.

3. This is clearly the case for Murakami-sensei. It isn't so clearly the case for Ms. Weiss, who explains her deep desire to write only in terms of how much fun it is. It may be that Ms. Weiss's religious belief makes "creation as the assertion of one's existence" less compelling for her than it is for Murakami-sensei. On the other hand, in Ms. Weiss's books, her own life's transmutation into art is readily apparent (as she tells us, "You cannot help leaving your goddamn fingerprints all over what you write!"). She does seem to assert her existence through her creation, although she never directly says this.

Asano Kiyoshi (26)

(I first met Asano-san by chance: I asked him for directions to a house I was looking for, and he bombarded me with questions about my life. Our interviews were held in my apartment, so that he could escape his dreary company dorm room. He is a sturdy but homely young man, seemingly wounded, his pain showing itself in his face as he spoke. His refuge and salvation is clearly his faith; our last interview he spent proselytizing me, to no avail. A month after our interviews, I went drinking with him and several of his fellow bank employees. They talked about sexual escapades; he sat stiffly silent.)

I became a member of Sōka Gakkai when I was four; my parents were members.[4] When I was in high school, I didn't practice the religion faithfully, but I returned after a couple of years. Now, my father and sister participate, but not enthusiastically; my mother and I are pretty fervent. I've told my father and sister that they should take the religion more seriously, but you can't force religion on people. . . .

I went to a university run by Sōka Gakkai. My grades weren't too good in college; I played rugby, played too much, I guess. The career center suggested that a bank might be interested in me; a recruiter from Yamato Bank came to our college and somehow liked me. At the interview, they asked if my Sōka Gakkai activities would interfere with my work; I told them that that would never happen. I don't proselytize at the bank; I talk about my religion to my close friends, but never to my customers. Sōka Gakkai tells us that although faith is important, it's wrong to sacrifice your work for its sake. Sōka Gakkai has millions of members; if we were to devote ourselves only to religion, ignoring our work in society, other people would be troubled. That would be bad. There are Sōka Gakkai meetings [*zadankai*] in the evening, but I have to work late, so I can't go. They understand.

---

4. Sōka Gakkai is the lay organization associated with the Nichiren Shōshū sect of Buddhism. It is the largest "new religion" in Japan, founded in 1930 and now claiming six million followers (Kōdansha Encyclopedia 1983; Metraux 1988). It is disliked by many Japanese because of the aggressive proselytizing it has practiced.

Sōka Gakkai wants to send its talented members into society, so it's important for us to work for demanding companies like banks. I do attend Gakkai meetings Saturday night and Sunday mornings, unless I have to work.

I've been working for the bank for two years now. Through Gakkai activities, I try to develop a broader perspective than work gives me; if you devote yourself only to work, you won't know who you really are. The speeches made by Ikeda Daisaku, the honorary president of Sōka Gakkai, appear in Sōka Gakkai's daily newspaper, and I always read them; most important, I chant my prayers every morning and evening, about an hour a day. I don't need to drink after I come home to get rid of stress from work, like my coworkers do.

Sōka Gakkai teaches how to attain Buddhahood [*jōbutsu*], the state of absolute happiness; we chant the words *Namu Myōhō Rengekyō* [Hail to the Lotus Sutra] to attain it. Living in this world, our characters get warped. To purify ourselves, we chant. It's a lifelong discipline. Sometimes I want to skip it, but I don't. In chanting *Namu Myōhō Rengekyō,* I feel power and energy bubbling up inside me. While I chant, I pray in my heart about my work, that it will go smoothly, and I pray for all the people in my bank, for their happiness. (Sometimes I think of a woman I want to talk to. Sometimes an image of a naked woman appears, and I'm horrified, but that's only natural!) For me, Sōka Gakkai is more important than the bank; the root of my life is religion. But my work is also part of my religious practice.

I don't have any problem with nonreligious coworkers in the dorm where I live (almost all of us unmarried male company workers live in the dorm; we're expected to, and it's cheaper this way). I try to see their good points, deal with them as human beings. My room's on the second floor, where nobody else is living; if I chant loud, nobody'll hear. When I first moved there, that floor was full of people; they joked about the strange noise coming from my room! Still, nobody told me to shut up. When I go drinking with my coworkers, sometimes I get teased. They say, "This guy here, he chants sutras," or they ask if my chanting really does me any good. I laugh it off. When people are drunk, there's no point talking about religion. If they're serious I'll talk, but not if they just want to make fun of me.

Japan needs religion. Japan's become one of the main economic powers in the world, but as human beings, Japanese people are lacking. There's a possibility of "smiling fascism" in Japan—that's President Ikeda's term—we're immersed in our easy lives; we look down on other countries, thinking that all we have to do is loan them money. The Roman Empire was an economic power of its time, but it was destroyed from within and disappeared. Japan may be similar.

Sometimes I get depressed about work; my boss gets angry at me, and the young girls in the bank don't like me because I can't do my job well. I'll do better in a year or two, I'll work hard until I can do my job well, but I've had to go through a lot. When I make a mistake, my coworkers get mad at me and refuse to talk to me; it's really tough. When I played rugby in college, I could work out stress; now I can't. Sometimes I want to run wild and scream; if this kind of thing continues, I might beat someone up! . . . No, all I can do is hang on; I won't give up. . . .

It's been a year since I last saw my parents; these two years with the bank have been the first time I've lived apart from them. I didn't take my New Year's vacation this year to visit my parents: I didn't want to tell my boss I wanted it, because I was making lots of mistakes in my work. . . . I try not to think that I'm working for the sake of Yamato Bank. Bank employees tend to be closed-minded and too concerned with status. Still, by working for the bank, I can grow; by watching my boss deal with customers, I can learn a lot. I work hard because I want to be recognized as a member of society. Also, I've given a lot of trouble to people, so I feel I have to learn to do my job well. I don't want to think that I'm working only for the sake of the bank's profit; I want to think in bigger terms. That's one reason I chant my prayers each day.

The bank has a lot of control over its employees' lives. I can't drive to work; we're not allowed. If we had a traffic accident, it would cause trouble to the bank. I think the bank's afraid of gangsters [*yakuza*] trying to extort money after an accident. If I have an accident on my day off, I still have to report it to my boss; whatever I'm doing, I'm always an employee of Yamato Bank. Your bosses even visit you at home, to check on how you live. When I tell this to people, they're shocked; even for Japanese, this practice is strange. I feel like I'm a junior high school student again! Something's wrong with this; foreigners must think it's really weird. But to the extent that they manage our lives, they do take good care of us. . . . (Things *are* changing in the bank. Once a year everybody goes on a trip together, two nights at a hot springs resort. But lately, the company outing's become unpopular; now we have lots of people who want to spend their free time with their family or friends. But you're expected to go on these trips. . . .)

I never get enough sleep. At work I'm always tense; I can relax only in the restroom. Yesterday I went drinking with my coworkers. I sang *karaoke* like crazy; probably they thought I was singing to get rid of stress because I'm bullied. I never talk to them about it; it'd be bad to show my weakness. Once you're drunk, you can say your true feelings, but even then, I can't say to my boss, "Why do you get mad at me all the time?" There's a line I can't cross even when I'm drunk. . . .

Now's the hardest time of my life; it's been like hell. I believe I'll be happier in the future; it can't get any worse. But maybe now is the most important time for me. Because I'm going through such a tough time now, in the future I'll be able to understand others going through tough times; in that sense, I'm learning a lot from my problems. As iron gets stronger by being hammered, as Japanese swords are improved by being tempered through heat, human beings become stronger through pain. . . .

In the future, I want to be able to do good work. I want to be a section chief, and to be married with a family. (If the woman I wanted to marry wasn't a Sōka Gakkai member, I'd persuade her to join; if she wouldn't join, I wouldn't marry her. I might go through hell in giving her up, though.) But if all these things come true, I still wouldn't be completely satisfied, because they're material things. I also need to satisfy the spiritual side of my life. I want to help people in need; I want to spread the Sōka Gakkai teachings. It would be great if I could save people by telling them about this religion. I want to grow as a human being; that's more important than having a happy marriage or success in work. I'm a little different from other bank employees; maybe I'll be completely defeated, or maybe I'll grow into the banking business. I'm not worried about getting fired. I've heard that some guy got fired after he hit his section chief; I can understand that—sometimes I want to do that myself! Usually, though, if you don't do well, the bank just sends you off to obscure branches. If I found myself in such a position—well, I'd have to support my family, so I'd do my best. . . .

If I were to die now, there'd be a meaning to it; there are no accidents. I believe in reincarnation; that's our faith's teaching. Some people are born rich, others poor. It's unfair; that's why I believe in reincarnation. When you die, you can't take anything with you; no matter how rich and famous you are, you've got to leave it behind. That's why I'm trying to develop the spiritual part of myself. I want to be reborn as a human being, but I don't know if I could if I died now. I don't know if people who believe in Sōka Gakkai are reborn higher than those who don't; there are bad people among Sōka Gakkai members too. I believe that Sōka Gakkai is the true religion and other religions aren't, so it may be that Sōka Gakkai believers and nonbelievers end up in different places in the next life. But I don't think about that. I'm not in Sōka Gakkai because of the fear of death, but because of the pain of life. If I hadn't had religion, I might have killed myself by now. I can understand those who kill themselves. A boy who'd been bullied by his classmates killed himself in Tokyo recently; he left a note saying that he couldn't stand this living hell any longer. I can understand his feeling. But if he'd had a religion, he might have been able to overcome it. . . .

For me, praying is my *ikigai*. I'm trying to find *ikigai* in work too; I come home worn out and try to make myself ready to try again. But *ikigai* from religion is the root of my being. . . . *Ikigai* is the energy we need to live. We work to eat and to live, so work is that kind of energy, but it's not a very high energy. Maybe that's why Japanese have been called "economic animals." What we need is religion.

Dave Redding (34)

(I went to Dave Redding's police station for our first interview. With his scholarly mien and slicked-back hair, he could have been a high-school science teacher, except for the gun strapped at his side. In between phone calls and questions and orders from superiors, he spoke to me without missing a beat about his spiritual life, and how it was in many ways at odds with the police work he does for his living. I later interviewed his mother. She became critically ill a few days after our last meeting (later recovering); Mr. Redding called to tell me that her interview tapes might be the last words of hers he would ever hear.)

I'm a policeman. My grandfather was a policeman back East, and so were five of his brothers. It's the old Irish thing, you could be either a policeman or a priest. My father was a mailman, my mother a waitress; my father's dead, my mother's bedridden. She lives in an apartment near here; I go there three times a week, cooking and cleaning. My sisters and brothers help out too.

I was brought up a Catholic. I got kicked out of Catholic school in ninth grade for ditching classes and got a job as a hod-carrier's helper. I recommend that for anybody who doesn't think they want to be in school! . . . I remember going to a counselor in high school and saying that I wanted to study philosophy; her eyes glassed over: "We'll see if we can get you into carpentry training." People are always trying to squash your dreams; no matter how unrealistic they may sound, you should be allowed to dream those dreams! At seventeen I had a spiritual reawakening; I went to the seminary at nineteen. I kept studying part-time after I became a policeman and eventually got my degree. Of five children in my family, I was the only one who went to college. I didn't get much support from my family in that. My brother laughed at me a while ago because I had to go to spiritual direction. I took offense: spiritual direction is a tradition in Western culture since Augustine. I said, "Man, you sit here and watch fucking TV and take your cues off that: what's wrong with spiritual direction?" I never want to be like that, ridiculing people's ability to grow. . . .

A policeman wasn't something I always wanted to be; I just fell into it. I came on the force for two years and then resigned; two years later I returned, and I've been back seven years. I was getting too emotionally involved: one Thanksgiving I was working, and one brother shot the other over a turkey leg; and I'm just getting married and working with a guy with a wife and kids at home who's stopping in to see his girlfriend. There's a code in the police, of circling the

wagons: if a cop, say, uses more violence than necessary, they'd look
at you, "Are you one of us?" I was going, "This isn't my code. My
code's right and wrong." We caught a burglar and my partner started
pounding him; I intervened—I was ostracized for that, threatened. I
left because I felt my moral sense going down. I came back with
more self-knowledge; I'd learned to be more accepting. A policeman
starts off thinking, "I'm going to help people, I'm going to change
this," but you soon realize that once you go around the corner, everyone just goes back to doing their thing. . . .

I get teased now for my religious beliefs, a good-natured teasing.
I'm not trying to ram this down anybody's throat; I have enough
problems trying to work it out for myself. If people here want to talk
about it, I'll talk, but I'm not here to convert anybody; I'll let God do
that. My witness is my life, not what I say. For me it's not an option
but a necessity. How do you process the pain of the human situation
without having a faith? Without it, this is an awfully cruel world. . . .

There has to be a force that deals with violent people in society.
Take a kid who at eleven started pulling burglaries, at fourteen stick-
ing people up; it's hard to say that all he needs is a talking to. My
feeling is that with the nuclear family in disarray, we're in decay. We
need to get back to staying together as families. We've gotten into
moral relativism, so that the consequences of our behavior escape us.
People have to see that while you have all these rights, what about the
responsibilities that come with them? America's in a state of social
pathology now. But for a Christian, whatever happens to this world
in some ways doesn't matter. There's a concern for my children, but
God's world is what's real. . . . (God created all people in His image,
but in this job, that premise is challenged. "How could God create
this?" But there's also the sense that "I am you." I too could be living
in the projects. . . . I used to talk to people about the Lord when I'd
arrest them; they had to listen. I don't know if it worked: finally that's
God's work.)

I now deal with citizen complaints; before, I was a patrolman. When
you're a police officer, you're out there dealing with the things other
people don't want to deal with: the fights, the family violence. When
I was working the street, I worked alone, which I preferred because

I could control how I exposed myself to danger. Still, the radio says, "Go here," and you go; you can't say, "That doesn't sound like something I'd want to do!" I prayed sometimes in the squad car in the middle of the night. At three in the morning, I'd feel the sense of evil turned loose, the devil having his way with people at that hour. I'd arm myself with prayer: "Lord preserve me, I don't want to die here." I had a reputation for being able to handle myself, but they didn't realize I had a partner! It sounds hokey, but for me it was real. Through Christ, evil has no power; it is negated. . . .

What it came down to for me was when I finally internalized this feeling of right and wrong, so that I could say, "I don't care if these people knock the shit out of me, I'm right!" I've gone into parties by myself: "This is the law, people are being disturbed, the party's over, and if I come back, you're going to jail." You leave, come back, boot the door open, run through fifty people, grab the guy, throw him to the ground, put him in handcuffs, drag him out. . . . I've done this dozens of times. That's when you know you're a policeman, but it takes a few years. . . . I've never been shot at, thank God, and I've never fired a shot, though I've been in situations where there was shooting between a suspect and other cops. You can't just pull out a gun; a gun can be taken away from you a lot easier if you're waving it around. We've all been to the funerals of people whose guns have been taken away from them. You live in constant apprehension. It may be hard for ordinary citizens to understand it when policemen seem rude or tense, but. . . .

The promotional structure here is totally out of balance; you have to sacrifice your family to do well on the test. If you're a person for whom family and faith share an equal role with your profession, they say, "I don't know if you're the kind of person we want." I have to say, "No thank you." I find comfort in Scripture, where it talks about "seeking the low places"; in a real way, that's my desire. Above all in my life is my faith in Christ; from that, everything else grows. To see all this, the poverty, the crime, the dregs of humanity, people's spiritual emptiness, you kind of go, "wait a second, there has to be more."

At thirty-four, this is what I am: a Catholic Christian, police officer, father of four. I've been married ten years; my wife is Catholic. Yes, we're going to stay married all our lives! I'm just starting, as the sun hits high noon, to see it coming down the other side, and to see how neat it would be to share all that history with a person. She works one day a week and stays home the other days. I'm not always overflowing with joy when I come home. Lately I've been tired; I really love my kids, but it gets to me sometimes. More and more, the gravity of my responsibility is sinking in: "Here I am responsible for all these kids!" The things they'll be going through, I have to realize that I can't protect them from, but only provide the foundation. Then they're on their own. Now, I'm glad they're little.

I'm studying to be a Catholic deacon; I hope to have a voluntary ministry in the future, like working with AIDS patients or in a nursing home, apart from my job, bringing the living God to people. That would be the real meaning of my life. . . . Aging, death—yes, it bothers me, but that's the basic question of Christianity: Did Jesus in fact rise from the dead? Is death conquered? Or is death the final say? If Christ didn't rise from the dead, then He's just another guy. If there was no life after death, then all would be futile; you'd do whatever good you could do in this realm, but what would be the use? The promise of eternal life, of salvation through Christ—that's what it's all about. That takes faith, that's where everything else stops. You have to be willing to give up your life to it.

If I died now, I believe I'd go to heaven. John says that God is love; I think that heaven would be existing in total love. I hope to be with my father, my grandparents, my children. . . . I guess I doubt now; maybe ten years from now, I'll be able to say that I'm certain that when I die I'll be with the Father in heaven. The road to that kind of faith is prayer. I pray maybe an hour each day formally, but lots of other times too, in my workday, or while I'm sitting here talking. My kids might be yelling, but I feel that God honors my prayer in whatever way I can do it. I'm not into "Shut up, I'm praying! Thank you, Jesus. . . ." The goal in prayer is to pray always. I see my prayer life as becoming a center; I need to stay close to that center. . . .

As I understand it, Jesus died for all men. But of course I have to take into account my cultural biases: I've grown up a Catholic. I'd say Christianity is most true, but a Buddhist wouldn't. I'd hope that a Buddhist would realize that the key is for God to have sent His son to redeem us. But that's up to God. If you want me to speculate, I believe that all people will be saved: we are all saved through Jesus Christ. . . .

What's most important to me, work, religion, or family? In my study to become a deacon, the idea of balance is always brought up. I don't see these things as distinct, but integrated. The challenge is to give proper attention to each of them. But finally it's faith which gives meaning to my work and family. What are you working for? If you're working to get a nice house or a nice car, that's pretty empty. The idea of knowing God permeates all the areas of my life.

As I pray, my objective is to become more Christlike, as we come to know Him through Scripture, and as He reveals Himself in our hearts. I see Him as a radical, as someone who blew away the establishment. He's not the guy popularly depicted. He is God become man! None of our lives, held up to total illumination, can hold up as virtuous; that's where Christ's forgiveness comes in. One day when I was seventeen I got down on my knees and asked the Lord into my life; I asked God to show Himself to me, and He did. He still does today.

Asano Kiyoshi and Dave Redding: Analysis

These men are similar in that both hold their faiths to be key to their lives, and both have been thought "strange" because of their faiths. They differ in their faiths and their jobs, and in age. The conflicts that Asano-san now experiences at work seem parallel to those experienced by Mr. Redding a decade ago.

Both men find their *ikigai* in their religious beliefs, but their religions teach them to devote themselves to work and family as well. Sōka Gakkai, Asano-san tells us, encourages its members to work hard in society "for demanding companies like banks"; Mr. Redding says that in his study to become a Catholic deacon, "the idea of balance is always brought up" between work, family, and religion. In the tenets of their faiths, one may be a devoted believer, a devoted spouse and parent, and a devoted employee; in fact, one's religious devotion makes one a more devoted spouse, parent, and employee.[5] One reason for these tenets is that both Catholicism and Sōka Gakkai have to exist within societies that don't adhere to these faiths. For the sake of "other people," believers such as these two men are encouraged to devote themselves to society's dominant *ikigai* of work and family.

Both men's work is structured so as to insinuate itself into their lives as *ikigai*. Asano-san's bank regulates his life in various ways, from the expectation that he live in the company dormitory, to home visits by his boss, to quasi-compulsory company trips; as Asano-san is well aware, work must take first priority in his daily life. Mr. Redding tells us that passing the police promotional examination demands total devotion to work; because he deeply values family and faith, he will "seek the low places" and remain at low rank in the police. (In ten or so years, when his bank begins selecting future executives from men of Asano-san's seniority, he may face a similar conflict.)

The conflict of family with faith hasn't been fully experienced by these men. Mr. Redding's wife is Catholic, and she understands, he told me, his spiritual aspirations; aside from dealing with his brother's scorn, his conflict is one of balancing the attention his children require with his study and prayer. Asano-san's family is split between fervent adherents and more casual adherents, but all are members of Sōka Gakkai. He says he wouldn't marry a woman who couldn't be persuaded to join Sōka Gakkai, although "I might go through hell in giving her up."

Despite the tuggings of work and family, both men hold their religious beliefs to be most essential in their lives. One obvious explanation for this is that both were brought up in religious families. However, both have siblings less religious than they, and both turned away from their faiths as teenagers, only to return a few years later and attend religious colleges. In their work, their faiths have caused as much as solved problems for them. Because Mr. Redding couldn't

5. This is more true of Sōka Gakkai, which is an organization of lay believers, than of the Catholic Church, which has a priesthood, priests and nuns being those who give up family and work outside the aegis of the church. Mr. Redding, in studying to become a deacon—in rough terms, a lay priest—is affirming his religiously sanctioned choice to commit himself to his family and work as well as to his faith.

reconcile the gap between his Christian ideals and his brutalizing fellow policemen, he was ostracized and quit the force; following his reinstatement, he has become less idealistic—less religious—at work. Asano-san is made fun of when he goes drinking with his coworkers, and his chanting may have caused them to flee his floor of the company dormitory. His faith doesn't seem to be a direct cause of his being bullied at the bank, but may well be a contributing factor.

In the face of such strong pressures to abandon their faiths and become "members of the gang," why have these men persisted in their religious *ikigai?* The answer apparent from their accounts is that religion provides them a means of making sense of life in all its pain. As Asano-san tells us, "I'm . . . in Sōka Gakkai because of . . . the pain of life. If I hadn't had religion, I might have killed myself by now." Mr. Redding asks, "How do you process the pain of the human situation without having a faith? Without it, this is an awfully cruel world." Their faiths show them that despite life's pain, the awful work situation Asano-san must endure, the "dregs of humanity" Mr. Redding has nightly confronted, life is ultimately good and just.

Both men thus partake of a meaning that transcends this world. From the vantage point of that meaning, giving a higher meaning than this world alone can give, both look down upon the values of their nonreligious fellows. Work is "not a very high energy," holds Asano-san. "If you're working to get a nice house or a nice car, that's pretty empty," says Mr. Redding. This seems to be why they so diligently hold to their faiths as *ikigai,* despite the social frictions their faiths cause them: *their* deepest commitments, *their* deepest sources of meaning are not of this fleeting and illusory human world, but of ultimate truth.

But there's a problem with this commitment. Most of Asano-san's and Mr. Redding's coworkers don't believe in the ultimate truth that these men are committed to. Both men are wise enough not to proselytize at work, but if their faiths are indeed the only true faith, then maybe they should proselytize. As Asano-san says of his nonbelieving coworkers, "I try to see their good points, deal with them as human beings," and indeed, both men must hold such an attitude in order to be able to work harmoniously with their fellows. Yet they clearly believe that those who do not share their faiths are misguided and possibly even damned or doomed to be reborn as a lower form of life.

The problem is that these men's faiths and social worlds are at odds. If they insist too much on their faiths, they won't fit in their social worlds, particularly at work; if they insist on fitting in their social worlds, they may lose their faiths. They must balance the two, believing firmly in their faiths but keeping their faiths inconspicuous in their relations with nonbelievers; they must neither condemn nonbelievers nor allow their relations with nonbelievers to weaken their faiths. This is the tightrope that must be walked by those who believe deeply in an ultimate not fully shared by the world around them.

We've examined two different "minority" *ikigai: ikigai* as found in creation and in religion. Let's now turn to two people whose "minority" *ikigai* is less a matter of choice than of birth.

Yamamoto Shōji (55)

(I went to Yamamoto-san's Ainu Association headquarters with a Japanese newspaper reporter who was browbeaten for his Japaneseness, a browbeating I escaped. [At one point, Yamamoto-san put his forearm next to mine and said, "Look, we both have body hair! (unlike many Japanese) You're Ainu, too!"] At first I had trouble with Yamamoto-san; I heard in his voice a pleading victim's tone rather than the Ainu pride that his words indicated and that I wanted to hear. In a later meeting, when I spoke with him alone, he dropped this tone, as if he did not need to use it with a non-Japanese. I couldn't tell from his appearance that Yamamoto-san was Ainu, but Japanese tell me that they usually can distinguish Ainu from Japanese.)

There are about twenty-four thousand self-acknowledged Ainu; that includes anybody with Ainu blood.[6] Beyond this, many Ainu hide their identity at work and from their families, to avoid discrimination.

6. The Ainu are the indigenous people of northern Japan. Throughout Japanese history, culminating in nineteenth-century Hokkaido, the Japanese pushed northward and steadily appropriated Ainu land, destroying traditional Ainu culture.

Probably there are fewer than ten Ainu left of pure blood. What's left is only Ainu consciousness. Even if you're one-sixteenth Ainu, if you have pride in your Ainu ancestry, you're Ainu. We must abolish the idea that Japan is made up only of Japanese. There are only fifteen or so people who still use the Ainu language in their daily lives. I myself have to speak Japanese; I know lots of Ainu words, but I can't speak Ainu in full sentences. I grew up among Japanese, speaking Japanese; in that sense, yes, maybe I'm 80 percent Japanese. I want to raise the percentage of my Ainu identity to fifty, at least; I want to spend the rest of my life on that! It's dangerous to take a negative attitude toward the future of the Ainu; we'd lose our courage to create a society where Ainu culture will prosper. We have to be optimistic. . . .

I work for the Ainu Association. Most of my work involves raising the consciousness of teachers. Five years ago, a survey was conducted among public school teachers; one question asked what kind of life Ainu now lead. Of eight thousand teachers, 424 couldn't give any answer, 90 said that Ainu live as they did long ago, dwelling in pits in the ground and eating raw meat, and 622 held that Ainu in some places still live like that. So, 712 teachers seem to think that we Ainu have never worn a suit or leather shoes! We can't send our Ainu children to schools with such ignorant teachers!

Yes, there's discrimination against Ainu at school. When nobody's watching, other kids write on the blackboard that "so and so's Ainu," or scribble "Ainu" on the books of Ainu children. Schools do nothing about it. There are lots of Ainu children in the junior high school near here—this area has low-income housing—and they're harassed. When they walk in the hall, Japanese students say, "Here comes a dog!" or "You touched an Ainu! You're dirty!" Many Ainu children lose heart; no matter how hard we try to persuade them not to quit school, it's useless. . . .

Generally, two or three incidents of discrimination at schools are reported to us each year. This may not sound like many, but this is just the number of incidents brought to us. Many incidents are hidden from parents; many Ainu parents don't want to get involved in problems of bullying or discrimination. That's why discrimination against Ainu doesn't get much attention in schools. That's why it's such a problem.

When I was a child, the other kids wouldn't let me come near the heater in the classroom in winter; they said the school wasn't for Ainu, but only for Japanese. They also called me *chōsen*, "Korean". My father was Korean, my mother Ainu, with the tattooed mouth of traditional Ainu women. My father came to Japan in 1930 as the leader of a group of Korean laborers. In Korea he'd had a company that went bankrupt; he'd heard about the chance to make money in Japan, but those stories were lies. He was forced to dig a railroad tunnel, but couldn't bear it; he and six others fled into the mountains. They reached a village ten days later; by then, three of the men had died. The survivc s sought help, but no Japanese would open his door to them; only the Ainu families would help. I'm sure the same thing would happen now. When northern Japan was first being developed, failed Japanese settlers sometimes fled by night, leaving their babies outside the homes of Ainu families, who raised them as their own. Ainu people believe that human beings must live together in harmony regardless of the color of our hair or eyes; this is how we've been living for ages. No wonder the Ainu were helpless when the Japanese entered the Ainu land! There's a Japanese saying, *Hito o mitara, dorobō to omoe* [When you see a stranger, consider him a thief]; that was a reality to the Japanese! Another saying: "Where the people from Sendai [Japanese] have walked, no grass grows." That's what happened to the Ainu people!

The four men who survived were taken care of by Ainu families. At that time, my mother was living with her son after being divorced; she met my father and married him. But his family in Korea found out where he was and came to take him back. I don't remember my father's face or name; I've heard about him only in fragments. He left in 1937, when I was two. My mother died of a stroke when I was nine.

I went to school for just three years. Nobody in my class could beat me in math and Japanese in those years. When my mother died, my sister and I were adopted by different families. I couldn't go on in school after that; instead I took care of the children of my foster family. They were a *shamo* [Japanese] family; they adopted me only because they could use me as a worker. But I was grateful that they gave me food and shelter. . . .

It wasn't until twenty years ago that I really learned to read. Until then I could only work as a laborer. In my early teens, I lived in a road construction camp. I didn't have any family to go home to in the holidays; I stayed at the camp alone. Then, when I was fifteen, my half brother and I moved to an unsettled area to cultivate the land. When I was twenty-three, I had a terrible accident with a chain saw and was in the hospital for two years. After I got out, I couldn't do heavy labor, but found a job with a cooperative; I was hired to distribute flyers to members' houses. At the construction camp, I'd addressed women, whatever their age, as *onēsan* [literally "older sister"; generally a vulgar form of address used toward bar hostesses, etc.]; I'd never learned anything else, so I used that term when I talked to housewives as I distributed flyers. Lots of people complained, including the wives of the mayor and the police chief; they wondered why the co-op had hired such a rude person! So the co-op transferred me to the countryside, where I couldn't do any harm, and there I met my wife.

My wife is Ainu, and I'm half Ainu, half Korean; when we decided to marry, her whole village was opposed. It's terrible, but Ainu themselves are against marriage between Ainu; they believe that their children can escape discrimination by marrying Japanese and assuming Japanese identity. My wife had had several chances to marry Japanese men, but it was never finalized because their families were opposed: they didn't want Ainu blood in their families. We faced slander from the villagers; she so resented their attitude that she left her family and came to me. I realized around this time that one reason for the discrimination against me was my ignorance. I didn't know how to speak properly; I couldn't read or write. My wife taught me these things. She's an extraordinary woman. . . .

When my children reached school age, we traveled around northern Japan, and saw many Ainu wearing traditional costumes and posing for tourists' cameras. We could put up with that, but not with what we experienced at a museum of Ainu culture. The museum's photographer, who takes group photos of Japanese tourists, shouted as we walked by, "Look folks, here come some *real* Ainu!" My wife said to him, "What you just did was incredibly rude. You should apologize!" That incident helped make us what we are today, fighters against discrimination.

Two of my three children are married to Japanese. Even if we parents wanted otherwise, what could we do? When you face discrimination, you try to escape your own race. Young Ainu grow up in an environment that deprives them of pride in their heritage, so we really can't expect them to marry among themselves. We didn't expect our children to marry Ainu; we just didn't want them to marry while hiding the fact that they're Ainu, lying about their origins.

We held an Ainu wedding for my eldest son. The bride's family was opposed, but that's what the bride decided. She knew we wanted to hand down the Ainu cultural heritage. Actually, it was my son who most strongly resisted having an Ainu wedding. When my daughter's fiancé's family found out she was Ainu, they opposed the marriage. It was my daughter's fault, too; I'd always told her that if she was seriously dating someone, she should tell him her racial identity. But before she did, his family found out. They came to visit us; we live in a Japanese-style house, but inside, there's a room of Ainu implements, which they saw. The marriage took place only after a lot of difficulty.

Ainu now follow Shintoism and Buddhism, like the Japanese. When I die, though, I believe I'll be welcomed by our tribal ancestors. They'll accept us because we've fought against discrimination. The world after death I'm talking about is a different world from that of the Japanese; it's only for Ainu, a world we couldn't realize in this world.

My *ikigai* is to help liberate the Ainu and other minorities in Japan. I was born half Ainu, half Korean, both groups victims of discrimination; it took fifty years, but at last I can feel proud. I used to feel resentment toward my parents. Now I can feel joy, not the joy you might feel from making money, but real joy.

It would be great if we could create a community in the Kurile

Islands under UN supervision,[7] where people who seek real happiness could learn to live in peace and harmony with nature and to appreciate different cultures. I want to create this land of peace; I don't want to leave it as a dream! I also want to create a sanctuary where children—Japanese, Ainu, Korean—can experience life with cows in the pasture, hear the murmuring of streams. Now, children are glued to computer games; company employees play golf. People don't know how to enjoy themselves outside except by putting a ball in a hole! Rivers are encased in concrete now, mountains denuded. When I saw that new ski resort near here, I was shocked to see the mountains stripped of trees! Mountains are for growing trees, not cutting them down! In Japan today, land turns to money in people's eyes. But the land on the earth is for everybody, not just for some people to make a profit on! If people listened to the Ainu and understood our culture, they'd treasure nature more than they do now. Japan needs to learn from the Ainu.

Carol Jackson (54)

(I met Ms. Jackson in her classroom. She is a thin, unsmiling, fearlessly honest woman, uttering opinions that are "politically incorrect" as well as personally painful. After she had described the effects of her integrated classroom on students, I blurted out, "If I had kids, I'm not sure I'd want them to come here!" She replied, "I wouldn't either. I sent my kids to private schools." After talking at length with her, however, I changed my mind: I could not imagine a better teacher for one's children than Ms. Jackson.)

I teach third grade. The way I live is pretty middle-class: I have a job, I pay my bills. For a black person to be successful, that part of her must be white—this society's not mine. (Still, when I was in Africa a few years ago, it was my nationality that I identified with more

7. The Kuriles are a chain of islands extending from the northeast coast of Hokkaido to Russia's Kamchatka peninsula. They have been occupied by Russia since the end of World War II, but are claimed by Japan.

than my blackness; everybody was black, but I still didn't belong. My experience in Africa—I wouldn't talk about it for a long time. I felt glad my ancestors had been taken to America as slaves. . . .) Many people I know, like my cousins, live on welfare. When I had to quit teaching when my kids were born, I went back to cleaning houses. I didn't know how to get food stamps, cheat on my electric bill; I had to learn, to be able to feed my kids.

The kids in my class: you can just about pick out the ones that'll wind up in jail. I have two kids now like that. Their older brothers and sisters are in gangs; they already have value systems from the streets. We talk about the two value systems: either clothes, money, and big cars, or reading, writing, and arithmetic: delayed gratification. One of them was coming to school with a beeper; his brother would call him to pick up cocaine after school. Some of the black kids feel envy. Most of the white kids don't know what's going on. They're not at risk; they don't live in that kind of environment. . . . I said to him, "James, I'm going to call your mother!" He said, "You ain't gonna get her; she's in jail." And she is—for crack. We were making Christmas things; he was crying the whole time because his mother was in jail. . . .

For the kids at risk, you've got to talk to the parents. One parent came in with her fists balled up, ready to beat me up. I've never had a white parent do that; the whites try to beat you up intellectually, suggesting subtly that because you're black you're inferior, but I can hold my own. That woman who wanted to fight was high on crack. The problem is getting the parents to listen. Many, especially in the black community, are caught up in survival, getting the next meal on the table.

Before busing began, I was teaching almost all black kids. It was like being down south, except that we had almost all white teachers, and a lot of them didn't care. Integration really does make this a better classroom. That kid with the beeper—the white kids and some of the black kids too were asking him, "What do you use that for?" You could tell he was thinking about it; he knew that what he was doing was wrong. Keeping poor black kids and middle class kids away from each other isn't the answer; this is the way the world is. The first year we integrated, the problems were so different from now. You don't hear kids talk about black and white problems like they did when we first integrated. Now they're human problems. The gang stuff is here, though, influence as early as kindergarten; The kindergarteners play crips and bloods. . . .

I took my own kids out of the public schools. My son had a learning disability; I knew he'd be "the bad little black boy in the corner." Teachers in public school can be racist and get away with it, but in private school, if you confront that, they have to do something. There's still a lot of racism in this public school. We have two "gifted and talented" classes, just three blacks in each, all the rest white. When the kids were tested in the summer, they didn't even let the blacks know they were doing it. The PTA ladies, whites, were the ones whose kids got it.

I enjoy teaching; it's the other stuff—other teachers, attitudes from parents—that I don't like. It's a job; I do it well. I feel a lot of satisfaction from teaching, though no rainbows in the sky.

My grandmother raised me. She had four children from four different men, which she raised by herself. She never took welfare; she was a laundress, a cook. Her two girls both had babies out of wedlock, my aunt at fourteen, my mother at seventeen when she had me. They gave us to my grandmother. She did a lot of hitting, whipping; I ran away when I was thirteen, saying, "You're not going to hit me anymore!" After that I stayed with my mother and my aunt. I felt it was a big mess, and I had to survive. The women in my family had men, but they were appendages: they came in, had sex, and left. My mother had four husbands; the first two I tried to think of as fathers. The third, I had an incestuous relationship with; I got messed up by that for the rest of my life. It's been hard, because I don't trust anybody. Without the therapy I got later, I'd have been dead. . . .

My grandmother raised my cousin and me; we're teachers. My aunt raised six other kids; all of them are on welfare. My grandmother told me, "You got to get an education; you got to take care of yourself, your children." There was never any fairy tale stuff; on Christmas, she'd say, "These skates aren't from Santa Claus. They're from me: I saved the money." I'm grateful to her for that influence, but it took me a long time to appreciate it. . . .

My cousin and I went to the almost-all-white state university. We couldn't find a place to live; finally a lady said, "You can live in the basement. But if anybody moves out because you're here, you have to leave." When we graduated, she told the others, "Congratulations!" But to my cousin and me she only said, "Every quarter I didn't think you'd come back. . . ."

I got out of school, got married, started teaching. My husband wanted to be a flight engineer, but found out he couldn't; he had astigmatism. I remember our landlady, the epitome of a white middle-class stay-at-home-and-take-care-of-my-babies kind of lady, saying, "That's terrible! He won't be able to take care of you!" For a long time I wished I could be "a helpless lady," with the husband, the two kids, the white picket fence. Later I saw through it: the Norman Rockwell pretense, that everything's OK—I can't stand that phoniness. . . . My husband was devastated; for the rest of his life, he jumped from one job to another. He'd been raised in the South. His mother, his sister, they sucked him dry; but there was a control he had over them, that went with the patriarchal stuff. At the beginning of my marriage, I played into it, acted helpless and all that shit, but that was lying. I was mad all the time, from playing one role and living another. I paid the bills, but I pretended it was coming from him. . . .

We were married eighteen years. When Allen was five, we had to get some help for him; the therapist said we all should come in, but Bill resisted: "You don't have to go to the white man for help. I can help you." Bill felt like his kids and I were being taken away from him. I hate to remember it, but once when I was about to leave him, he grabbed Allen's leg and I had his arm; we were pulling that kid apart. I kept leaving and coming back. . . . (Now Bill's sick unto death. I thought, when I got divorced, that I was through; but my kids are still connected to Bill: when they bury him, I'm not going to let them do it by themselves.)

My kids, they're most important to me. I'm happy with where my children are; they're sensitive, respect other people, value education.

They're both finishing college now. When they were children, we lived in a black neighborhood because they needed to know about their blackness. Even so, Cheryl was identifying more with the white kids than with the blacks. When she went to public high school, for the first time she saw the black students who'd jump up and call the teacher a motherfucker. Later, she found some black friends who were like her. . . .

I'm trying to get Allen into a black college now. He thinks he loves this white girl; I'd like him to meet some black girls. I'd be upset if he married her; I'm in therapy trying to work it out. This girl has no understanding of black culture—I don't want to be her mother! Maybe he'll love her till she dies: who knows? But when their kid comes home after being called a nigger, if they haven't figured out how to deal with it, I don't want to teach them. It's too painful.

Has life been worth it? I don't know—it depends on the day. I've been able to get enough out of life to not die, to want to go on with it. I could have been a street girl, but somehow there was enough in life to keep me on the straight and narrow. Where it came from was my education, my belief in myself, and my family—my mother, my aunts, my cousins—it has a funny but real strength. We meet at Christmas, summer; it's not as strong as it was when my aunt was alive, and my grandmother, but there's still a family: love, caring, concern. . . .

Am I a Christian? I don't know. I've gone to all the churches, but I've never found one to meet my adult needs. I found people looking to a book to explain their lives; I found people telling me who I needed to be, but not asking, "Who are you?" I pray to God, about things I can't do anything about—I prayed when I thought they were going to send my son to the Persian Gulf—and I give thanks to God a lot. It's not just luck; sometimes the Good Lord really does provide. He's here. I see God as a force in the universe that makes things work. I can go to the mountains and feel that God, a force here to protect me. . . .

I don't look forward to any heaven. (What if St. Peter at the gate doesn't like black people?) I'd just as soon have it over when I'm done here; I've done most of the things I wanted to do in life. The center of my life has been my children, but it's time to let them go. It's been teaching too, but I'll be leaving soon—I have bad arthritis— I'm going to have to find another job, another purpose. I've considered working with the old folks in a retirement home. I'd like to do something new. The only problem is my health, which is going; that's the rub. . . .

I don't think I could have made it without therapy. I couldn't have hung in there. I'd have killed myself. Figuring out your life through therapy isn't black or white, it's beyond that. Therapy has made possible my finding my purpose in teaching and in my kids; it's allowed me to rise above survival, so that I could see my way clear to a little happiness. Church wouldn't have done it for me. Lord have mercy Jesus, that would have depressed me even more. If things get bad, I'll go to therapy; I'll find the money, even if I have to go hungry. Some people don't know that there's a way out; I found that way out. Here I am fifty-four years old—but I found that way out.

Yamamoto Shōji and Carol Jackson: Analysis

Yamamoto-san and Ms. Jackson are both members of minority groups; both have struggled to define themselves as Ainu-Korean in Japanese society and as African-American in American society. But whereas Yamamoto-san identifies himself with an all-but-extinct Ainu culture, Ms. Jackson finds her identity neither within the black American subculture nor within white culture, but in a balance of the two.[8]

Yamamoto-san's *ikigai* is the dream of resurrecting Ainu culture. Soon, however, there may be no Ainu culture left to resurrect. Yama-

---

8. In comparing Japanese and American minority groups, the Ainu, the original native people of northern Japan, most resemble the American Indians. African Americans in the United States somewhat resemble Japanese Koreans, in that both were taken from their native lands as slaves or forced laborers (African Americans from the seventeenth to the nineteenth centuries, Japanese Koreans before and during World War II). But these two American groups make up 13 percent of the American population (African Americans 12.1%; Native Americans 0.8%); the two Japanese groups make up only half a percent of the Japanese population (Koreans 0.5%; Ainu less than 0.1%).

moto-san admits that he may be "eighty percent Japanese"; there are, he says, fewer than ten pure-blooded Ainu, and only fifteen full speakers of the Ainu language. This may serve as an advantage in his formulation of *ikigai*, in that his dream of Ainu culture need not be tempered by reality's ambiguities; the lack of a real Ainu culture enables Yamamoto-san to hold an idealized image of the Ainu, an image he sees as a beacon showing Japanese the errors of their ways.

Ms. Jackson's *ikigai* may once have resembled Yamamoto-san's— I've heard that decades ago she was politically militant—following a similar logic: Black American culture exists because of enslavement by the dominant white culture; the problems of black America are due to good black culture's corruption by evil white culture. It was her visit to Africa that changed her perceptions: she now sees her troubled black students as victims of white racism but also of black familial dissolution. Underlying her own family as her *ikigai* is her therapy, allowing her to "see my way clear to a little happiness."

Yamamoto-san's and Ms. Jackson's *ikigai* represent alternative *ikigai* paths. Most members of minority groups, like most members of society at large, probably find *ikigai* in family and work. But it's difficult to find *ikigai* in family if, like the hidden Ainu Yamamoto-san describes, one must conceal one's racial identity; it's difficult to find *ikigai* in family if one is raised in an environment of the sort experienced by Ms. Jackson. It's difficult to find *ikigai* in work if one is denied an education, as was Yamamoto-san. For members of oppressed groups, a potential *ikigai* is the dream of political justice, whereby one's group will eventually triumph. Alternately, one may seek to remedy the effects of oppression through religion (or religion's variant, therapy), which may enable one to hold an *ikigai* such as family or work. Yamamoto-san's *ikigai* as political dream and Ms. Jackson's *ikigai* as based in therapy may represent different poles of personal response to the social deprivation they have experienced as members of minority groups.

The *ikigai* differences of Yamamoto-san and Ms. Jackson reflect, in part, the different situations of Ainu in Japan and African Americans in the United States. Only one in several thousand Japanese is a self-acknowledged Ainu. Even in northern Japan, where Ainu are concentrated, the movement for Ainu liberation has made few inroads, as Yamamoto-san admits in saying that he receives no more than two or three complaints a year about discrimination in schools. African Americans, in contrast, make up 12 percent of the American population and can be found at all levels of society. African Americans are far more numerous, racially distinct, and socioculturally diverse than Japanese Ainu, and can't easily be encompassed in a single political dream (which is not to say that some African Americans don't try). Yamamoto-san's *ikigai* dream of awakening dormant Ainu consciousness and Ms. Jackson's refusal to hold such a dream are consistent with these sociocultural differences.

There are also personal reasons for Yamamoto-san's and Ms. Jackson's *ikigai*. It was after the death of Yamamoto-san's Ainu mother that he was cast out, with no home to return to; later, it was his Ainu wife who taught him to read. Ainu seem to have been the source of the goodness and love in his life, Japanese the source of indifference and discrimination. Ms. Jackson, on the other hand, suffered as a child from her own black family's chaos, as well as from white racism; her *ikigai* reflects her disinclination to see the world in wholly black and white terms. This difference in *ikigai* is reflected in their formulations of identity. Yamamoto-san seeks to drive out the Japaneseness in himself: "I want to raise the percentage of my Ainu identity to fifty, at least!" Ms. Jackson holds that her pursuit of mental health transcends race. Therapy may be largely a white undertaking; however, for Ms. Jackson, "figuring out your life through therapy isn't black or white," but a matter of becoming fully human.

The issue of racial identity is explicitly raised through their children: two of Yamamoto-san's children have married Japanese, and Ms. Jackson's son is dating a white woman. Yamamoto-san says that being Ainu is a matter of consciousness more than racial background; thus intermarriage is not a problem. But this view may be overly sanguine: with enough intermarriage, Ainu consciousness as well as Ainu "blood" may disappear. It may be that privately his children's marriages have clouded his *ikigai* dream, but he would admit no such thing to me. Ms. Jackson has tried to raise her children to be proud of their black identity, but one "identified more with the white kids than with the blacks" as a child, and the other "thinks he loves this white girl." The values of her children are not surprising, considering

Ms. Jackson's own values. When she speaks of "black culture," she seems to signify the underclass; as a teacher, she seems to see herself as a representative of middle-class white culture. Yet that culture in its racism is what she has fought all her life, from college, to her school, to, perhaps, heaven.

The tension between black and white and, indeed, all the pain of Ms. Jackson's life by her account seems overcome through therapy, but this process has been exhausting for her. Yamamoto-san envisions a world after death only for Ainu, his *ikigai* dream transposed into a world beyond this one. Ms. Jackson, although she believes in and prays to God, looks forward to no heaven, but only to a bit of continuing peace in this world. That, for her, is all; she has no more dreams.

Ikigai and Significance

The Pursuit of Significance

In chapters 4 and 5, we looked at the lives of a few people who may embody a widespread pattern of *ikigai* in Japan and the United States: *ikigai* as dreams of future work or family for young people, as work or family for those in the prime of life, and as past familial roles and relations continuing into the present for old people. This chapter's accounts don't fit this pattern; the people in this chapter don't hold the *ikigai* of work and family, the *ikigai* apparently held by many, perhaps most Japanese and Americans, but rather the *ikigai* of creative activity, religious belief, or political dream. If work and family can be considered "conventional" *ikigai*, then these *ikigai* may be considered "unconventional."

Why do the people in this chapter hold such *ikigai?* The answer may lie in what I think of as "the pursuit of significance": a sense of one's life as fundamentally *mattering*. The key to Murakami-sensei's *ikigai* lies in his pursuit of significance through creation. "Through *shodō* I want to leave proof of my existence." Ms. Weiss's *ikigai* lies in her relation to her significance-bestowing God: "God gives the universe purpose." The key to Asano-san's and Mr. Redding's *ikigai* lies in their religious beliefs' explication of life's pain and celebration of life's transcendent significance. Yamamoto-san's *ikigai* is the political dream of seeing the Ainu granted significance by Japan; Ms. Jackson, the exception to this group, has found her *ikigai* in her family, on the basis of the therapy that has enabled her to survive. Thus, for five of the six people in this chapter, the overt pursuit of a sense of significance seems central to their *ikigai*.

This pursuit may mark an essential difference between this chapter's *ikigai* and family and work as *ikigai*. In both Japan and the United States, after leaving school one is expected to work, marry, and have a family. These *ikigai* may engender inner conflict, as the accounts in the preceding chapters clearly show, but intrinsically need not: one may conceivably hold such *ikigai* without doubt as to their worthwhileness. On the other hand, those who hold creative endeavor and religious belief as *ikigai* may have to consider why they don't hold the conventional *ikigai* of family or work, and carefully examine what their *ikigai* means to them and what kind of significance it offers them.

However, those whose accounts we examined in earlier chapters also seem to be pursuing a sense of significance through *ikigai*, although in less direct form. Miyamoto-san says that "while I'm working, I believe that without me the bank couldn't survive. . . . Asahi Bank is what it is because of me." Wada-san argues that being a mother allows for a more genuine sense of significance than working for a company. Ms. Pratt tells us that "I am . . . the solid rock for [my children]. . . . They know who they can rely on." Nakajima-san seeks significance through playing to perfection the role of wife and mother. Kinoshita-san seeks to become a doctor as his "mission," Mr. Isaacs, a trainer as his "calling"; they feel that these occupations can provide them a significance now lacking in their lives. Murakami-san emphasizes that she is needed by her family, and she finds her significance in being so needed; Ms. Tucker, in shifting *ikigai* from family to God, with whom she is on "a first-name basis," is shifting the pursuit of significance from this world to the next.

Indeed, all of those portrayed in our accounts seem in some way to be pursuing through *ikigai* a sense of the significance of their lives. But the difference between those in this chapter and those in earlier chapters is not only that the former are more self-conscious. Beyond this, whereas those portrayed in earlier chapters (eleven of the twelve) seek their significance through *ikigai* rooted within this

world, those portrayed in this chapter (five of the six) seek significance through *ikigai* that in some sense transcend this world. Let us
now consider these different varieties of the pursuit of significance.

The Pursuit of Significance Within One's Lifespan

The primary this-world *ikigai* of those I interviewed are work, family,
and personal dream. Those who adhere to these *ikigai* may have religious beliefs or practices (for example, Ms. Pratt and Wada-san) but
their *ikigai* seem centered in this world and life.

Work takes up a good half of the waking hours of the majority of
Japanese and Americans in their prime. In terms of personal happiness, it may be a very good thing if work is the source of one's *ikigai*
and sense of significance, since it seems obvious that one will be
happiest if one can spend one's time engaged in an activity to which
one is deeply committed. Miyamoto-san, judging from his account,
seems personally fulfilled in a way that Takagi-san is not: Miyamoto-
san spends most of his waking hours in an activity he lives for, as
Takagi-san does not. It may also be a very good thing for a society if
most of its working members find their *ikigai* in their work: it seems
plausible that on aggregate those who find their *ikigai* in work are
more productive workers than those who don't. Certainly many of
the symptoms of malaise in the American economy in the 1970s and
1980s, symptoms ranging from shoddy American merchandise to employees saying things like "It's not my responsibility, I only work
here," reflected workers' inability or unwillingness to find their *ikigai*
in their work.

But problems may arise from holding work as *ikigai*. Work doesn't
usually last through one's life. Mr. Murray tells us that he is afraid of
retirement; Miyamoto-san's wife urges him to find a hobby so that
he doesn't become senile after he retires. Both men now find *ikigai*
in work, but will soon enough have to give up that *ikigai*, their main
sources of significance; what they will do with themselves after that
is a question that neither can now answer. This is a problem for
selves, and for societies as well. As the gap between retirement age
and life expectancy grows ever wider, the problem of what people do
with themselves after retirement looms ever larger.

An even more fundamental problem with work as one's *ikigai* and significance in life may be seen in this statement by Miyamoto-san: "Do I feel like a cog in the corporate machine? Well, of course I'm a cog—the bank is a big organization; what I'm doing could be done by others just as well as by me—but while I'm working, I believe that without me the bank couldn't survive." Miyamoto-san admits to being alienated from his labor; it bears no intrinsic relation to him, in that innumerable others could do the same work he does, and it would make no difference to the bank, but he endeavors to overcome alienation through an act of will. He is apparently successful at this, but that he must engage in such willed self-delusion in order to sustain his *ikigai* of work is revealing. We need not believe in the romantic notion that everyone has a unique calling to see that if willed belief is necessary in order to find *ikigai* in work, then work as *ikigai* may indeed be precarious.

It is precarious for selves who must delude themselves with false senses of significance, and also for modern society, many of whose jobs may seem increasingly distant from the kind of work anyone feels "meant" to do in their lives. This problem may be greater in the United States, with its emphasis on "self-realization," than in Japan, with its emphasis on "commitment to group." After all, if Miyamoto-san can truly believe that he lives for Asahi Bank, then the fact that he himself may be merely a replaceable cog in its vast mechanisms need not trouble him.

Family as *ikigai* seems less precarious than work as *ikigai*. As opposed to Miyamoto-san above, Wada-san tells us that the false consciousness of men in finding *ikigai* in work is absent in women's finding *ikigai* in family: every mother has her own unique and irreplaceable role to play vis-à-vis her children, while a worker's indispensability to his company is only an illusion. Similarly, Mr. Eliot tells us that "there are many people who think that they live for work, but the reality is that it can't be a true commitment. . . . It's an animal instinct to have your deepest commitment to your family." To these people, work as *ikigai* is artificial, but family is natural; family is what everyone would live for, if only they understood their true priorities.

It seems a good thing that many people find their *ikigai* in family, since one's family is generally the site of one's most concentrated and sustained human relations. Surely it is more conducive to personal happiness to be deeply committed to one's family than not to be committed. It is a good thing for society as well. If, as discussed in chapter 4, people can't find their *ikigai* in their families and children, then society's reproduction may be threatened, as is to some degree the case in the contemporary United States, with its high divorce rate, and Japan, with its low birth rate.

But family as one's *ikigai* and source of significance may also be problematic. Many of those whose accounts we've examined—Ms. Pratt, Takagi-san, Ms. Tucker, Ms. Jackson, Wada-san, and Mr. Eliot—say that "my children shouldn't be my *ikigai;* they'll have their own lives to live." The situation of a mother who couldn't find an *ikigai* apart from her children was poignantly described by a young Japanese woman I spoke with: "My mother's *ikigai* was raising her children; my father's *ikigai* was his work. Now they're both home, with nothing to do; all they do now is fight over trivial things. My mother says that she misses the past, when she raised us children. That was the most fulfilling time of her life, it seems. Now it seems as if she herself is a child."

One's children should thus not be one's *ikigai,* these people say, both because of the transience of that *ikigai* and because it may place a burden on the children. However, one's relation to one's spouse is, ideally, neither transient nor burdensome to spouse or self, and indeed, Wada-san, Mr. Eliot, and Murakami-san (and to a lesser extent Ms. Weiss, Mr. Murray, and perhaps until recently Ms. Tucker) find *ikigai* in their relation to their spouses. But there are problems here too. As Mr. Murray, Ms. Pratt, and Ms. Jackson have found to their great regret, finding a spouse who can serve as one's deepest human link is a perilous task.[9] As Ms. Pratt says, "When you have a partner in your life, you have this best friend. Now I feel there's a void." Even if one has been fortunate enough to find a spouse to serve as *ikigai,* that relationship, particularly for women with their longer life

9. As earlier noted, the American divorce rate is far higher than the Japanese divorce rate. However, Japanese periodicals often discuss *kateinai rikon,* or "in-house divorce," where a husband and wife live in the same household but are estranged, showing that lack of marital happiness is hardly only an American problem—as attested to by several of the Japanese women I interviewed.

expectancy, may not last. As Ms. Weiss says, "What would I wish for at this point in my life? That I'd die first! I wouldn't want to be left alone without William."

Thus, although family as *ikigai* lacks the alienation inherent in work as *ikigai*, it shares with work a potential transience that makes it, too, seem problematic. If one can continue to have a close relation with one's children after they leave home (and then enjoy a close relation with one's grandchildren), they may serve as lifelong *ikigai*. If one can find a spouse embodying that "other half" for which, as Plato writes in his *Symposium*, each of us is passionately searching, and if one's spouse can live as long as oneself, then spouse as *ikigai* may be ideal; but reality may fall far short of this.

If one can't find one's significance in work or family, whether because of one's place in the life course (Nakajima-san, too young to yet be married and have a family) or one's view of the world (Takagi-san, rejecting the standard *ikigai* of work and family for the dream of finding himself), then one's dream may serve as what one lives for. Dreams of the future as *ikigai* may make bearable a less-than-fulfilling reality, such as the jobs at which Takagi-san, Kinoshita-san, and (to a lesser extent) Mr. Isaacs must daily labor.

Dreams may serve as safety valves for both selves and society: however unfulfilling one's reality may be, if one can hold a dream as *ikigai*, then reality may be bearable; however unfulfilling most people's realities may be, as long as their dreams' fulfillment seems possible, then their society will retain legitimacy in their minds. But for many of those who dream, the odds that their dreams will become reality are very long indeed. Takagi-san will almost certainly never find the self he dreams of finding; Kinoshita-san and Mr. Isaacs, although maybe not Nakajima-san, face formidable obstacles in attaining their dreams.

Paradoxically, however, it may be that personal dreams are more fulfilling as dreams than as attained reality; in dreams, the voice of reality—"Is this all there is?"—need never be heard. Takagi-san's dream, in particular, perhaps functions better as his personal protest against a constraining reality ("I could have ———, but I have obligations to my family, and so I must do what I must do") than as a realizable dream: would he even know himself if he found himself?

There are exceptions to the bleakness of realized dreams: Murakami-sensei followed his dream and appears truly to have found his *ikigai* and his significance. But others I spoke with have been more disappointed. An American retiree, who had apparently dreamed of long vacations through decades of working at an unfulfilling job, told me with considerable reluctance that he now felt bored much of the time. It may be that one's dream as reality often can't provide the sense of significance that it yielded as potentially realizable dream; and of course as dream it is subject to life's inevitable narrowing, the passage of dreams from possible futures to might-have-been pasts.

In short, all the *ikigai* that we have discussed are problematic because the sense of significance they offer may expire before the self expires. One will probably retire from work, see one's children leave home, or attain or surrender one's dream long before one dies. To fill that gap, unless one finds one's meaning in memories, one will have to find something new to live for and find meaning within.

The Pursuit of Significance Beyond One's Lifespan

The significance offered by the *ikigai* discussed in the last section is not necessarily confined to one's lifespan in this world. One may hope to influence the world beyond one's own life through work or dream, as perhaps Miyamoto-san does through his contribution to his company and Mr. Isaacs and Ms. Pratt in their desires to contribute to the world. One may also think of one's family as transcending this world. This familial transcendence is institutionalized in Japan in ancestor worship, as Murakami-san's and Wada-san's accounts illustrate, but also is felt by Mr. Isaacs and Ms. Weiss in communicating with loved ones beyond the grave (although they both acknowledge that they may be only imagining such communication).

Still, for most of those in chapters 4 and 5, the significance they seek through *ikigai* is essentially rooted in their lives in this world. The *ikigai* we've discussed in this chapter, on the other hand, seem to offer senses of significance that may transcend one's life in this world. In this sense, this chapter's *ikigai* seem more secure than the *ikigai* of work, family, or dream. One must retire from one's job, but one's creative work will remain when one is dead and gone; one's children may leave and one's spouse die, but one's God or ancestors will remain, as may oneself in heaven or paradise. However, although the significance offered by creation, religion, and political dream is not transient but in some sense transcendent, it is a transcendence that seems difficult for many people to believe in fully.

The transcendent significance that *ikigai* as creative endeavor may offer is that of posterity. Posterity's advantage is that it can't be defeated by this world; the artist can say (as perhaps Murakami-sensei's friend did) "this present world does not appreciate what I create, but the world of the future will!" Murakami-sensei himself seeks to leave his work as a "proof of my existence" that will remain as proof if his work endures. But the belief that one's creation will endure may be hard to sustain. The two creators whose accounts we examined claim to give little thought to the future of their creative works: Ms. Weiss denies thoughts of posterity, and Murakami-sensei makes of posterity a joke. It may be that even for these two, well-known and highly regarded as few of their fellow artists can ever hope to be, their own creative efforts, in a world teeming with meritorious others, are not sufficient to sustain belief in the enduring significance of their work.[10]

Significance extending beyond one's life may also be sought through religious belief, or through the dream of political justice. These are both extra-world *ikigai* based not in one's own self's creation, but in belonging to something larger than the self. Yamamoto-san will die (and perhaps go to a world only for Ainu) having done his bit to fight discrimination, but the larger struggle will continue, with triumph coming to pass only long after he has passed away. Ms. Tucker may strive to be personally worthy of heaven, and Asano-san and Mr. Redding may strive to lead religious lives, but finally their striving may be not for their own selves' enhancement alone, but so as to be united with that which is larger than the self, the ultimate of God or Buddha.

Religious significance has an advantage over the other forms of significance that we've examined, in that it promises a link with the ultimate meaning of things. This link most often involves the promise

---

10. For these two, posterity seems to have been something they have given thought to, but for other creators I interviewed, posterity seemed far from their minds. As an American jazz musician told me, "I don't play music thinking about whether my music will be known in the future. I play for the pleasure it gives me now."

of life after death (as Mr. Redding tells us, "If there was no life after death, then all would be futile"), but it may not, as is the case for Ms. Weiss and Ms. Jackson. What is key is not that *ikigai* in religious belief may provide a sense of personal immortality, but that it can provide a sense of the ultimate significance of one's life. *Ikigai* as work, family, personal dream, political dream, or creative activity can provide one with a sense of significance from one's social world, from one's family, or company, or society, or descendants, but not from anything beyond that social world (although these *ikigai* may be supported by the significance provided by religious belief). *Ikigai* as religion can provide a sense of significance that is perceived as being from beyond one's social world, from the cosmos; its meaning is not a provisional social meaning, but *ultimate* meaning.[11]

In this sense, religion as one's *ikigai* and source of significance may be highly beneficial to the selves who hold it (who of us would not want to believe that our existences are not ultimately meaningful?) and for society as well. Political thinkers from More ([1515] 1975, 54–55, 80–81) to Tocqueville ([1840] 1990, 149–51) have held that in a good society citizens must believe in God or in life after death, for this will lead them to behave virtuously. From the divine right of kings and the divinity of the emperor to today's far more pale attempts of the Japanese and American states to link themselves to Shinto and to the Christian God, states have attempted to cloak themselves in the mantle of religion to attain ultimate legitimacy.

But religious significance, too, is problematic in today's world. Despite the succor it offers, religious belief as *ikigai* is apparently held only by a minority of Japanese and Americans, who hold their *ikigai* in societies that are in most respects secular.[12] The difficulties of the

11. Religion too is a social creation; the ultimate significance it offers is a socially constructed significance. Whether religion offers an ultimate truth apart from its social creation is the fundamental premise that separates believers from nonbelievers.

12. Over 90 percent of Americans claim to believe in God (Harris 1987, 67; Stark and Bainbridge 1985); the vast majority of Japanese engage in religious practices such as ancestor worship (Smith 1974, 1987b). But for most Japanese, and perhaps for most Americans, religious belief doesn't seem to serve as *ikigai*. People have religious beliefs and engage in religious practices in the contemporary United States and Japan, but most don't seem to make their religion the most important thing in their lives.

committed religious believer in a secular social world are apparent in the accounts of Asano-san and Mr. Redding, who report on the teasing, ostracism, and scorn they have suffered because of their religious beliefs. These men, as we have seen, must walk a tightrope in being both members of their societies and believers in their religions. This may be the major reason why religious belief seems problematic as *ikigai*. There may, for many, be too great a gap between the reality postulated by religion and the secular social reality in which one lives: the latter, for many, cannot but erode the former.

The Precariousness of Significance

All of the above *ikigai* thus seem precarious as sources of significance. Work, family, and dream as *ikigai* may end before one's life ends: one may lose one's job, fail at one's relationships, suffer the death of loved ones, or see one's dream recede into the past. Religious faith and creative pursuits offer a transcendence that may seem difficult to believe in; to paraphrase Murakami-san, "I don't know about a world beyond this one. After all, no one's ever come back from there."

The precariousness of significance as sought through *ikigai* may be intrinsic to being human. As humans we dream of our futures, but we can't know them with certainty; as many religions tell us, life in this world is transient, its meaning opaque. Some of us may, by temperament, be better able to accept life's uncertainty than others of us. William James distinguishes between the "tough-minded" and the "tender-minded," between the materialistic and the idealistic, the irreligious and the religious, between those who seek no transcendent significance and those who crave such significance ([1907] 1981, 10). This is the distinction between tinker, tailor, soldier, sailor, doctor, lawyer, merchant chief on the one hand, and poet, monk, and mystic on the other; the distinction between those who accept this world as it is, and those who seek something more.

This distinction may be found to some extent in all societies, but it is culturally shaped. As we saw in the accounts of Murakami-san and Ms. Tucker, Japanese household religion may give one's family in this world a religious dimension; some strands of American religion may stress commitment to God as opposed to commitment to family. Indeed, it is perhaps not an exaggeration to suggest that in some of the accounts we've examined, the American God has its equivalent in the Japanese group. Just as Americans such as Ms. Tucker and Ms. Weiss find significance through their personal relationships with God, a religious significance not sought by their Japanese counterparts, Japanese such as Miyamoto-san and Murakami-san find their significance in the this-world groups to which they belong, company and family, more than their American counterparts. In allowing selves to feel significance and sustenance from beyond the self, God and group may, for some, be experientially equivalent.[13]

Japanese and Americans face their own culturally shaped underminings of the significance they seek. The Japanese corporate employee living for his company will face retirement from his work and his significance; the American religious believer may seek significance in God from within a social world that may scoff at such piety. However, the fact remains that *all* significance, however culturally shaped, is precarious in our world. This is partly due to our human condition, but it may also be due to our peculiar place in history: the state of late modernity common to Japan and the United States, rendering the pursuit of transcendent significance peculiarly problematic. Before proceeding to this final topic, however, let us discuss once again the formulation and negotiation of *ikigai* in the lives of part 2, to better understand the culturally shaped pursuit of a life worth living through *ikigai*.

---

13. This equivalence is apparent not only in the religious dimension given to family by ancestor worship, but also in the religious feelings employees may sometimes feel toward their companies. Rauch reports on an extreme but telling example of this, the 1979 suicide note of an executive whose company had been involved in a scandal: "The company is eternal. It is our duty to devote our lives to that eternity. Our employment may last for only twenty or thirty years, but the life of the company is eternal. I must be brave and act as a man to protect that eternal life" (1992: 69, citing Ishida Takeshi).

Part Three

Ikigai and the Meaning of Life

Chapter Seven

A Phenomenological Analysis
of *Ikigai*

Culturally and Personally Shaped Fate

At the close of part 1, I offered a theory of *ikigai:* "As the products of culturally and personally shaped fate, selves strategically formulate and interpret their *ikigai* from an array of cultural conceptions, negotiate these *ikigai* within their circles of immediate others, and pursue their *ikigai* as channeled by their society's institutional structures so as to attain and maintain a sense of the personal significance of their lives." Let us now examine this theory in light of what we have learned from the accounts of part 2.

Selves are "the products of culturally and personally shaped fate": we are shaped from beyond ourselves, by forces that we can neither control nor fully comprehend. We are shaped by the particular families in which we grew up, molding our individual personalities in ways that we can understand only partially, long after we have been so molded. We are also shaped by the particular society in which we grew up, giving us a language and a set of social practices through which we come to see our particular human world as the natural order of things.

Ernest Becker touches upon the inexorability of personal shaping when he writes that "since the child is partly conditioned before he can manipulate symbols, he is formed without being able to put any distance between himself and what is happening to him. . . . The result is that the person acts out his hero-style automatically and uncritically for the rest of his life" (1971, 149–50). People cannot really know why they live for what they live for, Becker is saying; they are, throughout their lives, servants of their early symbolic shaping.

I believe Becker to be correct, but it's difficult to see direct evidence of this in the accounts of part 2. The people therein, like all of us, seek to present themselves as coherent, rational beings (see Linde 1993, 3–19), whose *ikigai* makes sense given their stories—and (beyond a certain point, anyway) it hardly seemed appropriate for me to try to poke holes in their stories. The people in part 2 present the unfolding of their lives and *ikigai* in convincing fashion, but lurking beneath their reasoned tellings of themselves is a void. As our interviews (though not the edited versions) consistently revealed, none of these people could finally explain why they hold the *ikigai* they hold. They could say, "My *ikigai* is ———, because I love it." But the question this raised was, "Why do you love ———? Why not any of a dozen other things?" In trying to answer this question, the people I spoke with could cite biographical data of various sorts, but finally were left tongue-tied in trying to explain why they were themselves. It may be that such comprehension is humanly impossible.[1]

"Personal fate" has shaped these people in their earliest years beyond their comprehension, but it has also shaped them throughout their lives. Had Murakami-sensei's company not hired a *shodō* teacher for its new club, had Ms. Weiss been released from the mental hospital a year earlier, had Mr. Isaacs's brother not lost his footing on a certain rock ledge, these people might have different lives and different *ikigai* today. Those who find *ikigai* in work might, under slightly different circumstances—a job interview with different im-

---

1. Gregory Bateson has written that "Consciousness, for obvious mechanical reasons, must always be limited to a rather small fraction of mental process. . . . Consider the impossibility of constructing a television set which would report upon its screen all the workings of its component parts, including especially those parts concerned in this reporting" (1972, 136). The logical structure of consciousness, Bateson is saying, makes it impossible for us to understand the basis of our consciousness, and by implication the basis of our *ikigai*.

pressions made—have joined different companies in their youth; those who find *ikigai* in family might, under slightly different circumstances—a *omiai* meeting gone better or worse; a party attended or unattended—have married a different spouse. What then of their *ikigai?* The *ikigai* we hold in our lives seem the result of chance as much as desire, happenstance as much as will. They seem to be in large part the result of fate.

There was, among the people I interviewed, considerable resistance to recognizing the effects of fate.[2] I found that an easy way to irritate happily married Americans and younger Japanese was to suggest that they might have been equally happy had they married any of a hundred thousand other people instead of the person they happen to have married; an easy way to annoy Japanese and American religious believers was to suggest that had they grown up in different circumstances, they might have different faiths, which would seem just as true to them as the faith they hold now. The Japanese and Americans I interviewed, and perhaps all of us, want to believe that we fashion our own lives, rather than having our lives shaped for us by a world beyond our comprehension. This isn't true, but who among us can live truly believing that it isn't true?

Personal fate and cultural fate are inextricable, in that the cultural is personal, the personal cultural. But loosely speaking, we may make this distinction: the shapings of personal fate are what make us distinct from others in our society; the shapings of cultural fate mold us in common with others in our society. As children we emerge as selves not only through our particular personal world, but also through a particular language and set of social practices that ever after condition us in our comprehension of ourselves and our world. Pierre Bourdieu (1977, 166) discusses how our social world shapes us to see its structures and the parallel structures of our own minds as "natural" rather than as human-made and arbitrary (1977, 166). We can't comprehend ourselves and our world because we are

2. Lebra has noted that fate (*un*) is a common explanation in Japan for personal success or, more often, failure (1976, 175–76). I interviewed several Japanese who referred to *un* in explaining why they did not die in World War II. But the younger Japanese I interviewed, as well as almost all Americans, did not discuss "fate" as a force that had shaped their lives.

shaped in its image and it is shaped in ours. There seems, by Bourdieu's analysis, to be no way of escaping the hall of mirrors within which we live.

The shapings of cultural fate can be seen in the "taken-for-granted" language of our accounts. Because half the accounts are translated, the contrasting linguistic shapings of Japanese and Americans are less visible, but they are still apparent, particularly in the unthinking assumptions of individualism and sociocentrism. Japanese such as Wada-san say they raise their children "so as to not trouble others" in society; Americans such as Mr. Isaacs say they want to raise their children to be "the happiest human beings they can be." More particularly, in wordings throughout their accounts one sees Murakami-san's identity as located in her role in the family and Ms. Tucker's identity as located in her individual self. For example, Murakami-san's reaction to being ill was one of resolve: "I felt that I couldn't die, leaving my husband and child behind"; Ms. Tucker's reaction was one of resentment: "Every morning I had to get up with a smile on my face. I resented the fact that I was the one that had to make everything all right." Similar albeit subtler contrasts can be found in many of the accounts of part 2.

Cultural fate at this level is largely unconscious; selves may not recognize how they are shaped. But at another level, selves have considerable awareness of, although little control over, this shaping. They may fully accept or be utterly opposed to the social practices and institutional structures that they experience within their society, but regardless of what they think, they must to some degree conform. People must earn a living, fit, to some degree, gender and age-based roles, and worry, to some degree, about the opinions of the people around them, whatever they themselves may think.

Some Japanese in part 2, such as Kinoshita-san and Murakami-sensei, vociferously assert their individualism, their personal freedom against the norms of Japanese society; but, as is apparent between their lines, they nonetheless to some degree meet those norms: Kinoshita-san continues to be concerned about his mother's opinions (or else he wouldn't have spoken of them at such length); Murakami-sensei does what he must to remain in the good graces of the *shodō* world. In a similar way, Americans in part 2 such as Mr. Eliot vociferously assert commitment to family against the demands of work, but work half their waking hours all the same.

Others in part 2 don't vehemently oppose the prevailing norms of their societies, but they accept these norms only reluctantly. Wada-san, in discussing her mixed feelings about pressuring her son to study, says that "Japan really is a . . . society based on school credentials. Maybe that's bad, but that's the trend of Japanese society, and we have to flow with it." Ms. Peters tells us that "It's my life; I can do what I want!" but she also says that "I've got to have some career skills, because if [my] marriage didn't work out, I'd be left high and dry." She realizes that she can't altogether do what she wants.

These people, and all the people I interviewed, must conform to the pressure of cultural fate in their societies, fate that seems often to embody Japanese sociocentrism and American individualism. The Japanese and Americans I interviewed may be shaped by or shaped against these principles, and may agree with or vehemently oppose these principles, but they can't escape these principles in living their lives within their societies.

The Cultural Formulation of *Ikigai*

Our next phrase of theory is that selves "strategically formulate and interpret their *ikigai* from an array of cultural conceptions." At a deep level, we are shaped; at a shallower level, we shape ourselves. On the basis of personal and cultural shaping beyond our comprehension, we consciously formulate and interpret ourselves and our *ikigai*. At this level, selves are not victims of cultural fate, but canny consumers of culture, formulating their *ikigai* through their choices from the cavalcade of ideas "in the air" of their cultural world.

We see evidence of this in the diversity of *ikigai* in part 2, from Miyamoto-san's commitment to company to Takagi-san's dream of self, from Mr. Isaacs's ideal of therapy to Mr. Redding's faith in God, and from Ms. Pratt's commitment to her children to Ms. Weiss's sense of her art. Each of the life stories in part 2 reveal *ikigai* formed of personal reweavings of strands from the larger cultural world.

It's difficult to know exactly what strands from the larger cultural world are used by the people in part 2, but we can easily see larger

cultural parallels to the *ikigai* formulations in their accounts. Miyamoto-san's fervent defense of commitment to company as the Japanese ideal parallels recent popular books such as that of Saitō (1990),
entitled "What's wrong with liking work." His sense of the obsolescence of his *ikigai* ideal is reflected in media criticism of company-
centered *sarariimen* with no lives of their own. If Takagi-san's ideal
of self-realization parallels books such as Kobayashi's (1989), his account of his life emphasizes his obligation to his children, a theme
that appears often in Japanese mass media today.[3] Kinoshita-san's
sense of himself has certainly been influenced by the ubiquitous Japanese media commentary on the new values of the young; Asano-
san and Yamamoto-san clearly shape their identities in their personal
dialogue with the media of Sōka Gakkai and the Ainu Association.

Ms. Pratt tells us that she is of "two generations, the fifties and the
sixties . . . at war with each other," connoting for her commitment to
family as opposed to activism and feminism; her account and recent
American feminist writings (Faludi 1991, Hochschild 1989) depict
this war in parallel ways. Ms. Weiss's competing potential *ikigai* reflect her simultaneous commitment to a cultural tradition of artistic
self-expression and to her Judaic religious tradition. Mr. Isaacs's ideal
of therapeutic groups leading to a new America is the ideal of many
American self-help books influenced by the writings of Maslow. Mr.
Redding's deity is the God of Catholic tradition, but also of the 1960s
youth culture ("I see Him as a radical, as someone who blew away
the establishment"). These people, and all the people portrayed in
part 2, have gathered ideas of how to live from their cultures but
have rewoven these ideas to fit the warp of their own lives.

Despite the relatively "free" and individual nature of *ikigai*'s formulations, we can nonetheless compare the broad forms of *ikigai* and
plot out the accountings of *ikigai* on a continuum between "commitment to group" and "self-realization." Miyamoto-san in his commit-

---

3. For example, the television drama *Otōsan no sensō,* or "Father's war" (HBC
1990), is about a company worker who, late in his career, decides that his family is
most important to him. He resolves to spend more time with them but is rejected
by his wife and children, who feel more comfortable when he's away at work. The
drama questions men's devotion to work over family (this man being too late in his
newfound familial devotion), but may also serve to persuade viewers like Takagi-san
to value their families over their own dreams.

ment to company, and Murakami-san and Mr. Eliot in their commitment to family, stand near the "commitment to group" pole.
Kinoshita-san and Mr. Isaacs, valuing their dreams over work and
family, Takagi-san believing that the only valid *ikigai* is having an individual purpose, and Murakami-sensei, living for creative expression,
stand near the "self-realization" pole. Others stand in the middle: Ms.
Pratt and Wada-san try to balance commitment to family and self-realization, although they consider the former most essential. Ms. Weiss
values her own writing less than her commitment to God, but expresses surprise when she finds herself saying such a thing.

As we have seen in part 2, the cultural ambiguities and conflicts
between self-realization and commitment to group are linked to ideas
of gender, generation, and conventionality. Family as *ikigai* was
framed as commitment to group among both the Japanese and the
Americans I interviewed; work as *ikigai* was framed as commitment
to group for Japanese such as Miyamoto-san, but as self-realization
or personal attainment for most Americans. This division can be seen
in Takagi-san's and Mr. Eliot's accounts, Takagi-san conceiving of
self-realization as opposed to the "commitment to group" *ikigai* of
both work *and* family, Mr. Eliot giving up the personal attainment
of "making millions" at work for his "true commitment" to family. It
may also be seen in Ms. Pratt's and Wada-san's accounts, Wada-san
holding women's commitment to family as a truer commitment than
men's commitment to company, Ms. Pratt seeming to view commitment to family as less important than personal attainment through
work, although her *ikigai* finally is her family.

As for generation: for some of the younger Japanese I spoke with,
such as Nakajima-san, dreams involve future commitment to conventional roles, in accordance with the wishes of parents; for others,
such as Kinoshita-san, dreams involve self-realization apart from such
roles and in conflict with parents and other elders. Generally speaking, Japanese such as Miyamoto-san and Kinoshita-san seemed to
think of the generation gap as the younger generation's emphasis on
self-realization and their elders' emphasis on commitment to group.
On the other hand, Mr. Isaacs's conflict with his parents appears to
be over different forms of self-realization: their apparent valuation of
personal achievement through work, as opposed to his valuation of
personal growth transcending work.

Japanese and American elders and holders of unconventional *ikigai* in part 2 are given to seeing their societies as in decline, because of an excessive pursuit of self and a lack of commitment to God, Buddha, society, company, or family. Mr. Murray complains that his passengers have grown more rude over the past twenty years; America is in decay because the nuclear family is in disarray, says Mr. Redding; Miyamoto-san criticizes younger workers for their selfishness; Asano-san sees a complacent secular Japan going the way of ancient Rome; and Yamamoto-san castigates Japanese greed in praising Ainu harmony with nature. All these people seem to hold some form of selfishness as the root of present evil and some form of commitment as the source of past or future good.

The holders of unconventional *ikigai* in chapter 6 may seem, from the perspective of those who hold work or family as *ikigai*, to be pursuing their own self-realization, but they view their lives in a somewhat different light. Murakami-sensei and Ms. Weiss discuss their self-expression through their arts, but this pursuit they see as being within a community of artistic colleagues and forebears. Each mentions past artists, such as Rokumusai, Natsume Sōseki, Menotti, and Milton; their self-realization is in the context of their larger commitment to a tradition of art. Asano-san and Mr. Redding, and Ms. Weiss, pursue a transcendent commitment to their religious faiths and also a commitment to their community of believers: Asano-san discussed with me at length Buddha and Nichiren; Mr. Redding fends off his brother's scorn by invoking the Catholic tradition "since Augustine." Yamamoto-san discusses his commitment to the Ainu in terms of the history of Ainu oppression by the Japanese. Several of these people pursue commitments that put them in opposition to the more conventional commitments of their societies, but their commitments seem at least as intensely held as those more conventional ones.

The people in part 2 also use a variety of other cultural conceptions to justify and legitimate their *ikigai*. Such justification is apparent in terms like "ordinary people," "ordinary life," and "everybody" (*futsū no hito, heibon na seikatsu, minna*). Miyamoto-san says, "I'm an ordinary person living an ordinary life. . . . Being ordinary is being happy;

everybody thinks that way." It's as if his life is justified by being "ordinary," like "everybody's"; because he is "ordinary," he need not question his life. "Everybody" was indirectly invoked through the phrase *hoka no hito ni meiwaku o kakenai yō ni*, "so as to not trouble other people." Wada-san, as we've seen, tells us that she raises her children "so as to not trouble others"; Kinoshita-san criticizes his mother for raising him by that principle and repressing his spontaneity; Asano-san says that his religion teaches that believers should not trouble others by acting on their beliefs at the expense of society; and Murakami-sensei (and Kinoshita-san too) seems consciously to subvert the phrase when he says that he will live "without worrying about what others might think." Ms. Peters, too, uses "everybody"; she justifies the idea of living at home with her parents after college by saying: "You feel safe there, protected; that's how everybody feels."

"Everybody" and "other people" derive their power to legitimate from one's human world; "God" and "nature" derive their power from beyond that world. Many of the Japanese in part 2 speak of praying to their ancestors, but for most their ancestors don't seem to serve as primary sources of legitimation for their lives. In the American accounts, however, the legitimation offered by God figures prominently. Five of our nine Americans claim to pray regularly to God: Ms. Pratt says she has conversations with God; Ms. Tucker seems daily to speak with God; Ms. Weiss communicates with God "continually"; Mr. Redding, too, seeks to pray constantly, even "while I'm sitting here talking"; and Ms. Jackson tells us that she frequently gives thanks to God. For at least three of these people, God seems to be their ultimate source of legitimation.

For some of the people in part 2, Japanese more than American, "nature" may serve as a subtle, extrasocial legitimation of their lives. Miyamoto-san tells us that to feel a deep sense of obligation to his company is "natural"; Nakajima-san tells us that "it's only natural for people to marry";[4] Wada-san implies that although work is an artifi-

---

4. Of course, if marriage and commitment to company were "natural," then there would be no need to mention them (Bourdieu 1977, 167). It is because marriage isn't "natural" (some people don't marry) and because devotion to company isn't "natural" (the young people in Miyamoto-san's company lack such devotion) that these two seek, perhaps only semiconsciously, to justify their social claims by invoking nature as an extrasocial legitimation.

cial *ikigai*, family is natural; Mr. Eliot tells us that it is instinctive to be most deeply committed to one's family; and Yamamoto-san maintains that "if people listened to the Ainu and understood our culture, they'd treasure nature more."[5] I discussed last chapter how group may be a Japanese equivalent to Americans' God. Nature also may serve as a subtle Japanese equivalent to the American God, giving socially constructed *ikigai* an extrasocial legitimation.

Concepts such as "other people," "God," and "nature" may be used to justify how one lives; other concepts, such as "fairness," make comprehensible the difficulties of life. Mr. Murray first emphasizes life's unfairness ("Life isn't fair, but I didn't realize that until I was in my forties") but later reasserts his belief in fairness, at least in his own life: "I've certainly lived more than my share at this point. . . . I've had a very fortunate life." Mr. Murray can assert this belief only without knowing how his life may turn out and what it may finally mean, but Mr. Redding and Asano-san, bearing their religious theodicies, can assert their conviction more positively. Asano-san says that "some people are born rich, others poor. It's unfair; that's why I believe in reincarnation," whereby all eventually receive their just desserts. Mr. Redding views eternal life through Christ as rectifying the unfairness of this world's life and death.

Others justify life's difficulty not in terms of ultimate fairness but in terms of personal growth. Asano-san, miserable in his work, maintains that he will grow from his misery: "As iron gets stronger by being hammered . . . human beings become stronger through pain." This view is placed in a larger context by Ms. Pratt: "What would it be like if . . . people didn't go to war but treated each other with kindness, a perfect world. . . . we'd never learn anything in such a world. . . . I think you learn, grow through pain." It is as if, for their suffering to be justified, these people must feel that they can grow from suffering.

While many of the Japanese I interviewed stressed growth through

---

5. Kinoshita-san offers a fascinating contrast to these people in their invocation of "nature." They use "nature" to make their socially constructed *ikigai* seem more than social; Kinoshita-san uses it to emphasize that social mores are only social and fleeting: "I believe human beings will become extinct, like dinosaurs. When I think about that, I feel relaxed—I can do what I want instead of following others!"

suffering, a larger number of Americans emphasized *growth* through suffering, or simply growth. Mr. Eliot tells us that "I think I'm becoming more mature as I get older"; Ms. Pratt envisions herself as a wise old woman having compassion rather than cynicism. Mr. Isaacs's dream of personal development ("I just want to be the best human being I can be") is also one of growth, as has been Ms. Jackson's therapy, enabling her to grow beyond "survival, so that I could see my way clear to a little happiness."[6]

Ms. Pratt and Mr. Isaacs both modulate their emphasis on personal growth with an emphasis on contributing to society: Ms. Pratt speaks of her "mission orientation"; Mr. Isaacs ponders how he can best live so as to "make people's lives better in some way." If one's *ikigai* is framed as commitment to group, then contributing to the group is taken to be a matter of course. But if one's *ikigai* is framed as self-realization, then one's commitment to the world beyond oneself may be felt to require specific affirmation. "Contributing," for these two, seems to be a way in which the self and its growth are linked to the world, as if to say that through their own growth they can help make the world a better place.

The idea of personal growth may be in opposition to that of worldly success; this can be seen in the accounts of Mr. Isaacs, Mr. Redding and Mr. Eliot. Personal growth in the pursuit of self-realization is a vague ideal. As Baumeister has noted, "Everyone wants to be self-actualized, but no one is sure quite what it means or how to go about it" (1991, 109). Occupational achievement, on the other hand, is concrete: one can see how much one has or hasn't achieved. Takagi-san tells us that "I feel sad when I think about how old I am. I feel a chill when I realize that I haven't done much in my life yet." This conception is that of life as a race against the clock: in one's

---

6. Some of those I interviewed seemed well aware of the contrast between the certainty of physical decline and the possibility of mental growth. Takagi-san, despite his dream of self-realization, tells us that after forty life is all downhill. Mr. Eliot, on the other hand, sees the possibility of mental vigor, enabling one to both fight and accept physical decline as one ages. Both Murakami-sensei and Ms. Weiss discuss sardonically their aging (as Ms. Weiss says, "Aging is melancholy because you crumble to bits: things fall off you") but also see for themselves greater creative resources (Murakami-sensei) and a greater appreciation for life and what life means (Ms. Weiss).

limited span, one must achieve all one can. As Murakami-sensei tells us, "In the time before I die, I've got to do some work. I've got to do all I possibly can while I'm alive."

Mr. Isaacs seems to hold a similar conception ("If you're going to make a contribution . . . you don't want to dick around, waste time"), but more Japanese than Americans I spoke with accounted for themselves in this way. However, whether one justifies one's existence in terms of concrete personal achievement or vague personal growth, some key underlying questions remain unanswered. Why is achievement or growth so important? Why so strenuously pursue such things, given the fact that soon enough you die? But as I earlier noted, these aren't questions that I felt I could ask many of those I interviewed, my job as interviewer being to understand how people construct their senses of their lives, not to undermine those constructions.

The cultural conceptions we have looked at in this section are used to frame and justify one's life and *ikigai*. These conceptions include how one formulates what makes life seem worth living through self-realization or commitment to group; how one legitimates one's life, through "everybody," "nature," or "God"; how one justifies one's suffering in life; and how one conceives of the direction and goal of one's life. The Japanese and Americans I interviewed used these and other conceptions to assure themselves that their lives are indeed worth living, to formulate and legitimate the meaning of their lives.

The Social Negotiation of *Ikigai*

The next phrase of our theory is that "Selves . . . negotiate . . . *ikigai* within their circles of immediate others." The most pivotal area of *ikigai* negotiation seems to be with one's spouse. At one extreme, a few of the accounts show no *ikigai* negotiation with one's spouse. At the other extreme, the accounts of the three divorced Americans seem to show a rupture in *ikigai* negotiations, as if, because *ikigai* negotiation was no longer possible, divorce was the only option.[7] Be-

---

7. I suspect that failure of *ikigai* negotiations is a dominant factor in many divorces. This may, of course, take a variety of specific forms, from arguments over finances to arguments over extramarital affairs, but these are matters of *ikigai*. Con-

tween these extremes, there may be crises in the *ikigai* negotiations between spouses involving a shift or threatened shift of the *ikigai* status quo, crises that must be weathered if their marriage is to survive.

Of the fifteen married or previously married informants, four—Miyamoto-san, Mr. Redding, Ms. Weiss, and Yamamoto-san—give no indication of *ikigai* negotiation between spouses. It seems from my interview with Miyamoto-san and from passing conversation with his wife that they never discussed their familial division of *ikigai* whereby he finds it in work, she in family. This may not entirely be the case (Did his wife never once complain about his late hours and his absence from the family? Did he never once complain about the dinners she cooked for him?) but it may indeed be that their familial division was so taken for granted as to require little discussion. As for Mr. Redding, Ms. Weiss, and Yamamoto-san, it seems that because Mr. Redding and his wife share a deep faith in Catholicism and live their lives by that faith, there is comparatively little ground for basic *ikigai* conflict between them. It seems that because Ms. Weiss's husband married her in large part *because* of her ambition to become a writer, and because he supported her in this endeavor throughout their marriage, doing much of the housework decades before it was socially acceptable for men to do housework (as he told me in my interviews with him), there was little ground for *ikigai* conflict between them as well. Because Yamamoto-san and his wife are united as Ainu against the oppressive Japanese majority, here too there is little basis for *ikigai* conflict.

The *ikigai* negotiations and crisis points in the accounts of my married informants range from the implicit to the starkly obvious. Ms. Tucker seems to have shifted her *ikigai* from family to God. I sensed that this shift may have been met by the subtle resistance of her husband, but in interviewing them both I was able to detect only hints of this negotiation. For Wada-san, the point of *ikigai* crisis is

---

sider the following. Wife: "If you want this marriage to continue, you've got to break off with X. Who's more important to you, me or her?" Husband: "That's the problem. I just don't know." The participants in this dialogue would consider it a discussion about infidelity, but it is also a discussion about *ikigai*.

clearer, occurring when her husband was unable to work. "I really didn't know if he *couldn't* go or just didn't *want* to go," she tells us. She worried that he was no longer willing to work and support his family and thus carry out his end of the *ikigai* familial role agreement. A potential *ikigai* crisis in Takagi-san's marriage occurred when he told his wife that he wanted to quit his company, thus threatening their *ikigai* role division. He didn't quit, but Murakami-sensei, after a similar consultation with his wife, did, whereupon she went to work to support the family. The wives of these men staved off potential *ikigai* crises by acceding to their husbands' desires to quit work to pursue greater personal fulfillment.

The crisis in Mr. Eliot's marriage was in a sense the opposite: rather than the husband seeking to abandon his commitment to work, it was Mr. Eliot's wife who pressured him to abandon that commitment, to spend more time with his family. His openness to renegotiating the *ikigai* role division apparently saved his marriage. Kinoshita-san and Mr. Isaacs, like Takagi-san, say that their *ikigai* is their dream rather than their marriages. They are too new in their marriages to have yet tested their *ikigai* priorities, but they may face serious challenges if their spouses oppose their dreams (as may Kinoshita-san's wife) or unintentionally block them (as may Mr. Isaacs's wife).

The three divorces among the Americans may be interpreted as failed *ikigai* negotiations. The failure of Mr. Murray's first marriage was due largely, he says, to his being concerned with "just the mechanical aspects of raising a family, not the emotional things." Had he offered the deep commitment to family in his first marriage that he offers to his second, perhaps there would have been no divorce. Ms. Pratt tells us that her marriage ended because "I take my family responsibilities very seriously, and he's the kind of man who never wants to grow up." Her husband, by her account, did not deeply commit himself to his family and to supporting it, and the marriage ended because she couldn't prevail upon him to change. Ms. Jackson's *ikigai* negotiations in her marriage appear to have been more complicated. "For a long time I wished I could be 'a helpless lady,'" she tells us, making her deepest commitment her family, while her husband devoted himself to work and to supporting the family. But although her husband couldn't support his family, he insisted that it appear as if he could, and it was the lie of this appearance that by her account destroyed their marriage.

The second most pivotal area of *ikigai* negotiation is negotiation with one's parent or child. The younger people in chapter 5 all face or have faced the problem of establishing their own values. For Nakajima-san, personal independence is not an issue, in that she wholly adheres to the values of her parents; Ms. Peters seeks at present to avoid such independence. Kinoshita-san and Mr. Isaacs, on the other hand, have staked their *ikigai* on their personal independence in opposition to their parents. Kinoshita-san tells us that his mother opposes his dreams and his marriage; he tells his mother, " 'If you gave me two lives, then I could follow your advice this time, and live my own life next time. But I have only one life to live.' " Mr. Isaacs tells us that his parents worry about his personal development courses, "but I'm getting to the point where I don't care as much what they think. They live their lives, I live mine." Kinoshita-san's mother and Mr. Isaacs's parents seem to realize that if they object to their sons' *ikigai* dreams too strenuously, their relationship may be sundered, and so they accept, however reluctantly, their sons' *ikigai*.

Virtually all the parents in part 2 have concerns about their children's futures that are at least indirectly concerns over *ikigai*. Wada-san and Ms. Pratt worry about whether their eldest sons will go to college (and thus perhaps be able to find a future career which can serve as their *ikigai*). Takagi-san is concerned about his son conforming too much (and thus not being able to find and live by his true *ikigai*). Mr. Eliot hopes that his son will develop the social skills that he himself lacked as a youth and that his daughter will be able to overcome her gender conditioning to live up to her potential. Ms. Tucker agonizes over whether her youngest son will accept God into his life. Yamamoto-san and Ms. Jackson are concerned about their children's possible rejection of their cultural and racial heritages in their marriages. As a number of Japanese and American parents said, they raise their children to have their own independent values, but on the basis of a common "yardstick" of values shared by parents and children. What this seems to mean is that the *ikigai* negotiations between parents and children tend to be of a basically different nature than the negotiations of spouses. The former negotiation may be on the basis of an eventual mutual independence, while the latter may be on the basis of a continuing mutual interdependence, thus requiring more intense negotiation and commonality of values (although this may be truer in the United States than in Japan, given the continuing presence of three-generation families in Japan).

A third arena of *ikigai* negotiation is that of negotiation within and across "subcultures." As a general rule, the more distant the personal relationship between two people, the less likely *ikigai* will emerge as a topic of discussion. Thus, for example, Miyamoto-san can only speculate as to the *ikigai* of his subordinates at work, having never discussed the matter with them, and Mr. Murray speculates about his coworkers' commitment to work on the basis of their staring at their feet on the employees' bus rather than on the basis of direct conversation. Many of those I interviewed, such as Kinoshita-san, speculate as to their friends' and acquaintances' *ikigai*, but few claimed to have actually spoken about such a personal matter.[8]

The exception to this rule seems to occur in "*ikigai* subcultures." Artists, it appears, may indeed discuss *ikigai* with one another. For example, Ms. Weiss mentions a writer's conference at which an aspiring writer was advised not to make writing her life; Murakami-sensei discusses with his fellow calligrapher whether or not one should write for posterity, thus touching on the meaning of commitment to *shodō*. The same seems to be the case for religious believers: Mr. Redding's deaconite classes and Asano-san's Sōka Gakkai meetings are sessions devoted in part to the explication of religious belief as one's *ikigai* and of the balancing of religious commitment with commitments to work and family. (Ms. Jackson's relation with her therapist isn't necessarily linked to her membership in a subculture. But it seems that one's therapist [or alternatively, one's minister] is the one person, aside from spouse or parents or children, with whom matters of

---

8. This *ikigai* reticence with non-kin seems due not to the abstraction of *ikigai*, but to the fact that what one lives for is viewed by most people as a private matter, which nonintimates have no business prying into (unless they are therapists, or perhaps anthropologists—although one American I interviewed insisted on keeping his inner life private: "I'm not going lie on your couch and get my head shrunk.").

"what one lives for" may be most freely discussed in the United States, if not in Japan.)[9]

Creative endeavor, religious belief, and political dream as *ikigai* may thus be exempt from the reticence that characterizes the *ikigai* of family and work. This may be because of both the minority status of these unconventional *ikigai*, necessitating overt explication of why they are held, and the fact that these *ikigai*, in their focus beyond this life, may be more self-consciously formulated, maintained, and negotiated than the *ikigai* of work and family.

This negotiation may take place not only within these subcultures of unconventional *ikigai*, but also between these subcultures and the larger culture with which they coexist. Yamamoto-san describes the unthinking discrimination that many Japanese practice toward the Ainu; the confrontations he has with such people are in a sense his demand that they recognize his *ikigai* as an Ainu. Creators such as Murakami-sensei have to negotiate their identities and *ikigai* as creators with the larger world whose *ikigai* is work and family. But *ikigai* negotiation with the larger culture is most explicit in the accounts of Asano-san and Mr. Redding. The attitude of some of Asano-san's fellow bank employees and Mr. Redding's fellow policemen toward them seems a microcosm of the general attitude of many of those who find *ikigai* in work or in family toward those who find *ikigai* in other areas: "Why can't you find *ikigai* where the rest of us find it?" (By the same token, their attitude, although they don't express it to their coworkers, seems to be, "Why can't you find a better, higher, truer *ikigai* than the ones you hold?") Those who have such *ikigai* must to some extent negotiate with and entreat their fellows to accept it as valid and worthy.

A final form of *ikigai* negotiation is the communication of religious believers with the objects of their devotion. I've noted that five of our

---

9. In Japan, there is no cultural figure comparable to that of therapist with whom one may discuss what one lives for. This may be because commitment to group, being already defined, is inherently less problematic for the self than is self-realization, and may thus require little therapeutic discussion. If this is true, then with the emergence of self-realization as an *ikigai* ideal in Japan, Western modes of therapy should be gaining importance there, as appears to be occurring, to judge from works such as that of Ōhira 1990.

nine Americans pray to God; for two of them, God seems explicitly to answer back. As Ms. Tucker tells us, "I've had days where I've forgotten to say, 'God, this was a wonderful day, thank You,' and He's forgiven me"; Ms. Weiss says, more jocularly, "What'll happen if I lose my gift? You know, God once said to me, 'You're going to get old and stupid anyway, what are you worrying about?' " The equivalent of this for many Japanese (and for Americans such as Mr. Isaacs and Ms. Weiss) was discussion and negotiation with their ancestors or departed intimates. Although many Japanese I interviewed expressed skepticism that they "really" talk with their ancestors, these ancestors may nonetheless appear in their lives, as, for example, for Murakami-san: "Last night in a dream I saw my grandmother. . . . I wonder if she wants to tell me something?" As Ms. Weiss playfully implies, it may be difficult to understand what is truly "self" and what is "other" in conversations with departed intimates, but these conversations do appear to involve direct or indirect *ikigai* negotiation between the self and some entity felt to be beyond the self.

The Institutional Channeling of *Ikigai*

The next phrase of our theory is that "Selves . . . pursue their *ikigai* as channeled by their society's institutional structures." All cultural formulations and social negotiations of *ikigai* are structured by the institutional world within which it must be sought. The *ikigai* of part 2 are channeled in accordance with a number of basic principles, some common to Japan and the United States and some distinct to each.

The most basic institutional reality is that one must have money to survive. The two young women in chapter 5 state this plainly. "My father always says that money can solve 80 percent of the problems you face in this world," says Nakajima-san. "Love doesn't make the world go round, it's cash," says Ms. Peters. Their desire for money and all it can buy both contrasts with and echoes our middle-aged Japanese and Americans' concerns over supporting their families. Ms. Pratt says that "I have three kids I have to educate, collegewise. I have no idea how I'm going to do that!" Ms. Jackson tells us that when she quit teaching to bear her children, she had to learn "how to get food stamps, cheat on my electric bill . . . to be able to feed my kids"; Takagi-san tells us that despite his desires, "I can't quit my company because I have to support my kids." This concern about money is most pronounced among those in part 2 who have children, but it seems to exist to some degree for everyone, from the two young women dreaming of a wealthy adulthood to those near death, such as Ms. Tucker, planning her demise so that her family can afford it.

I've discussed how concern with commitment to group seems linked to difficult economic conditions and concern with self-realization to more relaxed economic conditions, as was the case in the United States in the 1960s and 1970s and in Japan in the 1980s. As part 2 reveals, large-scale economic trends by no means determine individual formulations of *ikigai*, but they do channel *ikigai* along certain general paths. One can't quit one's job to pursue one's dreams if one has no money and there is no new employment to be had. When the economy is booming and "self-realization" is emphasized, the economic channeling of *ikigai* may seem less apparent; but regardless of economic ups and downs, the fundamental necessities of survival have channeled many of the *ikigai* considerations of those I interviewed.

This is true in both Japan and the United States, but there are significant differences between the two nations in the ways economic structures channel *ikigai*. As we have seen, Japanese institutions seem structured in accordance with commitment to group, American institutions with individual freedom and responsibility, and this may mean, as in the accounts of Takagi-san and Mr. Eliot, that Americans may be generally freer to change jobs than Japanese and thus more able to pursue personal fulfillment through work. Of course this American emphasis on "individual freedom and responsibility" also means that companies may feel free to lay off workers whenever they choose. Still, it does seem that the institutional constraints on means of earning a livelihood are generally greater in Japan than in the United States (at least for those Americans in the middle class).

Japanese workers work longer hours than their American counterparts, and may be required to spend considerable time on company activities apart from work.[10] However, as Miyamoto-san's and Asano-san's accounts indicate, there is resistance among younger Japanese to giving all their time and energy to their companies; young people like Kinoshita-san are unwilling to commit themselves to working for a single company for long.[11] Maybe Japan is gradually becoming less economically constraining of workers' pursuit of *ikigai*. At the same time, American companies, according to Schor (1991), have become progressively more demanding of their employees' time over the past two decades, progressively more constraining of their employees' pursuits of *ikigai*.

A second institutional reality shaping accounts is that of gender roles: Men are institutionally channeled to bear the primary responsibility for wage earning and financially supporting the family, women for child-rearing and emotionally nurturing the family. Women in Japan and the United States earn no more than between half and three fourths of what their male counterparts earn (Smith 1987a, 14; Faludi 1991, 363–99). This difference clearly illustrates the large-scale institutional channeling of women to make their deepest commitment to home and family rather than to work and of men to make their more remunerative deepest commitment to work—although there are, of course, millions of individual exceptions to this.

This channeling too seems somewhat more pronounced in Japan than in the United States. Although there is much debate in the United States as to how much the progressive cultural ideal of men and women finding equally their deepest commitments to work and to family is being realized (Hochschild 1989, Faludi 1991), it does seem that the employment situation of women is more restricted by

10. Lummis and Saitō cite 1986 statistics showing that Japanese workers work on average 2,150 hours per year, American 1,924 hours, a difference of close to an hour each working day (1991, 1). Schor notes that in manufacturing, "Japanese workers put in six weeks more each year than their counterparts in the United States"; a similar gap exists between Japanese and American office employees (1991, 153, 154). But Schor also notes that Japanese and Americans in common work far longer hours than French and Germans, who average just 1,650 working hours per year.

11. See Sengoku 1991 on the lack of perseverance among the Japanese young. A 1990 *Asahi Shinbun* editorial urged recent school graduates not to quit their work at the first sign of difficulty, but to attempt to persevere for at least a few years (1990a).

gender in Japan than in the United States. Among other indications of this is the fact that Japan's 1985 Parity in Employment Law, intended to grant women equal opportunity with men in the workplace, is in fact only advisory; thus in the current economic downturn in Japan, many large companies are ignoring the law and refusing to hire women for career-track positions (Sanger 1992). Indeed, although I interviewed divorced Japanese women who labored to support their children, I interviewed no Japanese woman who was able to balance a commitment to personally fulfilling work and a commitment to her children as does Ms. Pratt. By the same token, I interviewed no Japanese man who took a path such as that of Mr. Eliot, abandoning a lucrative career to be with his family. (Murakami-san does, however, depict her son-in-law in such terms.)

A third institutional reality is that in most cases one's work ends years or decades before one's life ends; one's children begin to lead more or less independent lives long before one dies. I noted in chapter 1 how Japanese men and women may have two or three decades to live after retirement from work or children leaving home. The same seems true for Americans, if not so much for men (who have a later retirement age and a lower life expectancy than their Japanese counterparts), then certainly for women: American women have on average twenty-seven years to live following the departure of their last child from the home (McCullough and Rutenberg 1989, 286). This means that for Japanese and Americans, especially women, their roles in work or in child-rearing, and perhaps their *ikigai* as found in work or in children, may end long before their lives end.

But this situation is mitigated differently in Japan and the United States. In Japan, the three-generation household continues to be the living arrangement of some 65 percent of elderly Japanese (Misawa and Minami 1989, 221). We may add to this figure its contemporary variant, as experienced by Takagi-san and Murakami-san, the adjacent residences of grandparents and parents-children. This arrangement may lead to tension, as expressed by Takagi-san, but may also enable the continuation of an elderly person's *ikigai* in family. Murakami-san, for example, seems to find great happiness in being able to interact with her grandchildren.

In the United States, the three-generation household has become atypical. "In 1900," writes Fitzgerald, "some 60 percent of all Americans sixty-five and over lived with an adult child. Today, only about 17 percent live with one" (1987, 209). Although communication between parents and children, via telephone and visits, may remain frequent, an elderly person's *ikigai* of family may not be sustained by such contact. The patternings of household arrangement thus seem to encourage lifelong *ikigai* of family in Japan and to discourage this in the United States.[12] When Wada-san, in speaking of women's *ikigai* as found in children, says that "what women live for . . . lasts all their lives," she may be speaking more of Japanese women than of American women.

In the United States, as I have noted, working hours are considerably shorter than in Japan; indeed, Japanese mass media often state that Japanese need to learn from Americans how to use leisure and enjoy life. Americans, too, may be overworked, as Schor (1991) argues, but I interviewed no American who said, as did Miyamoto-san, "If I had more free time, I don't think I'd know what to do with it." Just as the three-generation household in Japan may institutionally support the lifelong retention of family as *ikigai* for many Japanese, the institutional emphasis on leisure and its productive use in the United States over the past half-century may enable many Americans to find more easily a new purpose in life upon retirement or "empty nest."

A fourth example of the institutional channeling of *ikigai* involves religion. In societies such as seventeenth-century Plymouth or twentieth-century Saudi Arabia, religious observances have been a mandatory part of daily life, and admitted agnostics or believers in other faiths are not tolerated. This isn't the case in Japan and the United States at present. Both societies mandate the separation of religion and state, and prohibit discrimination on the basis of religious belief,

12. This refers to *ikigai* as found in children and grandchildren rather than in spouse; *ikigai* as one's spouse may be more common in the United States than in Japan. Studies in the United States have shown that marital satisfaction tends to increase following the departure of children from the home (Gormly and Brodzinsky 1989, 470). But the difference in life expectancy between men and women may make *ikigai* as found in spouse difficult to sustain: "Old age, the final phase of the family life cycle, has almost become a phase for women only" (Carter and McGoldrick 1989, 12).

although informal discrimination is practiced in both societies. Asano-san and Mr. Redding mention social harassment, but they have suffered no job or housing discrimination or government persecution because of their religious beliefs. (This lack of religious discrimination contrasts with the racial discrimination suffered by Ms. Jackson and Yamamoto-san, although even this discrimination has been more informal than formal, more social than institutional.)

However, it seems that the distinct institutional presence of religion is often greater in American lives than in Japanese lives. Those Americans who regularly attend church or synagogue—whether some 40 percent of Americans (Harris 1987, 67; Stark and Bainbridge 1985, 76–80) or no more than 20 percent, as more skeptical recent surveys show (Hadaway, Marler, and Chaves 1993)—focus specifically on their religion for at least an hour or two most weeks. The percentage of Japanese involved to an equivalent degree in the religious activities of their shrines or temples is doubtless far smaller. The most common form of religious observance in Japan is in the home, in offerings of food to the household ancestors (Smith 1974, 90–91). These offerings are likely to be daily and thus to involve a significant commitment by at least one member of the household, most often the wife, but they are for the sake of the family and its continuity (Plath 1964) and don't involve religious practice distinct from the family. Religious practice in the United States, on the other hand, is distinct from family, and sometimes opposed to it, as we saw in Ms. Tucker's account. Accordingly, if Japanese household religion reinforces family as *ikigai*, American church religion may reinforce religious belief as opposed to nonreligious work and family as *ikigai*.

There is, finally, a fifth point to be made about the institutional channeling of *ikigai:* the general absence in both societies of overt coercion by the state of their citizens' *ikigai. Ikigai*, as a matter of individual consciousness, cannot be altogether coerced: police, priests, or party officials can't compel the members of a given society to hold certain *ikigai* and reject others. Religious states may compel religious behavior by their members, but they cannot compel belief. Totalitarian political regimes may require constant expressions of support from their citizens' mouths but can't ensure support in citizens' hearts. At this stage of technology, anyway, there remains the possibility of resistance in one's consciousness, if not in one's watched words and actions.[13]

Despite this incoercible core of *ikigai*, states throughout history have tried to mold their subjects' *ikigai*, through education and propaganda as well as coercion. Compared to such states, today's Japan and United States are noncoercive in their molding of *ikigai*. Japanese and Americans may be encouraged in innumerable ways to find *ikigai* in work and family, as supported by conventional religious practice, but anyone who refuses such an *ikigai*—such as Takagi-san, Murakami-sensei, Kinoshita-san, Mr. Isaacs, Asano-san, Mr. Redding, Ms. Weiss, and Yamamoto-san—will not be jailed or shot by the state.

This lack of *ikigai* coercion is revealed most clearly by the Japanese government's response to Japan's plummeting birth rate. In the late 1930s, giving birth was made a patriotic duty (an official slogan of this period was *Umeyo Fuyaseyo*, "Bear Children, Swell the Population" for the sake of Japan), and "laws against birth control were rigidly enforced" (Wagatsuma 1983). Japanese women responded with such fervor that the birthrate rose to thirty-one births per thousand people per year. The Japanese birthrate is now below ten births per thousand people, considerably below replacement level, and the government has been hard pressed to find a solution to the problem. Judging from recent reports, both appeals to patriotism and offers of cash rewards for bearing children are met merely with disdain by many women (Reid 1990; Weisman 1991; McArthur 1991; Yoshihiro 1991). Institutional changes in Japan—more day-care facilities, cheaper land prices, more career opportunities for women who have borne children—might lead to a rise in the birth rate, but without such structural changes, the government seems impotent to shift by exhortation and bribery the *ikigai* of young women toward the raising of children.

Most of the accounts of part 2 reflect this absence of coercion. There seem, in some of them, to be social and psychological penalties

13. With genetic engineering and ever more skillful conditioning, the unsubtle attempted *ikigai* coercion of the gun barrel and torture chamber may at some point be replaced by more effective modes of coercion. Huxley [1932] 1969 and Skinner 1971 provide, from very different points of view, premonitions of such an age.

to be paid if one works but does not make that work one's *ikigai* or has a family but does not make it one's *ikigai*, but these *ikigai* are not coerced by the state or by any other institution. Marcuse has written of "the overwhelming, anonymous power and efficiency of the technological society" in shaping individual desires (1964: 226), but the accounts of part 2, in my reading, don't reveal this domination, but rather show the exercise of a definite, albeit conditioned, freedom.

Society as an organized set of socioeconomic institutions does not appear to coerce selves' choices of *ikigai*, but in a more inchoate sense, society as "other people" may to some degree do so. We've seen how "other people" and "everybody" are invoked in some accounts as personal justification, but such terms may also connote pressure to conform. Several of the Japanese in part 2 mentioned *sekentei* (appearance, what people think) as a force compelling their conformity to social norms. For Nakajima-san in particular, *sekentei* seems to shape her *ikigai*. In opposition to this, the accounts reveal a more defiant advocacy of self-realization among some of the Japanese I interviewed than among the Americans, a defiance perhaps due to the greater social suppression of dreams of self-realization in Japan. It seems that although attempted state coercion of *ikigai* seems minimal in contemporary Japan and the United States, general social coercion of *ikigai* is greater in Japan than in the United States. But for Japanese such as Kinoshita-san, Murakami-sensei, and Asano-san, this coercion seems resistible.

In chapter 6, we considered the final phrase of our *ikigai* theory, that selves seek "to attain and maintain a sense of the personal significance of their lives." We looked at significance as sought within one's life, through the *ikigai* of work and family and, beyond one's life, through the *ikigai* of creative endeavor and religious belief. However, almost all of those portrayed in part 2 have some sort of religious sense, whether vague or explicit. Even those whose *ikigai* is not religious belief still seem to grope for the ultimate significance that such belief offers. They still seem to seek, beyond their own meaning of life, a sense of *the* meaning of life. This pursuit will be the subject of our next and final chapter.

Chapter Eight

Ikigai and the Meaning of Life

My Informants' Sense
of the Meaning of Life

We examined in part 2 the sense some Japanese and Americans have of the meaning of their lives: their work, family, or personal dream, creative endeavor, religious belief, or political dream. But if these senses of personal meaning are not linked to a sense of larger, transcendent meaning, then they may be seen as merely futile. What use is living for work or family if you'll be in the ground and oblivious in just a few years or decades? What use is living for your children if their lives are no more intrinsically meaningful than your own? What use is the pursuit of self-realization if, after the attainment of such an exalted state, you merely drop dead and are forgotten, no different from a housefly? What use is living for your political dream if, as Kinoshita-san suggests, in short order "human beings will become extinct, like dinosaurs"? If nothing that we do has any meaning beyond our own tiny lives, then why bother?

I discussed in chapter 6 the precariousness of the significance sought through *ikigai*: work and family because of their transience, creation and religion because of their questionable transcendence. The ultimate source of this precariousness seems to be that one's own meaning of life cannot securely be linked to an enduring larger meaning. Our own small meanings pass, and we know that the larger meanings we posit might not be real. The Japanese and Americans portrayed in part 2 seem in varying degrees aware of the meaninglessness of this world if it is not linked to anything larger and seem in varying degrees to think about what the larger meaning of life might be (although the extent to which their expressed thoughts are a reflection of their lives, as opposed to only our interviews, remains an open question). Takagi-san, Kinoshita-san, Ms. Weiss, and Mr. Redding, among others, seem to have devoted considerable thought to the question of what life means; Nakajima-san, Ms. Peters, and Mr. Murray, among others, seem to have thought about this question very little. As a whole, the people of part 2 gave a variety of answers to the question of what life means, answers sometimes explicit, sometimes implicit and ambiguous.

Some of them, those who find their *ikigai* in their religious beliefs, seem to see their own lives as being meaningful only if they are linked directly to what they see as the ultimate meaning of life. For Ms. Tucker, Ms. Weiss, Asano-san, and Mr. Redding, their own meaning of life and their sense of the meaning of life coincide.

The opposite pole is that of those who deny any ultimate meaning of life, such as Miyamoto-san, Takagi-san, Mr. Eliot, Kinoshita-san, and Mr. Isaacs. Kinoshita-san, and to a lesser extent Takagi-san, are existentialist in their steadfast denial of transcendent human significance; as Kinoshita-san says, "Sure, humans can feel *ikigai,* but maybe spiders feel *ikigai* when they're eating their prey." Miyamoto-san and Mr. Isaacs seem to hold a this-world sense of the enduring, larger meaning of their lives. Miyamoto-san links his sense of commitment to group to the cultural specialness of the Japanese ("If we can prove we're still competitive working just eight hours a day, we may really be able to say we're superior as a race"). Mr. Isaacs says, "I don't think that human beings have any divine purpose. I just want to be the best human being I can be, and help other human beings to be the best they can be," thus locating his larger meaning in a vision of human improvement. Mr. Eliot, too, seems wholly immersed in his life in this world ("I haven't thought much about death. My brain's too filled with what I'll do tomorrow!").

Mr. Murray, Yamamoto-san and Murakami-sensei also are very much this-worldly types, but unlike the men discussed above, each does envision something beyond this world. Mr. Murray, after speculating as to life's larger meaning ("If there's anything of spirit that runs through us all, it's the thread that runs through life"), says, "But damned if I know! How should I know all this?" Murakami-sensei feels that "death isn't the end," but he devotes no thought to death. His sense of meaning lies in his *shodō; shodō* is of this world, he holds, the other world being unknowable. Yamamoto-san dreams of a "land of peace" in this world for Ainu, but also dreams of a world after death for Ainu, as if to hedge his bets: if this world's Ainu paradise does not come to pass, the next world's Ainu paradise nonetheless awaits.

The eight men in the preceding paragraph deny or don't much concern themselves with a meaning of life beyond the human. On the other hand, our six mothers in part 2 all link their lives to a larger meaning beyond this human world. Aside from Ms. Tucker and Ms. Weiss, who find their *ikigai* in their religious beliefs, Ms. Pratt regularly converses with God, and Ms. Jackson prays to God about her family; Wada-san and Murakami-san, although both somewhat skeptical about the reality of ancestors beyond the grave, nevertheless practice ancestor worship. The American women seem certain of God's existence. Ms. Pratt tells us that "there's a part of me that believes absolutely that there's a God." Ms. Jackson says, "It's not just luck, sometimes the Good Lord really does provide. He's here." Ms. Tucker says that "I know completely that God and Christ are real"; Ms. Weiss says that "the beauty of things makes God completely apparent." The Japanese women, on the other hand, focus on religious form rather than faith: as Wada-san tells us of ancestor worship, "I guess it's only a formality, but I have to respect it and convey it to my sons"; as Murakami-san says, "I speak to my parents at the *butsudan* [altar], and offer them rice, but I still can't believe in that stuff." However, practice, too, is a form of obeisance to the other world; the essence of Japanese religion, as often noted, is not faith but practice (Davis 1992, 236; Reader 1991, 15–20), and these two women do indeed practice.

For these six women, their belief in God or their practice of ancestor worship seems in large part rooted in their desire to protect their families—the *ikigai* of all these women—from the misfortunes that may befall them in this world. Our two young women, Nakajima-san and Ms. Peters, don't yet have families to protect, but although they are fearful about death and about what might lie beyond, they both can imagine heaven as "in the sky, above where airplanes fly," "having lots of clouds, and misty," a heaven that may yet offer protection for their families to come.

Thus, although many of the men in our accounts seem to devote little thought to the larger meaning of life, the women do involve themselves in that larger meaning, whether through a sensed personal link to God or through the practice of ancestor worship. The accounts of part 2 may reflect the apparent fact that women are, on average, more concerned about religion than are men.[1] But this is too simple; it doesn't address the ambiguities and contradictions running through Part 2.

The two people who most deny any transcendent meaning of life are Kinoshita-san and Takagi-san. But Kinoshita-san tells us that "basically I don't believe in life after death, but I guess I do believe, like a child, when I see TV programs about psychic phenomena"; Takagi-san says, "Every summer we visit [my father's] grave. I talk to him: 'Dad . . . Are you OK?' I don't think he's OK—he's dead! But I tell him about the kids, tell him the things I'd tell him if he were alive." Both men thus indicate a hope or at least a yearning for a world that transcends this one.

Mr. Isaacs seems to base his sense of the meaning of life in human progress, yet he also wonders, "Where is my brother now? Rationally I have no idea, but emotionally I do sometimes sense that he's near." Murakami-san practices ancestor worship, but doubts its Buddhist meanings. "Priests are only human. They've never been to the other world; what they preach they've only learned from books!" Yet she also receives messages from that world: "Last night in a dream I saw my grandmother. . . . I wonder if she wants to tell me something?" Emotionally, both imagine communication with a larger world and meaning that they rationally doubt. Similarly, Ms. Weiss speaks with her father in dreams, knowing that such communication may be only imagined, yet finding succor in it.

1. Harris notes that in the United States "women are far more religious than men"; 13 percent more women than men regularly attend church, by his statistics (1987, 68). In Japan, making daily offerings to the ancestors is generally the duty of the oldest woman in the household and is almost never performed by men.

Miyamoto-san seems to find his largest meaning in his this-world commitment to his company and his Japaneseness, and dismisses religion as the province of women; yet "in the bottom of my heart I may be seeking religion. . . . Maybe I'm afraid of death; maybe in twenty years I'll believe in life after death." Wada-san ("I believe fifty percent in life after death, but maybe I'll believe a hundred percent when I'm seventy-five!") and Mr. Eliot ("I don't believe in God at this point, but that's an area where I'd say I need more maturity. . . . Yeah, there's a good chance I'll come to believe") similarly say that although they don't believe now, they may believe in the future, when they may need such beliefs. For these people, their criterion of belief seems to be not the truth of religion but their need for religion.

Related to this is the fact that many of the people portrayed in part 2 seem well aware that they may be "making up" their religious meanings, that the transcendence they envision they may be only imagining. Ms. Peters, as well as Kinoshita-san, speaks dismissively about seeing television programs about heaven and yet imagines life after death on the basis of those programs. Wada-san ("We don't finally know what'll happen to us after we die . . . so all we can do is follow the forms handed down to us by our ancestors") and Ms. Pratt (who says that her "ongoing conversations with God" may be "mostly with myself") admit that their beliefs may be their own creations, and yet they seem to gain sustenance from them.

Furthermore, even those who believe in standard religious entities such as God or the ancestors don't believe in the same kind of God or ancestors. Ms. Tucker, Ms. Pratt, Ms. Jackson, and Mr. Redding all believe in some variant of the Christian God, but Ms. Pratt's universalistic God ("The commonalities of religion throughout the world: there's a reason they're there") seems quite different from Ms. Tucker's orthodox Christian God. Ms. Jackson's God, "a force in the universe," seems different from Mr. Redding's God, as found in salvation through Christ ("If Christ didn't rise from the dead . . . then all would be futile"). Mr. Redding's and Ms. Tucker's God offers eternal life as Ms. Jackson's God may not. Mr. Redding believes that Jesus saves people of all religions, while Ms. Tucker believes that God might not even save her own son. Ms. Tucker talks to God, she's certain, while Ms. Pratt acknowledges that she may be talking to herself. All four seem to have transcendent beliefs different from those of Ms. Weiss, whose Jewish God serves for her as the personification of the world's beauty.

Similar variances of belief may be seen in our Japanese accounts. Wada-san, Takagi-san, Nakajima-san, Murakami-san, and Yamamoto-san all discuss ancestor worship, but each have personalized views of what their worship means. Nakajima-san's ancestors aid people in this life, she feels ("when something bad happens to their families, they'll come down and help") as Wada-san's apparently will not. Yamamoto-san's world beyond this life, being only for Ainu, is different from Nakajima-san's world, and Takagi-san, Wada-san, and Murakami-san are skeptical about any such world, although each practices the forms of ancestor worship.

There is a large difference between the ways in which the Americans and the Japanese conceive of the meaning of life through their religions. The Americans often seem to conceive of God as both the ultimate source of meaning in the universe and as a being with whom they have an intimate personal relation (as Ms. Tucker tells us, "I'm comfortable with the fact that I'm on a first-name basis with God"). The uncharitable question to which this may lead is, why should a God who has the entire universe over which to worry concern Himself with one's own small individual problems and prayers? Japanese (with the exception of believers in non-mainstream religions such as Asano-san) don't tend to have such a grand conception of the spiritual beings with whom they relate. The ancestors to whom they pray are generally family members they have known personally; their ancestor worship is in this sense a continuation in the next world of conversations once had in this world. Their religious meaning is thus a meaning of life that applies only to one's family. But for its adherents, this smaller meaning too may serve as "the meaning of life," implicitly conveying the extramundane meaning of all human beings' lives on this earth, even though it's a meaning generally conceived on a far smaller scale than "God."

As the preceding analysis shows us, there are only a few committed religious believers among the people in part 2, just as there are only a few committed nonbelievers. Most are in the middle, basing their lives in practical, this-world meanings, seeking larger meanings yet not at all sure of their larger beliefs and their truth. Many seem to yearn to believe but are skeptical; they pray to God or speak with departed loved ones, rationally doubting yet emotionally gaining sustenance from their relations with a world and a meaning beyond this one. Their formulations of that meaning often seem hypothetical (along the lines of "Well, maybe there's a world beyond this one") and subjective, owing less to received doctrine than to their own personal formulations of life, which many know may be "made up" and yet adhere to hopefully all the same.

This seems a strange situation: those I interviewed seem to seek a link to the transcendent meaning of life, and yet most of them have only their own private, tenuous, subjective senses of what that meaning might be. Maybe it's always been this way in different eras and cultures: between overt religious belief and overt unbelief lie most people, making up their own vague versions of reality's ultimate meaning while struggling to get by in this immediate practical reality. But I suspect that the root cause of my informants' ultimate uncertainty lies less in their humanity than in their recent history.

The Meaning of Life in the Late Modern Age

We've examined many of the cultural, social, and institutional differences between our Japanese and American accounts, but they also show a remarkable similarity. This similarity is due to the parallel personal cultures of the pairs of people whose accounts we've examined, and also to the underlying parallels in the larger cultures of Japan and the United States today. These two societies seem to be in similar states of "late modernity," which shape the ways in which the Japanese and Americans I spoke with are able to conceive the meaning of their lives and of life.

As everyone knows, Japan and the United States are advanced industrial societies based in capitalism and filled with ubiquitous advertising, mass media, and high technology. But they may also share certain common structures of "late modern consciousness." Berger, Berger, and Kellner describe such consciousness in terms of the fragmentation of values: "Through most of human history, individuals lived in life-worlds that were more or less unified. . . . For the individual this meant . . . that the *same* integrative symbols permeated the various sectors of his everyday life" (1974, 64). This, they say, is no longer the case: "Modern identity is *peculiarly differentiated.* Because of the plurality of social worlds in modern society, the structures of each particular world are experienced as relatively unstable and unreliable. The individual in most pre-modern societies lives in a world that . . . appears to him as firm and possibly inevitable. By contrast, the modern individual's experience of a plurality of social worlds relativizes every one of them" (77). They argue that this is due to the lack of any overarching symbol system providing a basis for such ordering, specifically religion: "Through most of empirically available human history, religion has played a vital role in providing the overarching canopy of symbols for the meaningful integration of society. . . . This age-old function of religion is seriously threatened by pluralization. Different sectors of social life now come to be governed by widely discrepant meanings and meaning systems" (79).

In a similar way, Giddens describes the erosion of a common sense of meaning in late modernity. This results, he argues, in the "fundamental psychic problem" of meaninglessness, "the feeling that life has nothing worthwhile to offer" (1991, 9). "Modernity is a post-traditional order, in which the question, 'How shall I live?' has to be answered in day-to-day decisions about how to behave, what to wear and what to eat—and many other things—as well as interpreted within the temporal unfolding of self-identity" (14). He describes the late modern world as one in which freedom of choice is ubiquitous as compared to previous eras, but which is "non-foundational," having no unquestioned basis in tradition, morality, or religion, from which such choices may be made (1991: 80).

Similarly, Lyotard defines "the postmodern condition" as involving "incredulity toward metanarratives" (1984, xxiv), arguing that the metanarrative of science, and progress through science, is no longer credible. In light of our discussion, we may use the term "metanarrative" to refer to all "overarching symbol systems" or "foundations for choice" such as nature or religion, as well as progress. "Metanarrative" may be conceived of as that which links the narrative of one's

own life and pursuit of significance through *ikigai* to larger principles
defining the direction and purpose of human life as a whole. Berger
and his coauthors, Giddens, and Lyotard (whether they label the contemporary world "modern," "late modern," or "postmodern") seem
to be discussing the same phenomenon, the loss of a common belief
structure in which most people in society find the meaning of life.

A number of theorists describe this phenomenon as it applies to
contemporary Japan and the United States. Shimizu Katsuo, for example, directly utilizes Lyotard in discussing how "metanarrative has
vanished" (*ōki na monogatari wa kieta*) in today's world (1987, 102).
He portrays a Japanese world in which some people seek the meaning of life through a multitude of *shinkō shūkyō* (new religions), others through private incursions into the occult and mysticism, others
through oblivious immersion in fashion, mass media, or computer
games, and still others in insanity. According to psychiatrist Miya-
moto Tadao, increasing numbers of Japanese mental patients now
"see themselves as the center of the universe, one with the sun and
the gods," that is, as "the meaning of life" (quoted in Shimizu 1987,
70). Walter Truett Anderson writes of a similar process taking place
in the United States. He discusses at length the battles in America
today between "constructivists" and "fundamentalists" over the nature of reality. "Fundamentalists," adhering to the metanarratives of
"religion, science, ideology, or cultural tradition" (1990, 19), are
"those who hold firmly to a set of truths that they declare to be *the*
cosmic reality" (13); "constructivists" "hold all truth to be a human
invention" (13). The struggle of these two groups Anderson sees as
underlying the more overt struggles in contemporary American life
in such areas as science, literature, religion, and politics; the American tide he sees as ineluctably turning toward "constructivism."

The above arguments seem to apply directly to those I interviewed
and their versions of the meaning of life. If late modern societies no
longer have integrated meaning systems explicating a meaning of life
common to all or most, if the question "How shall I live?" no longer
has, for many, firm, transcendently based answers, if metanarratives
no longer can provide common assurances that life is not, in Shakespeare's terms, "a tale told by an idiot, full of sound and fury, signi-
fying nothing," then the subjective formulations of meaning dis-

cussed by Shimizu and Anderson, and used by many of the Japanese and Americans portrayed in part 2, make perfect sense. Some thinkers hold that human beings fundamentally seek a sense of ultimate meaning (Tillich 1987, 32–38; Becker 1971, 1973), a sense of transcendent significance, enabling them to comprehend the meaning of their own lives within the framework of an enduring larger meaning. If in today's world such significance cannot be found within a common, taken-for-granted framework of larger meaning in Japan and the United States, then those I interviewed may have no choice but either to adhere to a disputed version of the meaning of life, through any of various religions, or to create their own senses of the meaning of life. And this, indeed, is what their accounts show us.

To understand how this contemporary state of fragmented meaning has come to pass in Japan and the United States, let us briefly examine the history of "the meaning of life" in the two societies, as shaped through the metanarratives of religion, nature, and human progress, the three larger meanings that those I interviewed most seemed to adhere to.

Progress, Nature, and Religion

Progress to human perfection was the dream of the European Enlightenment—as Condorcet wrote in 1794, "No bounds have been fixed to the improvement of the human faculties . . . the perfectibility of man is absolutely indefinite" (quoted in Baumer 1970, 441)—as well as thinkers of the Japanese Meiji Enlightenment such as Fukuzawa Yukichi. Today, however, Ellul (1964) writes of the monster of technology engulfing all human values, Heilbroner (1975) of the precarious "human prospect," given the realities of pollution, overpopulation, and nuclear weapons, and Lasch (1991) of the folly of the belief in progress that many Americans continue to hold despite all evidence to the contrary. In Japan, numerous recent works, for example, those of Hirooka (1986) and Sengoku (1991), focus on the dark ages into which a decadent Japan is certain to fall; Shimizu's (1987) vision of a gleaming, sterile, dehumanized Japanese future is intolerably bleak.

This hesitancy to hold progress as the meaning of life is reflected in several interviews. Miyamoto-san perhaps feels that the ongoing development of Japan is his larger meaning, while Yamamoto-san dreams of Ainu liberation as his meaning; but both are conflicted. Miyamoto-san says that if Japanese worked less, "we could recover our humanness," but he also rails bitterly against those young Japanese who don't make their companies their lives. Yamamoto-san dreams of resurrecting a culture now all but dead, he admits. Mr. Isaacs and Kinoshita-san base their larger meanings of life in the reform of their societies, but whereas Mr. Isaacs can dream of a potential utopia of human fulfillment, Kinoshita-san dreams of human extinction ("Human beings don't amount to much. . . . It wouldn't be any big deal if we became extinct") and seems to find personal solace in such a dream.

Such skepticism is less extremely but perhaps more tellingly expressed in the doubtful affirmations of an American man in his sixties whom I interviewed: "I like to think that the human species is . . . coming closer and closer to some form of perfection, though as I get older, I become a little more skeptical. . . . I think man is better now than he was in the past, though there are days when I think there's a good chance that man will destroy himself." This man, an atheist, seeks to believe in human progress but, given the reality of today's world, finds such belief difficult to sustain.

Nature was held as a guide for life by innumerable premodern Japanese writers, for example, the twelfth-century Japanese hermit Kamo no Chōmei (Keene 1968, 189) and the fourteenth-century writer Yoshida Kenkō (Yoshida [1431] 1981, 7), who compared human life in all its transience to bubbles of foam that form and vanish or to the dew on a summer morning, thereby making comprehensible that transience by placing it in a larger-than-human frame. In the West, God was long invoked more than nature, but by the late eighteenth and early nineteenth centuries, Enlightenment philosophes and romantic poets propounded nature as the source of all goodness and wisdom.

Today, however, Japanese and American writers emphasize the irrelevance of nature to the human world that increasingly has engulfed it. The Japanese philosopher Mori Arimasa writes of how, because people know nature only from television and postcards, "we cannot say that there is really any nature in Japan" (Mori 1970, 122); William Irwin Thompson's parallel writings (1991) emphasize "The American Replacement of Nature" by technology and mass media. Underlying this is the sense, emergent in the 130 years since Darwin, that nature can teach human beings nothing about how we should live. As the physicist Steven Weinberg writes, "the more the universe seems comprehensible, the more it also seems pointless." (1977, 154).[2]

I discussed last chapter how some of those in part 2—Mr. Eliot, Wada-san, Yamamoto-san, Miyamoto-san, Nakajima-san—invoke nature in justifying their lives. Some of these people may consciously or subconsciously link their own meanings of life to a larger meaning as found in nature, but it may also be that nature's invocation is no more than a linguistic convention. The relation of words to minds remains an open question. When those I interviewed said that something "is only natural," it may be that nature is indeed being thought of as the source of human significance, as, perhaps, the ultimate justification for a disputed social claim. But it is also possible that "nature" is invoked as no more than a casual figure of speech, bearing no larger implications whatsoever. Perhaps the truth, for those I interviewed, lies somewhere between these poles.

The meaning of life through religion is, as we've seen, believed, or yearned for by almost all of those in part 2. This metanarrative of meaning and its erosion in the history of Japan and the United States is particularly complex and ambiguous.

Religion seems to have once provided the standard frame of life's meaning in Japan, Europe, and the United States. Religious belief in past ages is largely unknowable, but it seems, according to many scholars, that there once was a generally accepted set of religious metanarratives in both Japan and the West. The European "medieval vision" may have been one in which angels and demons were, for most, as real as human beings and in which "religious truths [formed]"

2. Among others, Morris Berman (1984) has discussed quantum mechanics as revealing the inseparability of mind and nature, arguing that the new scientific view of nature can lead us to a return to "participating consciousness," a "reenchantment of the world." Perhaps nature may thus be reinvented as a metanarrative providing the meaning of life, but at present, such reinvention seems distant.

the ultimate logic of existence" (Erickson 1976, 27); medieval Japan's "basic map of reality" apparently consisted unquestionably, for most, of the six karmic levels of transmigration, including gods, humans, and "hungry ghosts" (LaFleur 1983, 26–59).

There no doubt were many in these earlier Japanese and Western ages who had no particular interest in religion.[3] However, apart from the degree of religious fervor a person may or may not have had, these religious backdrops seem to have provided most people in those worlds with a taken-for-granted transcendent reality that few would have any basis for doubting, a reality perhaps akin to today's taken-for-granted reality of electricity and gravity furnished by science.

In today's modern world, one may be passionately interested in science, or not interested at all, but if one were to express persistent doubt as to the truth of some scientific ideas (although not evolution in the United States), one's sanity might in short order be doubted. If I were to claim seriously that the light goes on when I flick the switch not because of electricity but because I am sending a personal signal to God, whose angels reside in the lightbulbs and ever await my signal, the people around me would soon conclude not that I was exercising my right to believe in whatever religion I wished, but rather that I was having schizophrenic delusions. Just as science provides the indubitable basis of Japanese and American everyday reality at present, religious doctrines may in the Japanese and American pasts have provided such a basis; they may have provided the meaning of life regardless of how much thought one devoted to them.[4]

It may be that the human beings who lived in these past worlds did not generally hold religious truths as their *ikigai;* rather, religious

---

3. Morris, for example, describes the religious indifference of Heian aristocrats (1979, 119), and Perry describes less-than-fervent fishermen in colonial New England (1984, 46).

4. If religion in the past may have provided most with a common framework of "the meaning of life," then why does science at present not provide such a framework? The answer seems to be that whereas religious doctrine directly linked human beings to transcendent meaning, science does not. Science depicts the universe without discussing the relation of human beings to it. Unless it is linked to a conception of human progress or offers a theory of the unity of mind and nature, science cannot serve as a successor to religion as a source of the meaning of life.

truths formed a taken-for-granted underlying reality that supported their this-world *ikigai*. Weber's Protestant Ethic ([1920–21] 1958) may have given work as *ikigai* an ultimate sanction for many over some two centuries in the West; the Meiji government's linkage of the values of filial piety and imperial loyalty (Smith 1983, 9–36) gave family as *ikigai* an ultimate sacred sanction in Japan until the end of the Second World War. In any case, as many scholars have discussed in various ways (Yanagawa 1977; Morioka 1984, 256–61, Endō 1989; and Davis 1992 on Japan; Baumer 1960; Turner 1985; Luckmann 1967; Berger 1969, 1970; Becker 1971, 1973, 1975; and Baumeister 1991 on Europe and the United States), this common, taken-for-granted meaning of life has apparently faded over recent centuries and seems no longer to exist in either Japan or the United States.

It faded in part for particular historical reasons. In Japan, the emergence of a money economy in the Tokugawa period served to erode the importance of traditional village festivals and shrines and the link to the sacred they provided (Davis 1992, 236); the Western-influenced rationalism of such Meiji thinkers as Katō Hiroyuki, Nishi Amane, and Fukuzawa Yukichi further eroded this religious sense; finally, the State Shinto that religiously linked family to state to cosmos from the late nineteenth century on, as mentioned above, lost its legitimacy with Japan's defeat in 1945. In the United States, James Turner pinpoints the loss of collective religious certainty and the emergence of "unbelief [as] a fully available option" as taking place between 1850 and 1870, years corresponding to the emergence of Darwinism (1985, 199, 4).

These particular reasons point to more general principles behind the fading of common religious meaning. The advance of science has rendered religion less necessary as a means of explaining the inexplicable. The French astronomer Laplace is reported to have said to Napoleon, "God? I have no need for that hypothesis," a detachment of religion from science that according to Turner echoed in nineteenth-century America. The Meiji apostle of Western science, Fukuzawa Yukichi, reports in his autobiography how as a teenager he secretly replaced with stones the sacred objects in several Shinto shrines to see if any harm might befall him for such blasphemous acts; when none did, he ceased believing in Shinto's claims (Fukuzawa [1899] 1966, 17). Beyond this, the increasing removal through technology of humans from any world beyond the human makes such a world shrink ever smaller in any realm beyond the private, as Shimizu (1987) and Thompson (1991) assert.

Finally, the increasing knowledge of other cultures and the rise of cultural relativism threatens each culture's traditional meaning of life, increasingly, as Anderson (1990) discusses, each person can pick and choose his or her own beliefs from among all the world's beliefs (among those I interviewed were a committed Japanese Jehovah's Witness and a committed American Tibetan Buddhist). When there are so many different meanings of life to choose from, why should one any longer believe that the meanings proffered by one's own culture are truer than any other?

Freud wrote of the "three blows to narcissism," and to the religious belief he saw as linked to narcissism, inflicted by science: "the cosmological blow," when human beings learned that their earth was not the center of the universe; "the biological blow," when human beings learned that they were not "different from animals or superior to them"; and "the psychological blow," as human beings realize that the human mind is beyond human beings' conscious control or knowledge (Baumer 1970, 690–91; see also Freud [1927] 1961). My candidate for a fourth blow to be added to Freud's list would be "the cultural blow," whereby human beings realize that their enculturated worldviews are not natural but arbitrary and perhaps fictional (Hatch 1983, 59).

This blow is dealt by the social sciences, which show us "the social construction of reality" (Berger and Luckmann 1967) and that our "webs of significance" are but webs of significance *we ourselves* have spun (Geertz 1973, 5). The best-selling work of anthropology ever written, Ruth Benedict's *Patterns of Culture*, delivers this blow in its call for cultural relativity (1934, 278), its message that one's own culture is but one more human construct among many.

This delineation of historical reasons for our loss of a common "meaning of life" should not be taken to mean something like, "Japanese and Americans used to believe in religion, but now believe no longer." In fact, as we have seen, almost all of those portrayed in part 2 do practice, believe in, or yearn for religion. But these Japanese and Americans don't seem to share a *common* religious vision. Each have different and often contradictory conceptions of what "God" or "the ancestors" consist of; many seem well aware of the subjective nature of their beliefs. Even fervent believers such as Mr. Redding become hesitant when asked if their beliefs apply to everybody, or only to themselves; they seem to subjectivize and thus undercut their faiths' claims to universal legitimacy, that their meaning of life is in fact everyone's meaning of life. As Mr. Redding tells us, "Of course I have to take into account my cultural biases: I've grown up a Catholic. I'd say Christianity is most true, but a Buddhist wouldn't."

It's perhaps not surprising that the Japanese I interviewed should have different, subjective conceptions of the ancestors: because my ancestors are not yours, my conception of the ancestors may also differ from yours. Furthermore, as Yanagawa argues, Japanese tend to think about life after death not in abstract universal terms but in the context of specific human relations: "Thanks to our ancestors, we can lead a peaceful life in this world; without our prayers, they cannot rest in peace in the other world. This notion is one of mutual aid between the living and the dead" (1977, 307).

However, both the Japanese and Americans I interviewed seem to lack common senses of what the ancestors or God consist of; there seems to be no clearly defined religious meaning uniting either group. Cultural difference can't explain this absence. Cultural commonality, a common erosion of collective meaning in the Japan and the United States of late modernity, perhaps can, and so this is the hypothesis I offer in trying to understand how those I interviewed explained, in their different private ways, the meaning of life.

Self, Society, and the Meaning of Life

Thomas Luckmann has described how the lack of a common meaning of life has affected the individual seeker of ultimate meaning in the contemporary United States:

To an immeasurably higher degree than in a traditional social order, the individual [in today's modern world] is left to his own devices in choosing . . . "ultimate" meanings. . . . The "autonomous" consumer selects . . . certain religious themes from the available assortment and builds them into a somewhat precarious private system of "ultimate" significance. . . . Syndicated advice columns, "inspirational" literature ranging from tracts on positive thinking to *Playboy* magazine, *Reader's Digest* versions of popular psychology, the lyrics of popular hits, and so forth, articulate what are, in effect, elements of models of "ultimate" significance. (1967, 98, 102, 104)

As we have analyzed at length, the Japanese and Americans of part 2 seem indeed to hold "private system[s] of 'ultimate' significance," which may be "precarious." The cultural sources of these ultimate beliefs (or perhaps cultural illustrations of beliefs these people already held) are often not clear, but seem to range from television programs (Ms. Peters and Kinoshita-san), to plays (Ms. Pratt) and operas (Ms. Weiss), to manuals on tea ceremony (Murakami-sensei), to newspaper speeches (Asano-san), to self improvement courses (Mr. Isaacs). Indeed, looking at contemporary Japanese and American societies at large, sources of "models of 'ultimate' significance" seem multifarious.

As has been said, these sources include the state: the Japanese state reasserted its Shinto tradition in the 1980s, with Japanese cabinet ministers visiting Yasukuni Shrine and thereby seeking to link, through the war dead, the Japanese state to the extramundane (Hardacre 1989, 133–63); the United States has long had its "civil religion" linking American state and society to transcendent religious legitimation (Bellah 1970), often overtly expressed in Christian terms, as in public prayers at presidential inaugurations. These invocations of religion seem to be efforts to give the this-world concerns of the state and its citizens a link to transcendent significance.

These sources of "models of ultimate significance" also include the vast mass media output describing a world beyond this one, whether in variations of Christian and Buddhist doctrines or in more amorphous terms, such as the many American "New Age" tracts now in bookstores. American bestsellers such as Raymond A. Moody Jr.'s *Life after Life* (1976), Kenneth Ring's *Heading toward Omega* (1984), and Betty J. Eadie's *Embraced by the Light* (1992), as well as Japanese bestsellers such as Tanba Tetsurō's *Reikai seikatsu no jissō* (The reality of life in the spiritual world, 1988), are a few of many recent books discussing the fate of the self upon its earthly demise. Movies and television, too, may enable the imaginative construction of the transcendent meaning of life: their depictions of a world beyond the grave may not be taken seriously by their viewers, but as several of those I interviewed said, "You never know. It *might* be true!"

Beyond this overt depiction of a larger transcendent meaning, movies and television dramas offer the implicit principle that life has coherence and "sense": a story is told in an hour or two that is resolved by its close, so that its viewers will feel dramatically fulfilled. The implication is that as drama, so too life: it all works out for the best in the end, and thus life has direction, purpose, and meaning. Those who watch such dramas may not explicitly believe in the truth of this metanarrative principle as it applies to their lives, but they probably entertain its possibility: the possibility that their lives are dramatically coherent, and thus meaningful. Indeed, Murakami-san was one of several people I interviewed who envisioned their lives as movies.

Similar latent principles of transcendent meaning may be found in Japan and the United States in areas ranging from money and social or professional rank ("If you're good enough, have enough, rise high enough, all will be forever well"—despite the fact that "you can't take it with you") to love ("all you need is love"; "love conquers all"; "love is eternal"). This construction of models of ultimate meaning thus extends to the most intimate of human relations. Mothers in the United States and Japan soothe their children with such words as, "Don't cry. Everything's all right" (*Nakanai de. Daijōbu yo.*) As Peter Berger has written, "*Is the mother lying to the child?* The answer, in the most profound sense, can be 'no' only if there is some truth in the religious interpretation of human existence" (1970, 55; emphasis in original). But whether the mother is lying or not, her words indicate her soothing of her child's anxieties through the invocation of the world's basic goodness: the primacy of good over evil, love over indifference, life over death.

We thus see a multiplicity of models of ultimate significance and of the meaning of life emerging from Japanese and American cultures today. Some of these, the mother's soothing words to her child, for example, may be universal, but others may reflect the present state of the soul in Japan and the United States. Given what may be the human need to see our lives as ultimately meaningful, and given what seems to have been the shattering of generally held visions of the meaning of life in Japan and the United States, people create their own such meanings from whatever materials they can find. Their cultures obligingly throw up a vast assortment of such materials.

The relation of self to society is often thought of in terms of power and resistance: the self's resistance to society's mechanisms of power, which continually threaten to subvert all resistance. The struggle of selves to resist the social and institutional pressures of society can certainly be seen in many of the accounts of part 2, but this isn't the most fundamental relation of self to society that I see in them. Rather, these accounts seem most basically to depict the subtle *complicity* of self and society in affirming the meaning of life, a complicity to mutually validate the transcendent significance of them both (Baumeister 1991, 360–65).

Thus, for example, our Japanese have been taught ancestor worship by "society," the world of others within which they live, the cultural, social, and institutional frameworks that constitute "reality" beyond the self. Their practice of ancestor worship then affirms society's teaching: by practicing it, they demonstrate that ancestor worship is right and true. Self thus affirms society's link to transcendent meaning as society affirms self's link to transcendent meaning. By the same token, our Americans in part 2 have been taught by "society" to pray to God; their praying then affirms that the God they have been taught by society is real. Society is justified to the extent that it can enable self to feel a sense of connection to larger meaning through its cultural forms; self is justified to the extent that it can believe these larger meanings. Self and society support each other in claiming, explicitly or implicitly, the transcendent significance of their mutually constructed values. All the potential metanarratives of meaning that I have described derive their power from this mutual legitimation of self and society.

But it may be that this is not enough. We've seen how there has emerged a multiplicity of ultimate meanings in Japan and the United States. This multiplicity, by its very nature, can never adequately take the place of what may have been the earlier, commonly held, and unitary ultimate meanings in Japan and the United States, meanings destroyed by the progress of science and by knowledge of and intermingling with other societies. When there are multiple visions of what life ultimately means, that very fact throws the ultimacy of each and all of them into question. The illusion of ultimate meaning that self and society create for each other no longer functions very well; increasingly, people see that "it's only us here, making it all up." Japanese and Americans such as most of those I interviewed cannot any longer know what life really means, and they know that they cannot know, as is apparent in their hesitant, subjective, self-doubting formulations of the meaning of life. We can't know the true significance of our lives, if any; so we utilize our social worlds to provide us with various models of possible significance, hypothetical significance, "as-if" significance, and we strive, with the help of our social world, to construct our senses of the meaning of life on the basis of this "as-ifness." But this "as-if" significance may not be enough, because we know that it is only "as-if"; we cannot help but know, many of us, that the meaning of life may be no more than the stuff of our fantasies.

What Makes Life Worth Living?

Let us now come full circle. What makes life worth living for most Japanese and Americans? It is *ikigai*, I have maintained, one's deepest sense of social commitment, most often to one's dream, family, work, or religious belief. My argument has been that selves in Japan and the United States seek through *ikigai* a sense of their social significance and, beyond that, hints if not assurances of their transcendent significance, linking their own meanings to the meaning of life. But it may be that Japanese and Americans are becoming progressively less able to make these connections.

Nietzsche, a century ago, presciently predicted this historical progression: "When we . . . reject the Christian interpretation, and condemn its 'significance' as a forgery, we are immediately confronted . . . with the *Schopenhauerian* question: *Has existence then a significance at all?*—the question which will require a couple of centuries even to be completely heard in all its profundity" (*The Gay Science,* cited in Baumer 1970, 594). By this interpretation, Japan and the United States may now be in a historical passage from assurance of significance to full awareness of absolute insignificance, from collective assurance as to the meaning of life to collective knowledge that life has no meaning. The current multiplicity of private, subjective, tentative versions of the meaning of life may represent a midpoint in that passage, a passage that, by Nietzsche's words, may take centuries, but that both Japanese and Americans may now in fits and starts be undergoing.

All of this may portend a dark future. Selves in Japan and the United States live by precarious *ikigai*, relying, to at least some extent, on the promise of a link to the ultimate meaning of things. This promise may be somewhat easier to sustain in Japan than in the United States, given the greater Japanese emphasis on the group beyond the self. However, the promise of transcendence may be increasingly difficult to maintain in both societies. Might the progressive erosion of all possibilities of knowing the meaning of life, and thus the ultimate meaning of one's own life, eventually create nations full of Camusian strangers, Laschian narcissists, Shimizian techno-drones lost in the fantasies of their computers?

Perhaps not. There is another, less dire interpretation of the subjectivizing of the meaning of life. In the same decade that Nietzsche wrote, William James advocated that since one cannot know with certainty the ultimate truth of one's beliefs, one should believe what is best for one to believe: "Believe that life *is* worth living, and your belief will help create the fact" ([1897] 1956, 62). This seems to be the tack taken by many of those I interviewed.

Anthropologists have sometimes argued that to know that one's deepest beliefs are no more than a social construction is intolerable for human beings. For example, in writing of ritual, Moore and Myerhoff argue that "underlying all rituals is an ultimate danger . . . the possibility that we will encounter ourselves making up our conceptions of the world, society, our very selves. We may slip in[to] that fatal perspective of recognizing culture as our construct, arbitrary, conventional, invented by mortals" (1977, 18). Nonetheless, several of those whose accounts we examined in part 2 seem to admit cheerfully enough that what they believe about transcendent meaning they may be only imagining, that when they talk to God, they may be only talking to themselves. These people acknowledge that they may be making up their conceptions of the meaning of life, because at some level they seem to realize that there is no perspective from which transcendent truth can be known: all knowledge is the product of social and cultural construction and can never be acquired except through this construction.

This idea may seem abstract, but it appears key to the lives of those I interviewed, and perhaps to Japanese and American lives in general. We have seen how Wada-san and Ms. Pratt acknowledge that their senses of the ancestors and of God may be but their own creations; Mr. Isaacs, Murakami-san, and Ms. Weiss acknowledge that their conversations with deceased loved ones may be products of their own imaginations; Miyamoto-san, Wada-san, and Mr. Eliot anticipate having religious belief in the future, when they will need it, rather than at present, when they are too busy to feel such need; Ms. Peters and Kinoshita-san invoke mass-media concepts of life after death that "may" be true. These people may have little intellectual conception of the social construction of all beliefs, but most of them do realize that the prevailing beliefs about ultimacy in their societies have no privileged status. (To cite Murakami-san's words once more, "Priests are only human. They've never been to the other world; what they preach they've only learned from books!") Thus they may, in Jamesian terms, believe what is best for them to believe in practically living their lives, knowing that those beliefs might not be true, but just *might* be true.

Instead of modern existentialism we may thus be seeing "late modern pragmatism," enabling the construction of personal senses of a transcendent meaning of life, after modernism has led to the destruction of any collective sense of such meaning. As we've seen, Japanese and American societies now offer a plethora of different possibilities of transcendent belief, and such beliefs, given the undeniable possibility of the truth of any or all of them, can provide a transcendent basis for one's deepest sense of social commitment, for that which most makes one's life seem worth living. They can offer no "truth," no unassailable "reason to believe," but they can at least offer a "reason to hope" that one's life has a larger meaning and significance beyond one's own tiny self—a hope that can never be completely destroyed.

What makes life seem worth living? I have discussed how Japanese and Americans may struggle to put up with jobs they dislike and relationships that are difficult because of *ikigai*, a deep commitment in their lives that makes them feel that life is indeed worth living. But this commitment, if it is not linked to a larger significance, may be untenable: life may, for some, be worth living strictly on its own fleeting terms, but for many of us it requires a link to something larger, a meaning that is in some way transcendent. This applies to most of those I interviewed, as we've seen, and to me as well. All through my interviews for this book, I kept hoping, subconsciously, that someone might indeed teach me what life ultimately means—only to find that, of course, nobody knew any more than I did. It was only later, as I pored over the transcripts of what these people had told me, that I gradually realized that the key lay not in knowledge but in ignorance, and in what we make of our ignorance.

If I knew with certainty that this book I now write would open no eyes and minds, but merely gather dust on a library shelf, would I have written it? If I knew with certainty that all the books I hope to write in the future would in no way shape the world's future but merely crumble to dust as all things crumble, would I bother even trying to write them? If I knew with certainty that I was but an animal with an oversized brain, thinking ceaselessly in the effort to deny this fact, would I live this life as I now live it? If I knew with certainty that the pain of life had no meaning other than itself, as dumb pain, would I bother living this life? Certainly not.

But these things I do not know, and cannot know. I do not know that my destiny is not to contribute to the growth of human understanding; I do not know that such understanding is not ultimately significant. I do not know that I'm not a nerve ending of the universe, my role to see and marvel at the moon and the stars. I do not know that my wife and I won't continue to be together in worlds beyond this one. All these possibilities seem slightly ridiculous to me, but I don't know, can't know, that they are illusions, and so I will live as if they might be true.

This attitude is that of those I interviewed, the people whose stories you've read in this book. It is what they have taught me. We can't know why we were put on the planet, to live out our lives, Japanese and American; we can only shape our shaped lives from the array of cultural conceptions around us, choose carefully our meanings and our potential transcendence, and live our lives as if those meanings were real. This is what underlies the *ikigai* of the Japanese and Americans I interviewed, the *ikigai* of I who write this, and perhaps of you who read these words. This, ultimately, is all that can make life worth living.

References

Amaki, Shihomi. 1989. "Chūkōnen josei no ikikata to byōri" (The lives and afflictions of middle-aged and older women). In *Gendaijin no raifukōsu* (Contemporary lifecourse), edited by Misawa Kenichi et al. Kyōto: Mineruva Shobō.

Amano, Yūkichi. 1990. "Mata mata pantsu" (Again pants). *Watashi no CM uotchingu* column, *Asahi Shinbun*, 1 June.

Anderson, Walter Truett. 1990. *Reality Isn't What It Used to Be.* San Francisco: Harper and Row.

Asahi Shinbun. 1990a. "'Sunao' na kimochi de daiippo o" (Take the first step with a tractable mind). Editorial, 1 April, morning edition.

———. 1990b. *Tensei jingo* column, 24 April, morning edition.

———. 1990c. "Kazoku no katachi kawari, ohaka wa dō naru" [With family structures changing, how will the grave change with them?] 10 July.

Ayer, A. J. 1990. *The Meaning of Life.* New York: Charles Scribner's Sons.

Baldwin, Stanley C. 1988. *Take This Job and Love It.* Downers Grove, Ill.: InterVarsity Press.

Barringer, Felicity. 1992. "Laid-Off Bosses Scramble in a Changing World." *New York Times*, "The Week in Review," 12 July.

Bateson, Gregory. 1972. *Steps to an Ecology of Mind.* New York: Ballantine Books.

Baumeister, Roy F. 1991. *Meanings of Life.* New York: Guilford Press.

Baumer, Franklin L. 1960. *Religion and the Rise of Scepticism.* New York: Harcourt, Brace.

———. 1970. *Main Currents of Western Thought.* 3d ed. New York: Alfred A. Knopf.

Becker, Ernest. 1971. *The Birth and Death of Meaning: An Interdisciplinary Perspective on the Problem of Man.* 2d ed. Harmondsworth, Eng.: Penguin Books.

————. 1973. *The Denial of Death*. New York: Free Press.

————. 1975. *Escape from Evil*. New York: Free Press.

Beeman, William O. 1986. "Freedom to Choose: Symbols and Values in American Advertising." In *Symbolizing America*, edited by Hervé Varenne. Lincoln: University of Nebraska Press.

Bell, Daniel. 1976. *The Cultural Contradictions of Capitalism*. New York: Basic Books.

Bellah, Robert N. 1970. "Civil Religion in America." In *Beyond Belief: Essays on Religion in a Post-traditional World*. New York: Harper and Row.

Bellah, Robert N., Richard Madsen, William M. Sullivan, Ann Swidler, and Steven M. Tipton. 1986. *Habits of the Heart: Individualism and Commitment in American Life*. Berkeley and Los Angeles: University of California Press, 1985. Reprint, New York: Harper and Row (page references are to reprint edition).

Benedict, Ruth. 1934. *Patterns of Culture*. Boston: Houghton Mifflin.

Berger, Peter L. 1969. *The Sacred Canopy: Elements of a Sociological Theory of Religion*. New York: Doubleday 1967. Reprint, Garden City, N.Y.: Doubleday Anchor Books.

————. 1970. *A Rumor of Angels: Modern Society and the Rediscovery of the Supernatural*. New York: Doubleday, 1969. Reprint, Garden City, N.Y.: Doubleday Anchor Books (page references are to reprint edition).

Berger, Peter L., Brigitte Berger, and Hansfried Kellner. 1974. *The Homeless Mind: Modernization and Consciousness*. New York: Random House, 1973. Reprint, New York: Vintage Books (page references are to reprint edition).

Berger, Peter L., and Thomas Luckmann. 1967. *The Social Construction of Reality: A Treatise in the Sociology of Knowledge*. New York: Doubleday, 1966. Reprint, Garden City, N.Y.: Doubleday Anchor Books (page references are to reprint edition).

Berman, Morris. 1984. *The Reenchantment of the World*. Ithaca: Cornell University Press, 1981. Reprint, New York: Bantam Books.

Bourdieu, Pierre. 1977. *Outline of a Theory of Practice*. Translated by Richard Nice. Cambridge: Cambridge University Press.

Buber, Martin. [1938] 1965. "What is Man?" In *Between Man and Man*. Translated by Ronald Gregor Smith. New York: Macmillan.

Camus, Albert. 1955. *The Myth of Sisyphus and Other Essays*. Translated by Justin O'Brien. New York: Vintage Books.

Carter, Betty, and Monica McGoldrick. 1989. "Overview: The Changing Family Life Cycle—A Framework for Family Therapy." In *The Changing Family Life Cycle*, edited by Betty Carter and Monica McGoldrick. 2d ed. Needham Heights, Mass.: Allyn and Bacon.

Caudill, William A., and David W. Plath. 1966. "Who Sleeps by Whom? Parent-Child Involvement in Urban Japanese Families." *Psychiatry* 29 (4): 344–66.

Caughey, John L. 1984. *Imaginary Social Worlds: A Cultural Approach.* Lincoln: University of Nebraska Press.

Comfort, Alex. 1978. "Aging: Real and Imaginary." In *The New Old: Struggling for Decent Aging,* edited by Ronald Gross, Beatrice Gross, and Sylvia Seidman. Garden City, N.Y.: Doubleday Anchor Books.

Crystal, Graef S. 1990. "The Great CEO Pay Sweepstakes." *Fortune,* 18 June.

Davis, Winston. 1992. "The Secularization of Japanese Religion." In *Japanese Religion and Society: Paradigms of Structure and Change.* Albany: State University of New York Press.

Dumont, Louis. 1970. *Homo Hierarchicus: The Caste System and Its Implications.* Translated by Mark Sainsbury, Louis Dumont, and Basia Gulati. Chicago: University of Chicago Press.

Eadie, Betty J., with Curtis Taylor. 1992. *Embraced by the Light.* Placerville, Calif.: Gold Leaf Press.

Edwards, Walter. 1989. *Modern Japan Through Its Weddings: Gender, Person, and Society in Ritual Portrayal.* Stanford: Stanford University Press.

Ehrenreich, Barbara. 1983. *The Hearts of Men: American Dreams and the Flight from Commitment.* New York: Doubleday Anchor Books.

Ellul, Jacques. 1964. *The Technological Society.* Translated by John Wilkinson. New York: Vintage Books.

Endō, Shūsaku. 1989. "Society Now Shuns the Aged." *Japan Times,* 23 October.

Erickson, Carolly. 1976. *The Medieval Vision: Essays in History and Perception.* Oxford: Oxford University Press.

Faludi, Susan. 1991. *Backlash: The Undeclared War against American Women.* New York: Crown.

Feinberg, Walter. 1993. *Japan and the Pursuit of a New American Identity.* New York: Routledge.

Field, Norma. 1991. *In the Realm of a Dying Emperor.* New York: Pantheon Books.

Fitzgerald, Frances. 1987. *Cities on a Hill: A Journey through Contemporary American Cultures.* New York: Simon and Schuster.

Frankl, Viktor E. [1959] 1984. *Man's Search for Meaning.* New York: Washington Square Press.

Freud, Sigmund. [1927] 1961. *The Future of an Illusion.* Translated by James Strachey. New York: W. W. Norton.

Fukuzawa Yukichi. [1899] 1966. *The Autobiography of Fukuzawa Yukichi.* Translated by Eiichi Kiyooka. New York: Columbia University Press.

Geertz, Clifford. 1973. *The Interpretation of Cultures.* New York: Basic Books.

Giddens, Anthony. 1991. *Modernity and Self-Identity: Self and Society in the Late Modern Age.* Stanford: Stanford University Press.

Gilligan, Carol. 1982. *In a Different Voice: Psychological Theory and Women's Development.* Cambridge: Harvard University Press.

Ginsburg, Faye D. 1989. *Contested Lives: The Abortion Debate in an American Community.* Berkeley and Los Angeles: University of California Press.

Goffman, Erving. 1959. *The Presentation of Self in Everyday Life.* Garden City, N.Y.: Doubleday Anchor Books.

Goldschmidt, Walter. 1990. *The Human Career: The Self in the Symbolic World.* Cambridge, Mass.: Blackwell.

Goleman, Daniel. 1985. *Vital Lies, Simple Truths: The Psychology of Self-Deception.* New York: Simon and Schuster.

Gormly, Anne V., and David M. Brodzinsky. 1989. *Lifespan Human Development.* 4th ed. Fort Worth: Holt, Rinehart and Winston.

Gornick, Vivian. 1978. "For the Rest of Our Days, Things Can Only Get Worse." In *The New Old: Struggling for Decent Aging,* edited by Ronald Gross, Beatrice Gross, and Sylvia Seidman. Garden City, N.Y.: Doubleday Anchor Books.

HBC (Hokkaido Broadcasting Company). 1990. Otōsan no sensō (Father's war). Television drama: Tōshiba Nichiyō Gekijō, 26 August.

Hadaway, C. Kirk, Penny Long Marler, and Mark Chaves. 1993. "What the Polls Don't Show: A Closer Look at U.S. Church Attendance." *American Sociological Review* 58(6): 741–52.

Halberstam, David. 1986. *The Reckoning.* New York: Avon Books / Yohan Publications.

Hamaguchi, Esyun. 1982. *Kanjinshugi no shakai: Nihon* [Japan: a society of interrelation). Tōkyō: Tōyō Keizai Shimpōsha.

———. 1985. "A Contextual Model of the Japanese: Toward a Methodological Innovation in Japan Studies." *Journal of Japanese Studies* 11(2): 289–322.

Hardacre, Helen. 1989. *Shinto and the State, 1868–1988.* Princeton: Princeton University Press.

Harris, Grace Gredys. 1989. "Concepts of Individual, Self, and Person in Description and Analysis." *American Anthropologist* 91(3): 599–612.

Harris, Louis. 1987. *Inside America.* New York: Vintage Books.

Hatch, Elvin. 1983. *Culture and Morality: The Relativity of Values in Anthropology.* New York: Columbia University Press.

Heilbroner, Robert L. 1975. *An Inquiry into the Human Prospect*. New York: W. W. Norton.

Hewlett, Sylvia Ann. 1986. *A Lesser Life: The Myth of Women's Liberation in America*. New York: Warner Books.

Hirooka, Moriho. 1986. 'Yutakasa' no paradokkusa (The paradox of affluence). Tōkyō: Kōdansha.

Hochschild, Arlie, with Anne Machung. 1989. *The Second Shift*. New York: Avon Books.

Hokkaidō Shinbun. 1989a. "Nihon no seinenzō, kojin seikatsu shikō ga medatsu" (Japanese youths' inclination toward individualism stands out). 15 January.

⸻. 1989b. "Teinen junbi seminaa ni setsujitsu na koe ga tsugitsugi— 'kokoro to karada ni ōki na henka,' 'ikigai o mistuketai' " [In a retirement preparation seminar, poignant voices, one after another: 'My body and mind are changing'; 'I want to find *ikigai*']. 11 December.

Hsu, Francis L. K. 1985. "The Self in Cross-cultural Perspective." In *Culture and Self: Asian and Western Perspectives*, edited by Anthony J. Marsella, George DeVos, and Francis L. K. Hsu. New York: Tavistock.

Huxley, Aldous. [1932] 1969. *Brave New World*. New York: HarperPerennial.

Iwao, Sumiko. 1993. *The Japanese Woman: Traditional Image and Changing Reality*. New York: Free Press.

James, William. [1897] 1956. "Is Life Worth Living?" In *The Will to Believe and Other Essays in Popular Philosophy*. New York: Dover.

⸻. [1907] 1981. *Pragmatism*. Indianapolis: Hackett.

Japan Statistical Yearbook. 1991. 42nd ed. Tokyo: Statistics Bureau, Management and Coordination Agency.

Japan Times. 1994. "Birthrate Will Drop to 1.3 in 2011 from 1.45 This Year, Think Tank Says." 16 September.

Johnson, Sheila K. 1991. *The Japanese through American Eyes*. Stanford: Stanford University Press.

Kamiya, Mieko. 1980a. *Ikigai ni tsuite* (About *ikigai*). Vol. 1 of *Chosakushū* (Collected works). Tōkyō: Misuzu Shobō.

⸻. 1980b. *Ningen o mitsumete* (Looking closely at human beings). Vol. 2 of *Chosakushū* (Collected works). Tōkyō: Misuzu Shobō.

Keene, Donald, ed. 1968. *Anthology of Japanese Literature to the Nineteenth Century*. Harmondsworth, Eng.: Penguin Books.

Klein, Joe. 1992. "Whose Values?" *Newsweek*, 8 June.

Kobayashi, Tsukasa. 1989. *"Ikigai" to wa nanika: jiko jitsugen e no michi* (What is '*ikigai*'? The path toward self-realization). Tōkyō: Nihon Hōsō Shuppan Kyōkai (NHK).

⸻. 1990. "Ikigai—jibun no kanōsei, kaikasaseru katei" (*Ikigai*: the process of allowing the self's possibilities to blossom). Kokoro no nazo (Riddles of the heart), no. 20. Nihon Keizai Shinbun, 4 April, evening edition.

Kōdansha Encyclopedia of Japan. 1983. "Sōka Gakkai." Tōkyō: Kōdansha.

Kōjien [Japanese dictionary]. 1986. Tōkyō: Iwanami Shoten.

Kokusai Josei Gakkai (International Women's Society). 1980. Gendai Nihon no shufu (Contemporary Japanese housewives). Tōkyō: Nihon Hōsō Shuppan Kyōkai (NHK).

Kondo, Dorinne K. 1990. Crafting Selves: Power, Gender, and Discourses of Identity in a Japanese Workplace. Chicago: University of Chicago Press.

Kuroi, Senji. 1990. "Kishi gūdas." In Jikan. Tōkyō: Kōdansha.

Kurowassan [magazine]. 1990. "Tsumatachi no hontō no honne" (The true feelings of wives). 25 February.

LaFleur, William R. 1983. The Karma of Words: Buddhism and the Literary Arts in Medieval Japan. Berkeley and Los Angeles: University of California Press.

Lasch, Christopher. 1979. The Culture of Narcissism: American Life in an Age of Diminishing Expectations. New York: W. W. Norton. Reprint, New York: Warner Books (page references are to reprint edition).

————. 1991. The True and Only Heaven: Progress and Its Critics. New York: W. W. Norton.

Lebra, Takie Sugiyama. 1976. Japanese Patterns of Behavior. Honolulu: University of Hawaii Press.

————. 1984. Japanese Women: Constraint and Fulfillment. Honolulu: University of Hawaii Press.

Leinberger, Paul, and Bruce Tucker. 1991. The New Individualists: The Generation after "The Organization Man." New York: HarperCollins.

Levinson, Daniel J., with Charlotte N. Darrow, Edward B. Klein, Maria H. Levinson, and Braxton McKee. 1978. The Seasons of a Man's Life. New York: Ballantine Books.

Linde, Charlotte. 1993. Life Stories: The Creation of Coherence. Oxford: Oxford University Press.

Louv, Richard. 1992. Childhood's Future. Boston: Houghton Mifflin 1990. Reprint, New York: Doubleday Anchor Books (page references are to reprint edition).

Luckmann, Thomas. 1967. The Invisible Religion: The Problem of Religion in Modern Society. New York: Macmillan.

Lummis, Douglas, and Saitō Shigeo. 1991. Naze Nihonjin wa shinu hodo hataraku no desuka (Why do Japanese work themselves to death?). Iwanami bukkuretto, no. 198. Tōkyō: Iwanami Shoten.

Lynd, Robert S. [1939] 1967. Knowledge for What? The Place of Social Science in American Culture. Princeton: Princeton University Press.

Lyotard, Jean-François. 1984. *The Postmodern Condition: A Report on Knowledge*. Translated by Geoff Bennington and Brian Massumi. Minneapolis: University of Minnesota Press.

Marcuse, Herbert. 1964. *One-Dimensional Man: Studies in the Ideology of Advanced Industrial Society*. Boston: Beacon Press.

Maslow, Abraham. 1970. *Motivation and Personality*. 2d ed. New York: Harper and Row.

McArthur, Ian. 1991. "Traditional Japanese Family Facing Extinction." *Daily Yomiuri*, 7 August.

McCullough, Paulina, and Sandra Rutenberg. 1989. "Launching Children and Moving On." In *The Changing Family Life Cycle*, edited by Betty Carter and Monica McGoldrick. 2d ed. Needham Heights, Mass.: Allyn and Bacon.

Mead, Margaret. 1970. *Culture and Commitment: A Study of the Generation Gap*. Garden City, N.Y.: Natural History Press / Doubleday.

Metraux, Daniel. 1988. *The History and Theology of Sōka Gakkai: A Japanese New Religion*. Lewiston, N.Y.: Edwin Mellen.

Minami, Ikuhiro. 1989. "Chūnen dansei no seikatsu to ikikata" (The ways of life of middle-aged men). In *Gendaijin no raifukōsu* (Contemporary lifecourse), edited by Misawa Kenichi et al. Kyōto: Mineruva Shobō.

Misawa, Kenichi, and Ikuhiro Minami. 1989. "Rōnenki no seikatsu" (Life in old age). In *Gendaijin no raifukōsu* (Contemporary lifecourse), edited by Misawa Kenichi et al. Kyōto: Mineruva Shobō.

Mita, Munesuke. 1984. *Gendai Nihon no seishin kōzō* (The spiritual structure of contemporary Japan). 2d ed. Tōkyō: Kōbundō.

Moody, Raymond A., Jr. 1976. *Life after Life: The Investigation of a Phenomenon—Survival of Bodily Death*. St. Simon's Island, Ga.: Mockingbird Books, 1975. Reprint, New York: Bantam Books.

Moore, Sally F., and Barbara G. Myerhoff, eds. 1977. *Secular Ritual*. Assen, Netherlands: Van Gorcum.

More, Sir Thomas. [1515] 1975. *Utopia*. Translated and edited by Robert M. Adams. New York: W. W. Norton.

Mori, Arimasa. 1970. *Ikiru koto to kangaeru koto* (Living and thinking). Tōkyō: Kōdansha.

Morioka, Kiyomi. 1984. *Ie no henbō to senzo no matsuri* (Ancestor worship and the transformation of the household). Tōkyō: Nihon Kitoku Kyōdan Shuppankyoku.

Morris, Ivan. 1979. *The World of the Shining Prince: Court Life in Ancient Japan*. Middlesex, England: Penguin Books.

NHK (Nihon Hōsō Kyōkai). 1992. *Shin Nihonjin no jōken* [Conditions of the new Japanese). Television documentary series broadcast at intervals through 1992. Premiere broadcast, 3 January.

Nagashima, Hidesuke. 1989. "Effort Made on Vacation Law: Workaholism Tackled over Employers' Objections." *Japan Times*, 6 December.

Narita, Yasuaki. 1986. *"Kōkando ningen" o kaidoku suru* (Interpreting the "media-sensitive human being"). Tōkyō: Kōdansha.

Needleman, Jacob. 1991. *Money and the Meaning of Life*. New York: Doubleday Currency Books.

Newman, Katherine S. 1989. *Falling from Grace: The Experience of Downward Mobility in the American Middle Class*. New York: Free Press 1988. Reprint: Vintage Books (page references are to reprint edition).

Nihon Keizai Shinbun. 1990. "Shigoto igai ni ikigai o, nioroshi utsubyō" [Have an *ikigai* outside of work; otherwise, the possibility of depression]. 21 April.

Nihon kokugo daijiten [Unabridged Japanese dictionary]. 1972. Tōkyō: Shōgakkan.

Nihongo daijiten [Japanese dictionary]. 1989. Tōkyō: Kōdansha.

Nikkei Sangyō Shinbun. 1990. "Josei no kizoku ishiki, ikigai motome bunsangata ni" [Women's senses of belonging: seeking *ikigai* in many areas]. 29 October.

Niwano, Nikkyō. 1969. *Ningen no ikigai* (Human *ikigai*). Tōkyō: Kōsei Shuppansha.

Noda, Masaaki. 1988. *Ikigai shearingu: sangyō kōzō tenkanki no kinrō ishiki* (*Ikigai* sharing: the attitudes of workers in a time of structural transition in industry]. Tōkyō: Chūō Kōronsha.

————. 1990. "Shakai no shimesu mokuhyō yori ikiru imi o motomeru" [Beyond the goals that society provides, seeking a life meaning of one's own]. *Nihon Keizai Shinbun*. 15 July, morning edition.

Ōhira, Ken. 1990. *Yutakasa no seishin byōri* (The psychopathology of affluence). Tōkyō: Iwanami Shoten.

Ono, Yumiko. 1991. "Reluctant Feminists: Woman's Movement in Corporate Japan Isn't Moving Very Fast." *Wall Street Journal*, 6 June.

Peck, M. Scott. 1978. *The Road Less Traveled*. New York: Simon and Schuster.

Perry, Lewis. 1984. *Intellectual Life in America: A History*. New York: Franklin Watts.

Plath, David W. 1964. "Where the Family of God Is the Family: The Role of the Dead in Japanese Households." *American Anthropologist* 66 (2): 300–317.

————. 1980. *Long Engagements: Maturity in Modern Japan*. Stanford: Stanford University Press.

————. 1983. "Old Age and Retirement." *Kōdansha Encyclopedia of Japan*. Tōkyō: Kōdansha.

Powell, Bill. 1990. "Japan's Big Spenders." *Newsweek* (Far East Edition), 6 August.

Rauch, Jonathan. 1992. *The Outnation: A Search for the Soul of Japan.* Boston: Little, Brown.

Reader, Ian. 1991. *Religion in Contemporary Japan.* Honolulu: University of Hawaii Press.

Reich, Charles A. 1970. *The Greening of America.* New York: Random House.

Reich, Richard B. 1990. "Why the Rich Are Getting Richer, the Poor Poorer." *Utne Reader,* January-February. Reprint from *The New Republic.*

Reid, T. R. 1990. "Low birthrate Is Seen as Serious Threat." *Japan Times,* 31 October.

Reynolds, David K. 1983. *Naikan Psychotherapy: Meditation for Self-Development.* Chicago: University of Chicago Press.

Ricoeur, Paul. 1979. "The Model of the Text: Meaningful Action Considered as a Text." In *Interpretive Social Science: A Reader,* edited by Paul Rabinow and William M. Sullivan. Berkeley and Los Angeles: University of California Press.

Riesman, David, Nathan Glazer, and Reuel Denny. 1953. *The Lonely Crowd.* New Haven: Yale University Press, 1950. Reprint, abridged by the authors, New York: Doubleday Anchor Books (page references are to reprint edition).

Ring, Kenneth. 1984. *Heading toward Omega: A Scientific Investigation of the Near-death Experience.* New York: William Morrow.

Rohlen, Thomas P. 1974. *For Harmony and Strength: Japanese White-collar Organization in Anthropological Perspective.* Berkeley and Los Angeles: University of California Press.

———. 1983. *Japan's High Schools.* Berkeley and Los Angeles: University of California Press.

———. 1989. "Order in Japanese Society: Attachment, Authority, and Routine." *Journal of Japanese Studies* 15 (1): 5–40.

Roland, Alan. 1988. *In Search of Self in India and Japan: Toward a Cross-cultural Psychology.* Princeton: Princeton University Press.

Rosow, Irving. 1982. "Intergenerational Perspectives on Aging." In *Aging and the Human Condition,* edited by Gari Lesnoff-Caravaglia. New York: Human Sciences Press.

Saitō, Kōichi. 1990. *Hatarakizuki de nani ga warui* (What's wrong with liking work). Tōkyō: Manejimentosha.

Sakurai, Tetsuo. 1985. *Kotoba o ushinatta wakamonotachi* (Young people who have forgotten language). Tōkyō: Kōdansha.

Sanger, David E. 1992. "Women in Japan Job Market Find the Door Closing Again." *New York Times,* 2 December.

Sato, Ikuya. 1991. *Kamikaze Biker: Parody and Anomy in Affluent Japan.* Chicago: University of Chicago Press.

Schor, Juliet B. 1991. *The Overworked American: The Unexpected Decline of Leisure.* New York: Basic Books.

Schutz, Alfred. [1940] 1978. "Phenomenology and the Social Sciences." In *Phenomenology and Sociology,* edited by Thomas Luckmann. Harmondsworth, Eng.: Penguin Books.

Sengoku, Tamotsu. 1991. *"Majime" no hōkai: Heisei Nihon no wakamonotachi* (The destruction of seriousness: Japanese youth today). Tōkyō: Saimaru Shuppankai.

Sheehy, Gail. 1977. *Passages: Predictable Crises of Adult Life.* New York: E. P. Dutton, 1976. Reprint, New York: Bantam Books (page references are to reprint edition).

Shimizu, Katsuo. 1987. *Bunka no henyō* (The transmutation of culture). Kyōto: Jinbunshoin.

Skinner, B. F. 1971. *Beyond Freedom and Dignity.* New York: Alfred A. Knopf.

Slater, Philip. 1976. *The Pursuit of Loneliness: American Culture at the Breaking Point.* 2d ed. Boston: Beacon Press.

Smith, Robert J. 1974. *Ancestor Worship in Contemporary Japan.* Stanford: Stanford University Press.

———. 1983. *Japanese Society: Tradition, Self, and the Social Order.* Cambridge: Cambridge University Press.

———. 1987a. "Gender Inequality in Contemporary Japan." *Journal of Japanese Studies* 13 (1): 1–26.

———. 1987b. "Popular Religion in Japan: Faith, Belief, and Behavior." In *Tradition and Creativity: Essays on East Asian Civilization,* edited by Ching-I Tu. New Brunswick, N.J.: Transaction Books.

———. 1991. "Memory and Time in the Formation of the Not Entirely Sociocentric Self." Keynote Address, "Conference on the Self and the Social Order in China, India, and Japan." East-West Center, Honolulu, Hawaii, 5 August.

Sorita, Takeshi. 1981. *Ikigai no tankyū* (The search for *ikigai*). Tōkyō: Dai Nihon Tosho Kabushikigaisha.

Springsteen, Bruce. 1982. "Reason to Believe." From the record album *Nebraska.* New York: Columbia Records TC38358.

Stacey, Judith. 1990. *Brave New Families: Stories of Domestic Upheaval in Late Twentieth Century America.* New York: Basic Books.

Stark, Rodney, and William Sims Bainbridge. 1985. *The Future of Religion:*

Secularization, Revival, and Cult Formation. Berkeley and Los Angeles: University of California Press.

Statistical Abstract of the United States. 1992. 112th ed. Washington, D.C.: U.S. Bureau of the Census.

Steiner, George. 1975. *After Babel.* Oxford: Oxford University Press.

Sugimoto Yoshio, and Ross Mouer. 1982. *Nihonjin wa "Nihontekika"* (Are the Japanese "Japanese"?]. Tōkyō: Tōyō Keizai Shimpōsha.

Suntory Company. 1990. "Tondemonēme ni attemitei" ["I want to have an extraordinary experience!"]. Advertisement in *Asahi Shinbun,* 15 April.

Swindoll, Chuck. 1991. *The Strong Family: Growing Wise in Family Life.* Portland, Ore.: Multnomah Press.

Takayama, Hideko. 1990. "Japan's New Woman." *Newsweek* (Far East Edition), 15 January.

Tanba, Tetsurō. 1988. *Reikai seikatsu no jissō* (The reality of life in the spiritual world). Tōkyō: Tsuchiya Shoten.

Tergesen, Anne. 1990. "Historian Sees No End to City's Slide." *Japan Times,* 22 July.

Terkel, Studs. 1972. *Working.* New York: Avon Books.

Tevlin, Jon. 1992. "Why Women are Mad as Hell." *Glamour,* March.

Thompson, William Irwin. 1991. *The American Replacement of Nature.* New York: Doubleday Currency Books.

Tillich, Paul. 1987. *The Essential Tillich.* Edited by F. Forrester Church. New York: Macmillan.

Tocqueville, Alexis de. [1835, 1840] 1990. *Democracy in America.* 2 vols. Edited by Phillips Bradley. New York: Vintage Books.

Tōkyō Yomiuri Shinbun. 1989. " 'Ko ga ikigai' kara nukedasō. 'Kodomo no jiritsu to kazoku no kizuna' shinpojiumu" [Breaking free from 'children as a mother's *ikigai'*: symposium on 'children's independence and the family's bonds']. 16 September, evening edition.

———. 1990. "Jikka e nigeru otto, matsu no wa 'kahogo no oya.' Kosodate yamerarenai 'bosei koshitsu shō' " [Husbands who escape to their overprotective parents—the 'mother who can't let go' syndrome]. 14 May, morning edition.

Traube, Elizabeth G. 1992. *Dreaming Identities: Class, Gender, and Generation in 1980s Hollywood Movies.* Boulder, Colo.: Westview Press.

Turner, James. 1985. *Without God, Without Creed: The Origins of Unbelief in America.* Baltimore: Johns Hopkins University Press.

Ueno, Chizuko. 1987. "The Position of Japanese Women Reconsidered." *Current Anthropology* 28(4): 75–84.

Updike, John. 1982. *Rabbit Is Rich.* New York: Alfred A. Knopf 1981. Reprint, New York: Fawcett Crest (page references are to reprint edition).

Varenne, Hervé. 1977. *Americans Together: Structured Diversity in a Midwestern Town.* New York: Teachers College Press.

Wagatsuma, Takashi. 1983. "Family Planning." *Kōdansha Encyclopedia of Japan.* Tōkyō: Kōdansha.

Wagner, Helmut. 1970. Introduction to *Phenomenology and Social Relations,* by Alfred Schutz. Chicago: University of Chicago Press.

Watson, Lawrence C., and Maria-Barbara Watson-Franke. 1985. *Interpreting Life Histories: An Anthropological Inquiry.* New Brunswick: Rutgers University Press.

Weber, Max. [1925] 1964. "The Fundamental Concepts of Sociology." In *The Theory of Social and Economic Organization.* Translated by A. M. Henderson and Talcott Parsons. Oxford: Oxford University Press, 1947. Reprint, New York: Free Press (page references are to reprint edition).

———. [1920–21] 1958. *The Protestant Ethic and the Spirit of Capitalism.* Translated by Talcott Parsons. New York: Charles Scribner's Sons.

Weinberg, Steven. 1977. *The First Three Minutes: A Modern View of the Origin of the Universe.* New York: Basic Books.

Weisman, Steven R. 1991. "In Crowded Japan, a Bonus for Babies Angers Women." *New York Times,* 17 February.

Whorf, Benjamin Lee. [1941] 1988. "The Relation of Habitual Thought and Behavior to Language." In *High Points in Anthropology,* edited by Paul Bohannon and Mark Glazer. 2d ed. New York: Alfred A. Knopf.

Whyte, William H., Jr. 1957. *The Organization Man.* New York: Simon and Schuster, 1956. Reprint, New York: Doubleday Anchor Books (page references are to reprint edition).

Wilson, P. B. 1990. *Liberated through Submission: The Ultimate Paradox.* Eugene, Ore.: Harvest House.

Wolfe, Tom. 1983. "The Me Decade and the Third Great Awakening." In *The Purple Decades: A Reader.* New York: Berkley Books.

Yamazaki, Masakazu. 1987. *Yawarakai kojinshugi no tanjō: shōhi shakai no bigaku* (The birth of soft individualism: the aesthetics of consumer society). Tōkyō: Chūō Kōron.

Yanagawa, Keiichi. 1977. "Gendai ni okeru seishi no mondai" (The contemporary problem of life and death). In *Nihon ni okeru sei to shi no shisō: Nihonjin no seishinshi nyūmon* (Japanese conceptions of life and death), edited by Tamura Yoshiro and Minamoto Ryōen. Tōkyō: Yūhikaku.

Yankelovich, Daniel. 1982. *New Rules: Searching for Self-fulfillment in a World Turned Upside Down.* New York: Random House, 1981. Reprint, New York: Bantam Books (page references are to reprint edition).

Yoshida, Kenkō. [1431] 1981. *Essays in Idleness (Tsurezuregusa)*. Translated by Donald Keene. New York: Columbia University Press. 1967. Reprint, Rutland, Vt.: Charles E. Tuttle.

Yoshihiro, Kiyoko, ed. 1991. *Onna ga kodomo o umitagaranai wake* (The reasons why woman don't want children). Tōkyō: Bansei Shobō.

Index

affluence. *See* Japan: affluence of; United
States: affluence of
aging: *ikigai* dreams as influenced by, 144–
47, 152–54; and mental growth, 217–18,
217n6. *See also* generational differences;
elderly
Ainu, 180n6, 190–93, 190n8, 200
Amaki Shihomi, 95
Amano Yūkichi, 98–99
Anderson, Walter Truett, 240, 241, 246
anthropology: and conceptions of culture,
47–49; philosophical, 11, 11n3. *See also*
culture
art. *See* creation as *ikigai*
Asada Akira, 101
Asahi Shinbun [newspaper], 14, 16,
226n11; on dissatisfaction of women,
98–99, 99n12
Ayer, A. J., *The Meaning of Life*, 27

Bainbridge, William Sims, 201n12, 229
Baldwin, James, 153–54
Baldwin, Stanley C., 36
Barringer, Felicity, 31
Bateson, Gregory, 208n1
Baumeister, Roy F., 5n1, 104, 245; *Mean-
ings of Life*, 27; on significance of self,
217, 250
Baumer, Franklin L., 241, 245, 246, 252
Becker, Ernest, 5n1, 7, 207–8; *The Birth
and Death of Meaning*, 11n3; on mean-
ing of life, 241, 245
Beeman, William O., 29
Bell, Daniel, 40
Bellah, Robert N., 248; *Habits of the
Heart*, 28, 35–36, 37, 42
Benedict, Ruth, *Patterns of Culture*, 246

Berger, Brigitte, 238–39
Berger, Peter L., 238–39, 245, 246, 249
Berman, Morris, 243n2
Birth and Death of Meaning, The (Becker),
11n3
bōsōzoku [motorcycle gangs], 72n7
Bourdieu, Pierre, 209–10, 215n4
Brodzinsky, David M., 228n12
Buber, Martin, "What is Man?," 11n3

Camus, Albert, 3
Carter, Betty, 228n12
Caudill, William A., 23, 84n9
Caughey, John L., 4
Chaves, Mark, 229
children: childrearing patterns, 23–24; effects of divorce on, 103–4; *ikigai* conflict
of children and parents, 213; *ikigai* negotiation between children and parents,
221–22. *See also* parent-child relationships
Comfort, Alex, 153
commitment to group: and conformity, 29–
32, 145; cultural formulations of, 212–
14; dreams and maturity in, 145–47; and
economic conditions, 25, 33–35, 40, 225;
in future of Japan, 21–26; Japanese print
media on *ikigai* as, 17–18, 19–26; ordinariness as happiness in, 214–15; U.S.
print media emphasis on, 34–36. *See
also* companies, Japanese; Japan
companies, Japanese: commitment to, 20,
24, 26, 31–32, 203n13; group emphasis
in, 39; *ikigai* plans for employees by, 14–
15, 16, 18; in interview interpretations,
67–70; time demands by, 225–26,
226n10. *See also* Japan; work

CPSIA information can be obtained
at www.ICGtesting.com
Printed in the USA
FSOW01n0710121215
14156FS